WHEEL BOATS ON THE MISSOURI

Wheel Boats on the Missouri, *by Curtis Peacock, 1997.*

Nebraska State Historical Society, Lincoln

WHEEL BOATS
ON THE
MISSOURI

THE JOURNALS AND DOCUMENTS OF THE
ATKINSON-O'FALLON EXPEDITION, 1824–26

EDITED AND WITH AN INTRODUCTION BY
Richard E. Jensen and James S. Hutchins

Montana Historical Society Press, *Helena*
Nebraska State Historical Society, *Lincoln*

Designed by Arrow Graphics, Missoula, Montana
Typeset in Sabon

Printed by Thomson-Shore, Inc., Dexter, Michigan

Printed in the United States of America

Montana Historical Society Press
225 North Roberts St.
P. O. Box 201201
Helena, Montana 59620-1201

Nebraska State Historical Society
1500 R Street
Lincoln, Nebraska 68508

01 02 03 04 05 9 8 7 6 5 4 3 2 1

Library of Congress Cataloging-in-Publication Data

Atkinson, Henry, 1782–1842.
Wheel boats on the Missouri : the journals and documents of the Atkinson-O'Fallon Expedition, 1824–1826 / edited and with an introduction by Richard E. Jensen and James S. Hutchins.
p. cm.
Contains the journals of Brig. Gen. Henry Atkinson and Maj. Stephen Watts Kearny.
Includes bibliographical references and index.
ISBN 0-917298-69-1 (cloth : alk. paper)
1. Atkinson-O'Fallon Expedition (1824–1826). 2. Missouri River—Description and travel. 3. West (U.S.)—Description and travel. 4. Atkinson, Henry, 1782–1842—Diaries. 5. Kearny, Stephen Watts, 1794–1848—Diaries. 6. Indians of North America—Missouri River Region—Government relations. 7. River boats—Missouri River. I. Kearny, Stephen Watts, 1794–1848. II. Jensen, Richard E. III. Hutchins, James S. IV. Title.

F598.A83 2000
978'.02—dc21 99-086485

CONTENTS

ILLUSTRATIONS

INTRODUCTION

The Atkinson-O'Fallon expedition was authorized in response to attacks by Indians on American fur traders and trappers in present-day Montana and the Dakotas. The Americans blamed Canadian fur companies for inciting the Indians and for trading with those who lived south of the international boundary, thus usurping a portion of a valuable resource the traders regarded as theirs. To protect the nation's interests, President James Monroe directed Brig. Gen. Henry Atkinson and Indian Agent Benjamin O'Fallon to negotiate peace treaties with tribes along the Missouri River, and also to secure their promise to trade exclusively with American citizens.[1] Approximately 475 soldiers of the First and

1. Henry Atkinson (1782–1842), a North Carolina native, entered the army in 1808. He saw limited action in the War of 1812 but his administrative talents enabled him to survive the army's dramatic reduction after the war. He was the commander of the Sixth Infantry Regiment in 1819 when it embarked on the so-called Yellowstone Expedition, which halted at the Council Bluff. There the troops built Cantonment Missouri, which was washed away by a flood in the spring of 1820. New quarters were built on higher ground, which was officially named Fort Atkinson a year later. In 1824, Atkinson began organizing a second expedition up the Missouri, from which this journal comes. He died in service in 1842 with the rank of brevet brigadier general. Born in Lexington, Kentucky, Benjamin O'Fallon (1793–1842) moved to St. Louis at age fourteen to live with his uncle, William Clark. In 1816, after a brief stint in the milling business, O'Fallon was appointed a special Indian agent by William Clark and served at Prairie du Chien, where he exhibited a tendency to be forceful, even belligerent, in his dealings with the Indians. In 1819 he became the Upper Missouri agent responsible for the tribes above the mouth of the Platte River. In 1825 he was appointed special commissioner with General Atkinson to represent the president at the signing of fifteen treaties of peace with tribes within his jurisdiction. Health problems forced O'Fallon to resign in December 1826. After many years of poor health, he died in 1842 at his home in Jefferson County, Missouri. Roger L. Nichols, *General Henry Atkinson, A Western Military Career* (Norman: University of Oklahoma Press, 1965); John W. Steiger, "Benjamin O'Fallon," *The Mountain Men and the Fur Trade of the Far West,* 10 vols., ed. Leroy R. Hafen (Glendale, Calif.: Arthur H. Clark Co., 1965–1972), 5:255–81; John W. Steiger, "Benjamin O'Fallon and the Indian Frontier, 1815–1830" (Master's thesis, San Diego State College, 1963).

Sixth Infantry regiments accompanied Atkinson and O'Fallon to impress the Indians with the U.S. Army's ability to enforce the treaties. It was hoped this combination of military power and proffered friendship would put an end to further hostilities and to the suspected British meddling.

While the expedition was on the river, both General Atkinson and Maj. Stephen Watts Kearny kept diaries. These journals describe the trip from St. Louis to Fort Atkinson in the fall of 1824, the expedition from the fort to the Yellowstone River and back in 1825, and the return of a portion of the troops to St. Louis in 1826. Although the two officers' daily entries are generally terse, they cover a broad range of topics. Daily events and problems faced by a small army on the move are discussed. The councils with the Indian tribes are described in detail. There are notes on landmarks, flora, and fauna, as well as ethnographic observations. The performance of the unusual and experimental man-powered, paddlewheel boats in which they traveled received considerable attention. Occasionally the journalists found time to delve into arcane subjects, such as the relative palatability of black bear meat versus that of the grizzly bear. The orders issued by Atkinson and his staff concerning the management of the expedition are included with the diaries.

American officials were apprehensive about a commercial invasion from Canada into the upper Missouri country long before the Atkinson-O'Fallon expedition. James Wilkinson, the first American governor of Louisiana, arrived in St. Louis in June 1805, and within days summarized his views of the territory's political and economic situation in a letter to Secretary of War Henry Dearborn:

> It is well known that the Indian trade, from Hudsons Bay and the St. Lawrence, to the remotest streams of the lakes, the Mississippi and the Missouri is nearly monopolized by British Traders, their factors, Agents and Engagees, and that their goods are imported and their furs exported through British Posts; the privation We Suffer from this diversion of our rightful commerce, is a trifling ill, when compared to the transcendent influence, which is thus acquired and perpetuated by a foreign power, over the aborigines within our national limits.[2]

Americans involved in the fur trade probably felt the monetary losses were decidedly more than a "trifling ill," but westerners in general agreed wholeheartedly with Wilkinson's belief that the British were in control of the Indians.

Wilkinson began to formulate a strategy to bring the region safely under the mantle of the United States. He proposed to establish a line of military forts westward from the Great Lakes, to prevent aliens and contraband goods from entering the United States.[3] Wilkinson suggested the westernmost fort be located either at the falls of the Missouri or near the Mandan villages north of present Bismarck, North Dakota. From the villages major British posts on the Assiniboin River could be easily monitored. This location was also favored by the fur traders, who realized the important role the tribe would play in the trade. The Mandans were the northernmost sedentary people on the river and since they did not entirely desert their villages to go on buffalo hunts, traders were assured of some protection from the more aggressive tribes. There was also a trade system that had been in place since prehistoric times involving the Mandan and their nomadic neighbors, which was carried on under a flag of truce. The whites recognized the potential profits to be gained by joining this trade.[4]

Secretary Dearborn was not in complete agreement with Wilkinson's proposed line of forts. Dearborn felt the garrisons might be useful in the future, but for the present he wanted to keep the troops consolidated near St. Louis, where they would be better able to protect white settlements should the need arise.[5] He sent an order to Wilkinson to this effect, but it had not reached St. Louis before the governor had an opportunity to carry out part of his plan. A party of

---

2. Clarence Edwin Carter, ed., *The Territorial Papers of the United States*, 29 vols. (Washington, D.C.: GPO, 1934), 13:196–200. British traders, as well as traders from St. Louis, were regularly visiting the Mandan villages at this time. W. Raymond Wood and Thomas D. Thiessen, *Early Fur Trade on the Northern Plains: Canadian Traders among the Mandan and Hidatsa Indians, 1738–1818* (Norman: University of Oklahoma Press, 1985), 42.

3. Carter, *Territorial Papers*, 13:172–75. In this letter Wilkinson suggested a fort at the falls of the Missouri as an alternative to one at the Mandan villages. For an overview of the complex history of the Mandan, see W. Raymond Wood, ed., *Papers in Northern Plains Prehistory and Ethnology: Ice Glider 32OL110*, Special Publication No. 3 (Sioux Falls, S. Dak.: South Dakota Archeological Society, 1986).

4. Wood and Thiessen, *Early Fur Trade on the Northern Plains*, 19–20.

5. Carter, *Territorial Papers*, 13:239–40.

Arikara leaders was visiting St. Louis and when they were ready to return to their homes, Wilkinson ordered twenty-six soldiers to accompany them. After the Arikaras were safely escorted to their village, the soldiers were instructed to return to the mouth of the Platte River and build a fort, either there or at the Oto Indian village about forty miles upstream. Wilkinson was also worried about intrusions from Mexico and believed the Oto fort would counter foreign influences from the southwest. By the time Wilkinson received the order prohibiting just this kind of troop deployment, other events had foiled the mission. A Kansa war party threatened to attack the soldiers, forcing them to turn back long before reaching the Platte River.[6]

While Wilkinson was trying to establish a fort near the Oto, Meriwether Lewis and William Clark were well on their way to the Pacific Ocean. They had the difficult assignment of convincing the Indians to acknowledge the supremacy of the United States and accept the president as their "Great Father." During the winter of 1804–5 the explorers built a temporary fort near the Mandan villages, where they were able to assess what was then a very real threat posed by British traders to American interests. Lewis and Clark concluded that military support was necessary to secure the American frontier and to prevent the valuable fur trade from being lost to the British. Clark outlined a plan for a chain of forts along the Missouri and in the upper Mississippi area, which he felt would assure U.S. domination. His westernmost fort was to be at the falls of the Missouri and be manned by thirty-three soldiers.[7] Although the forts recommended by Wilkinson and Clark were never built, the plan received wide support from westerners, and similar strategies were still being considered twenty years later as an alternative to the Atkinson-O'Fallon expedition.

Although Lewis and Clark worried about the British usurping the trade, they showed little concern when they met Francois-Antoine Larocque, a North West Company employee, who came from his post on the Assiniboine River to trade with the Mandans. Upon his arrival Larocque chatted briefly with Lewis and described the American as "very friendly." The explorers warned Larocque that he must

6. Ibid., 13:243–44, 297–99, 235–37.

7. Ernest Staples Osgood, ed., *The Field Notes of Captain William Clark* (New Haven, Conn.: Yale University Press, 1964), 188.

not give the Indians any flags or medals as these were "the Sacred Emblem" of the U.S. Government. Larocque assured them he would not. The trader was also told, "that it was not the policy of the United States to Restrain Commerce & fetter it . . . & all persons who should Come on their territories, for trade or for any other purpose, will never be molested by an American Officer." Perhaps Lewis and Clark wished to demonstrate their sincerity, because two of the expedition's soldiers were allowed to trade eleven wolf and fox skins to Larocque for tobacco. Then, just before Larocque left for his post, Captain Lewis spent a day repairing the Canadian's broken compass.[8]

Lewis and Clark's impact on the fur trade in the upper Missouri went far beyond the congenial meeting with Larocque. While returning from the Pacific coast in 1806, Lewis and several of the expedition's soldiers met a Blackfeet party (probably Piegans) and a dispute arose over the possession of some guns. As the controversy escalated, shots were fired and two Indians fell dead.[9] The Blackfeet neither forgave nor forgot this ignominy, and would seek revenge on Americans for years to come. On a more positive note, the explorers confirmed long-held rumors about rich beaver streams in the upper Missouri country. Fur traders had suspected the presence of such streams, but prior to 1806, only a handful had ever ventured above the Mandan villages. Within weeks of the explorers' return, two corporations were formed to tap that source of potential wealth. One of the companies was under Pierre Chouteau, Sr. and the other enterprise, which would later evolve into the Missouri Fur Company, was led by Manuel Lisa.

In the spring of 1807 Lisa and his employees set out for the upper Missouri River country. They stopped at the Arikara village, but found the Indians in a cantankerous mood, demanding exorbitant gifts before allowing the whites to continue. Lisa took an aggressive approach and aimed a swivel gun at the Indians. The Arikaras decided a fight under these circumstances was not in their best interest

---

8. Wood and Thiessen, *Early Fur Trade on the Northern Plains*, 137–40, 150–52.

9. Gary Moulton, ed., *The Journals of the Lewis and Clark Expedition*, 11 vols. (Lincoln: University of Nebraska Press, 1986–1997), 8:134. One of the Piegans may have survived. Ibid., 136, n.2.; John C. Ewers, *The Blackfeet, Raiders on the Northwestern Plains* (Norman: University of Oklahoma Press, 1958), 45–48; Reuben Gold Thwaites, ed., *Original Journals of the Lewis and Clark Expedition*, 8 vols. (New York: Dodd, Mead and Co., 1905), 8:335.

and called for a council instead. To placate the chiefs, Lisa told them that two more boats would arrive in a few days with trade goods specifically for the Arikaras. This, and Lisa's valuable gifts, including guns and ammunition, convinced the Arikaras to allow him to continue his journey. His party ascended the Yellowstone to the mouth of the Bighorn, where they built a trading post.[10]

A few days after Lisa's departure, Pierre Chouteau and his men arrived at the village. The Indians prohibited Chouteau from continuing and demanded he remain with the tribe because Lisa had told them the white men were coming to trade. Chouteau offered to barter for half of his goods, but it was not enough. His predicament only grew worse when the Arikaras learned he was escorting a Mandan chief back to his village after a trip to Washington. Not only were the tribes at war, but an Arikara who went to Washington at the same time had died there. If the Arikaras had learned of Chouteau's plan to build a permanent trading post for the Mandans, it would have been one more justification for treating him harshly. Tempers flared as the negotiations broke down and gunfire erupted, killing three whites and wounding seven. The attack compelled Chouteau to retreat downstream and dashed his dream of a fortune for the present.[11]

The following spring Lisa sent his lieutenant, John Colter, to seek out Indians and bring them to trade at the post on the Bighorn. Colter fell in with a friendly Crow hunting party and when it was attacked by their old enemies, the Blackfeet, Colter had little choice but to participate on the side of the Crows.[12] The Blackfeet had not forgotten the injury they suffered at the hands of Meriwether Lewis two years earlier, and Colter's assistance to the Crows only reinforced the tribe's resolve to avenge those losses. Blackfeet intimidation and persistent threats of an all-out attack soon made Lisa's post

---

10. Richard E. Oglesby, *Manuel Lisa and the Opening of the Missouri Fur Trade* (Norman: University of Oklahoma Press, 1963), 48–49.

11. Janet Lecompte, "Auguste Pierre Chouteau," *The Mountain Men and the Fur Trade of the Far West*, 9:65; Raymond W. Settle, "Nathaniel Pryor," ibid., 2:279–80; Roger L. Nichols, "The Arikara Indians and the Missouri River Trade: A Quest for Survival," *Great Plains Quarterly* 2 (1982): 77–93. Army ensign Nathaniel Pryor, the Mandan chief's attendant, learned about Lisa's duplicity from an Arikara captive. Elliott Coues, ed., "Letters of William Clark and Nathaniel Pryor," *Annals of Iowa* 1 (1893–95): 616–17.

12. Aubrey L. Haines, "John Colter," *Mountain Men and the Fur Trade*, 8:80.

untenable, and the company was compelled to retreat to the Mandan villages. In addition to the troubles with the Indians, Lisa was suffering financial reversals and was soon forced to withdraw even farther downriver to conserve the firm's dwindling capital.[13]

The American retreat from the upper Missouri contributed to a growing anti-British feeling, which was especially prevalent in the West. British traders were blamed for instigating every hostile act committed by Indians, and these were reported at length in the newspapers, especially those in St. Louis.[14] Other factors soon united eastern and southern Americans with their frontier kin in a growing contempt of Great Britain. An economic depression, especially severe in the South and West, was blamed on the British blockade of Europe during the Napoleonic Wars. About the same time, seamen were being abducted from American ships and carried off by British warships. This affront to U.S. honor could not be ignored and provided a rallying cry for the Americans. On June 18, 1812, President James Madison signed a declaration of war against Great Britain.

During the War of 1812 the United States had a thin line of defense in the West, but for additional protection the army acquired boats and equipped them with swivel guns and other armament to defend the Mississippi River above St. Louis. In the closing weeks of 1812, William Clark, now governor of the new Missouri Territory, had two boats "made Bullet proof," which were large enough to carry forty or fifty men.[15] Two years later Clark sent 200 men in five barges from St. Louis to Prairie du Chien to build a fort. One of the boats was stationed there, but when the British

---

13. Ewers, *The Blackfeet*, 50-51; The Missouri Fur Company's financial problems are discussed at length in chap. 5 of Oglesby, *Manuel Lisa*. It was probably at this time that Lisa built the fort a short distance below the future site of Fort Atkinson. Richard E. Jensen, *The Fontenelle and Cabanné Trading Posts: The History and Archeology of Two Missouri River Sites, 1822–1838* (Lincoln: Nebraska State Historical Society), in press.

14. Steiger, "Benjamin O'Fallon," 29.

15. Carter, *Territorial Papers*, 14:632–33. On June 16, 1813, Clark was named governor of Missouri Territory by President James Madison. Ibid., 679. Shortly after Clark returned from the Pacific coast, Secretary of War Henry Dearborn appointed him "Agent of Indian Affairs to the Several Nations of Indians within the Territory of Louisiana excepting the Great and little Osages." Ibid., 109–10. At the time of the Atkinson-O'Fallon expedition Clark was superintendent of Indian affairs at St. Louis and was Benjamin O'Fallon's immediate superior.

attacked a few weeks later it could not prevent the capture of the new installation.[16] Other boats on the Mississippi were more formidable. They carried four- and six- pounder cannons and one hundred fighting men in addition to the oarsmen. Governor Ninian Edwards of Illinois Territory was a proponent of these large, armed river boats that he believed would be as much use to the nation's defenses as the gunboats patrolling the Great Lakes.[17] Col. Daniel Bissell, who was in charge of some of the river boats, agreed saying, "These kinds of boats, strike a great Terror on our Savage Enemies, as I am informed, in fact they are in my Opinion formidable machines of Defence."[18]

Even after the war, American officials remained wary of Great Britain's intentions. President James Monroe recommended "a few strong posts" high on the Mississippi River and near the boundary line between the United States and Canada.[19] Three forts were established on the upper Mississippi in 1816, but the cost was substantial. These forts, combined with support from posts farther east, eased Americans' fears about British meddling in that area and, for a time, forestalled serious troubles with the Indians.[20]

With these difficulties resolved, or at least under control, the focal point of the Americans' concern began to turn again to the upper Missouri country. While no battles had been fought there in the War of 1812, the conflict had significantly curtailed the fur trade. Indian hostility just prior to the war, and the belief that British agents were lurking nearby, convinced the Americans that trading was simply too hazardous. Thomas Forsyth, an experienced fur

---

16. Ibid., 762–63, 784–86.

17. Julius W. Pratt, "Fur Trade Strategy and the American Left Flank in the War of 1812," *American Historical Review* 40 (1935): 236; Carter, *Territorial Papers*, 16:289.

18. Quoted in Kate L. Gregg, "The War of 1812 on the Missouri Frontier," *Missouri Historical Review* 33 (1939): 188.

19. Benjamin Franklin Cooling, *The New American State Papers: Military Affairs*, 19 vols. (Wilmington, Del.: Scholarly Resources, Inc., 1979), 1:80.

20. Edgar B. Wesley, *Guarding the Frontier: A Study of Frontier Defense from 1815–1825* (Minneapolis: University of Minnesota Press, 1935), 136. Fort Edwards near Hamilton, Illinois, Fort Armstrong near Davenport, Iowa, Fort Crawford near Prairie du Chien, Wisconsin, and Fort Howard near Green Bay, Wisconsin, were founded in 1816. Francis Paul Prucha, *A Guide to the Military Posts of the United States* (Madison: State Historical Society of Wisconsin, 1964).

trader, described the trade during the War of 1812 in bleak terms. "After the war with Great Britain commenced our Indian trade almost ceased to exist, except where it was continued by some few hunters who got up among the Indians and would, in the spring season, bring down a few furs."[21] Even at the war's end, fur traders were not immediately ready to gamble on a renewed assault on the upper Missouri country, in part because no action had been taken on President Monroe's hint that forts might be established there. In 1815 the government attempted to reaffirm alliances with tribes along the Missouri, but this effort was limited to councils primarily with tribes from the lower Missouri River. Officials met with representatives from the Osage, Iowa, Kansa, Missouri River Sac and Fox, and several Lakota bands. Parties to these agreements promised to forget past hostilities and each tribe recognized the supremacy of the United States.[22]

Westerners in general had little faith in mere treaties. They felt more was needed to claim this enormous land and to make it safe for white citizens. William Clark concurred, and in May 1816, he called for added military protection in the West. As Wilkinson had done a decade earlier, Clark argued for the construction of a fort on the Platte River, but no action was taken.[23] Thomas L. McKenney, head of the Office of Indian Trade, discussed the future of government-owned trading posts or factories noting, "It may not be out of place to remark that I have contemplated an establishment at Council Bluffs on the Missouri and the River St. Peters, near St. Anthony's Falls, in the erection of which the policy of the Government would be promoted."[24] Although the army was not mentioned in the letter, it was understood that trading establishments at these distant points would require military protection.

While forts and government factories would have been a great help in extending American interests, it was difficult to convince a

---

21. Hiram M. Chittenden, *The American Fur Trade of the Far West*, 3 vols. (New York: Francis P. Harper, 1902), 2:921.

22. Charles J. Kappler, ed., *Indian Affairs, Laws and Treaties*, 3 vols. (Washington, D.C.: GPO, 1904), 2:80–86.

23. Wesley, *Guarding the Frontier*, 144.

24. Carter, *Territorial Papers*, 15:363. The government's trading posts were abolished in 1822. Richard Peters, ed., *Public Statutes at Large of the United States of America* (Boston: Little Brown and Co., 1861), 3:682.

budget-minded Congress to appropriate funds for outposts so far from any white settlements. Instead, Congress passed legislation aimed at excluding foreigners from the trade. In April 1816 a law was enacted specifying that only American citizens could be given licenses to trade with Indians. The military was authorized to arrest and seize the trade goods of aliens found violating the act, but the law had little effect because the army did not have the manpower to enforce it.[25]

In October 1817 President Monroe appointed John C. Calhoun to be his secretary of war.[26] Calhoun was an advocate of military expansion along the northwestern frontier, and one of his first recommendations was to build forts at the Mandan villages and at the mouth of the Yellowstone River. Although the president agreed, no immediate action was taken. Calhoun continued to offer similar proposals until 1818, when he succeeded in gaining authorization for the plan.[27] Brig. Gen. Thomas A. Smith was ordered to send a detachment up the Missouri River, marking the beginning of the popularly but erroneously titled Yellowstone Expedition. Smith was in favor of the plan and envisioned military establishments at the mouths of the Platte and Yellowstone rivers and at the Mandan villages noting, "the latter will be absolutely necessary in the event of any opposition from the English traders."[28]

The principal contingent of the Yellowstone Expedition, consisting of the Sixth Infantry, started up the Missouri in 1819. The army gambled on using steamboats to transport the troops, but for the most part the relatively new craft failed and the men concluded their journey in keelboats. Secretary Calhoun realized that delays could

---

25. Peters, *Public Statutes at Large*, 3:332–33.

26. John C. Calhoun was the secretary of war from October 8, 1817, until March 7, 1825. James Barbour assumed the post after Calhoun.

27. W. Edwin Hemphill, ed., *The Papers of John C. Calhoun*, 20 vols. (Columbia: University of South Carolina Press, 1964), 2:194–95, 3:60–61; Walter Lowrie, ed., *American State Papers, Documents, Legislative and Executive of the Congress of the United States; Military Affairs*, 38 vols. (Washington, D.C.: Gales and Seaton, 1834), 2:33. The president's agreement is found in ibid., 69.

28. Carter, *Territorial Papers*, 15:394–95. President Monroe also gave the expedition his full support, opting for an installation at the Yellowstone River. "James Monroe, Message to Congress, Dec. 17, 1819," U.S. Congress, *Annals of the Congress of the United States, 16th Cong., 1st Sess.* (Washington, D.C.: Gales and Seaton, 1855).

hinder the expedition's progress and gave his approval for a post at the Council Bluffs if the army could not reach the upper river.[29] Despite the best efforts of the troops, the approach of winter forced them to stop at the bluffs, where they built a cantonment. During the winter scurvy decimated the ranks and in the spring a flood destroyed the garrison. A site on higher ground was selected and a new fort was built, which would become Fort Atkinson.[30]

The fort at the Council Bluffs provided a modicum of safety for the six companies having licenses to trade on the Missouri. Although the companies had been content to remain on the lower river, three had licenses permitting trade as high as the Lakotas and one included the Arikaras.[31] With companies organized and the military on the river, a resurgence of the fur trade seemed imminent, but the Panic of 1819 spread a financial paralysis over the nation. The depression was at its worst in Missouri in 1820 and 1821, and the financial situation would have to improve before entrepreneurs would again be willing to gamble on the trade. In reaction to the panic, Congress became even more financially conservative.

The secretary of war favored a continuation of the Yellowstone Expedition and tried to convince Congress it would not be very expensive. The expedition was harshly criticized by fiscal conservatives because of the cost overruns, as well as for the failure of the steamboat experiment and the tardiness of the contractor hired to supply the expedition. The debate over funding continued to the end of the session, but when it came time to vote, Congress decided enough public funds had been expended and the Yellowstone

29. Hemphill, *Papers of John C. Calhoun*, 3:633–34.

30. Fort Atkinson was one of the largest military bases at this time. The barracks quadrangle enclosed a parade ground approximately 440 feet square. Nearly 1,000 troops could be quartered there. Soldiers spent much of their time working a large farm to make the post almost self-supporting. Gayle F. Carlson, *Archeological Investigations at Fort Atkinson (24WN9), Washington County, Nebraska, 1956–1971* (Lincoln: Nebraska State Historical Society, 1979); Sally Ann Johnson, "The Sixth's Elysian Fields: Fort Atkinson at the Council Bluffs," *Nebraska History* 40 (1959): 1–38; Virgil Ney, *Fort on the Prairie: Fort Atkinson on the Council Bluff, 1819–1827* (Washington, D.C.: Command Publications, 1978). The post was officially named Fort Atkinson on January 5, 1821. Carter, *Territorial Papers*, 15:688.

31. Elbert B. Smith, *Magnificent Missourian: The Life of Thomas Hart Benton* (Philadelphia: J. B. Lippincott Co., 1958), 1.

Expedition stalled at the Bluffs.[32] Proponents for still deeper reductions throughout the army began to argue their case in 1820. Their successful effort led to a bill signed by President Monroe on March 2, 1821, reducing the army by about 40 percent or approximately 6,100 men. The act also provided for some reorganization within the army and two military departments, Eastern and Western, were created.[33] Gen. Henry Atkinson was placed in command of the Right Wing of the Western Department, consisting of the region north of the Arkansas River and west of the Mississippi.[34]

Atkinson was not in favor of permanent posts on the upper Missouri. Instead, he recommended that every year about 400 men should ascend the river from Fort Atkinson to remind the Indians of the military might of the U.S. Army. The general felt the yearly expedition "would make as favorable impression on the minds of the Indians as if they [the troops] were to be at once located above." He pointed out that yearly expeditions would not require a special appropriation because the soldiers could provide their own rations from the surpluses produced on the large farm at Fort Atkinson. The army also had a sufficient number of keelboats at the fort to carry the men up the river. Atkinson repeated his recommendation again in 1821 and the secretary of war approved.[35]

There was some opposition to the plan within the military. Col. Henry Leavenworth, commanding Fort Atkinson at the time of the Atkinson-O'Fallon expedition, was not convinced an expedition would produce the desired results.[36] He doubted the Indians would

---

32. Dorothy B. Dorsey, "The Panic of 1819 in Missouri," *Missouri Historical Review* 29 (1935): 79–91; *Annals of the Congress, 16th Cong., 1st Sess.*, 545.

33. Peters, *Public Statutes at Large*, 3:615. The Western Department included everything west of a line roughly from the tip of Florida to the west tip of Lake Superior, including all of Tennessee and Kentucky. Bvt. Maj. Gen. Edmund P. Gaines was given the command with headquarters at Louisville, Kentucky. Wesley, *Guarding the Frontier*, 113.

34. Edmund P. Gaines to Henry Atkinson, July 26, 1823, Orders and Special Orders Issued by Bvt. Brig. Gen. H. Atkinson, June 1819–Jan. 1826, vol. 1:203–4, entry 5588, Records of Named Departments, Records of the U. S. Army Continental Commands, 1821–1920, Record Group 393, National Archives and Records Administration (NARA) (hereafter cited as Orders by Atkinson, RG 393).

35. Carter, *Territorial Papers*, 15:672–75, 720–21, 730–31.

36. Leavenworth assumed command of the Sixth Infantry stationed at Fort Atkinson on January 4, 1822. Order No. 2, Jan. 4, 1822, 205–6, Orders Issued, Sixth Infantry, Records of the Infantry, 1815–1942, Records of United States Regular Army

gain any respect for the army if soldiers merely visited their camps and then went "away again like wild geese." Visiting the Indians would not offer long term protection for American traders, nor would the troops be likely to encounter and evict foreign traders. Finally, Leavenworth concluded that the fur trade was generally not profitable and wondered if it was worth protecting in any case.[37]

The opposite view was taken by Thomas Hart Benton, the powerful senator from Missouri, whose constituents included many of the nation's foremost fur traders. In Benton's mind the fur trade was much more than a commercial enterprise. He saw the traders and trappers as the vanguards of westward expansion, and it was the senator's dream to see the United States extend its boundaries across the Rocky Mountains, evict the British from Oregon, and open a direct trade to the Orient by way of the Missouri and Columbia rivers. In 1819 Benton proposed the incorporation of an American fur company to operate in the Columbia basin and drive out the North West Company and Hudson's Bay Company. Benton found a strong ally in Representative John Floyd of Virginia, who was chairman of a committee to investigate the possibility of planting American colonies in the Columbia River valley. The expansionist-minded committee determined there should be colonies, and a bill was introduced in 1821 for that purpose, but Congress did not act on the proposal. Undaunted, Floyd reintroduced the bill the next year and it gained momentum when New England congressmen representing whalers and sea otter hunters realized the advantages of a safe and well-supplied American colony on the West Coast. Opponents argued that the bill's passage and implementation would force a confrontation with Britain over control of Oregon and possibly lead to another war. When the bill came to a vote in the House of Representatives, it was defeated by a substantial majority.[38]

It seems some of the expansion-minded officials were unaware of the problems involved in getting to Oregon or simply chose to

---

Mobile Units, 1821–1942, Record Group 391, NARA (hereafter cited as Orders Issued, Sixth Infantry, RG 391).

37. Henry Leavenworth to Thomas Jesup, Mar. 4, 1822, Consolidated Correspondence File, 1794–1890, Records of the Office of Quartermaster General, Record Group 92, NARA (hereafter cited as Consolidated Correspondence File, RG 92).

38. Smith, *Magnificent Missourian*, 80.

ignore them. Congressman Floyd remarked on the ease of taking wagons up the Missouri to the Three Forks, then west across the mountains and down the Columbia to the Pacific. It would have been a Herculean effort at best, but Floyd's claim that it could be done in less than six weeks was clearly a deception.[39] Secretary of State John Quincy Adams seems to have been unaware of the Rocky Mountains and the Great Basin when he described the branches of the Columbia that "almost mingle their sources with those of the Missouri, Platte and Arkansas."[40] Senator Benton also minimized the difficulties and dangers facing cross-country travelers, but the arguments he offered to support his expansionist goals were much more imaginative. In Benton's mind the fur traders and trappers were the original pioneers in the far west and their activities could be seen as an act of Christian benevolence. In a lengthy speech before the Senate, Benton explained that once the traders and trappers exterminated the wild game, Indians would have to support themselves by farming. This tangled logic was aimed at the many white Americans who believed it was their duty to "civilize" and Christianize the Indians, and one of the more important steps in this "civilizing" process was to change them from nomadic hunters to sedentary farmers. Benton was more rational when he argued that the fur trade was on a par with other major commercial ventures in the United States and deserved the same level of protection by the government. He lamented the cut in funds for the Yellowstone Expedition, and warned if a fort were not established in the Mandan country there would continue to be a gaping hole in the nation's defense.[41]

At Benton's request the Senate Committee on Indian Affairs sought information about conditions in the Missouri River country. A lengthy and detailed account was submitted by Joshua Pilcher, an experienced trader and a partner and field representative of the Missouri Fur Company. His opinions and the information he provided were biased in favor of traders and were exactly what Benton wanted to

39. James S. Hutchins, "'Dear Hook': Letters from Bennet Riley, Alphonso Wetmore, and Reuben Holmes, 1822–1833," *Bulletin of the Missouri Historical Society* 36 (1980): 208.

40. Samuel Flagg Bemis, *John Quincy Adams and the Foundations of American Foreign Policy* (New York: Alfred A. Knopf, 1956), 484–515.

41. *Annals of the Congress, 17th Cong., 1st Sess.*, 424.

although it was also of long standing. In 1807 they attacked Chouteau's company. Then in the mid-teens they killed another trader, and in 1820 robbed trading houses in the vicinity of the Great Bend. Early in 1823 they attacked the Missouri Fur Company's Fort Recovery and killed two traders.[52] Agent O'Fallon tallied the damages claimed by all the companies during the first half of 1823. He found that twenty-six Americans had been killed and an estimated $20,000 worth of supplies and furs had been lost in attacks by the Arikara and other Plains tribes.[53]

An attack by the Arikaras during the summer of 1823 greatly influenced Congress to fund the Atkinson-O'Fallon expedition. At the end of May, William Ashley and about ninety trappers arrived at the Arikara village. The initial meeting was cordial and Ashley bought several horses. The whites made camp on the riverbank, but that night two or three men slipped into the village. What these men did there was never explained, but their actions so angered the Arikaras that one white man was killed in the village and near dawn the Indians opened fire on the rest of Ashley's party. At least twelve trappers were killed before the whites were able to weigh anchor and retreat downriver.[54]

Ashley sent an express to Fort Atkinson with a demand that the army punish the Arikaras. Col. Henry Leavenworth, commanding the Sixth Infantry at the fort, agreed to mount a punitive expedition. On June 22 six companies of the Sixth Infantry, totalling about 230 men, embarked on board several keelboats. Many of these men would participate in the Atkinson-O'Fallon expedition two years later. They were joined by about 120 employees of the fur companies and 400 to 500 Lakota allies, who went along in the hope of plundering the Arikaras.[55] This latter group included Fire Heart

52. "Pilcher's Answers to Questions," *American State Papers: Indian Affairs*, 2:453–57.

53. *American State Papers: Military Affairs*, 2:579–80.

54. Among the better accounts of the Arikara war is Dale L. Morgan, *Jedediah Smith and the Opening of the West* (Lincoln: University of Nebraska Press, 1953). While the incident in the village may have been the immediate cause of the attack, Arikara animosity resulted from a complex series of real and imagined grievances. One cause of the trouble stemmed from whites who supplied guns and ammunition to enemies of the Arikara. Nichols, "The Arikara Indians and the Missouri River Trade," 86.

accused Tilton of "having two strings in his bow" for what appeared to be dealings on both sides of the border.[48] Despite appearances it became evident that Tilton and McKenzie were operating as loyal Americans.

A renewed American effort to open trade on the upper Missouri began as the effects of the Panic of 1819 began to fade, but the fur companies would be faced by increasingly hostile tribes. The Missouri Fur Company regrouped and Joshua Pilcher became the head of field operations. In 1822 he sent thirty trapper-traders under Michael Immell and Robert Jones into the Blackfeet country. It was a dangerous gamble, but there was the potential for enormous profits in this relatively untapped area. Although the Blackfeet had been instrumental in forcing Manuel Lisa's retreat a few years earlier, their first contact with Immell and Jones was congenial. Despite the show of friendship, the trappers' suspicions were not allayed, and they decided to return to their fort at the mouth of the Bighorn River. On the way they were ambushed by three or four hundred Blackfeet. Seven whites, including the two leaders, were killed and all of the furs from the winter's hunt, as well as guns, traps, and other gear valued at $15,000, were lost.[49] William Gordon, who survived, implicated the British traders whom he thought had "most probably" encouraged the Blackfeet to carry out the attack.[50]

The Blackfeet also besieged Andrew Henry's base camp near present Great Falls, Montana. Henry and his partner, William Henry Ashley, brought approximately 200 men to the area in 1822 to trap beaver. Within a relatively short time the Blackfeet killed four whites, while the rest fled for their lives.[51]

There were equally devastating losses at the hands of the Arikaras. Unlike the Blackfeet, Arikara aggression was not as predictable,

---

47. Ray H. Mattison, "Kenneth McKenzie," *Mountain Men and the Fur Trade*, 2:217–24. The Columbia Fur Company was also known as the Tilton and McKinsey Company.

48. O'Fallon to Atkinson, July 17, 1824, Benjamin O'Fallon Letterbook, 1823–1829, Beinecke Library of Rare Books and Manuscripts, Yale University Library, New Haven, Connecticut.

49. "Pilcher's Answers to Questions," *American State Papers: Indian Affairs*, 2:453–57.

50. *American State Papers: Military Affairs*, 2:583–84.

51. Chittenden, *American Fur Trade of the Far West*, 1:264.

Benton and his supporters were undoubtedly sincere in their beliefs concerning British meddling, but their fears had little, if any, basis in fact. Contact between white traders from the north and the Mandans and neighboring Hidatsas certainly had a long history, and by the 1790s the Hudson's Bay Company and the North West Company were in regular contact with the tribes. The Americans who began to enter the upper Missouri region after the return of Lewis and Clark proved to be ruthless competitors. In 1809 a Hudson's Bay Company trader complained of having been forced to give up his best trade goods in exchange for wolf pelts of the worst quality after Manuel Lisa's men had traded for the good furs. The situation did not improve. Three years later the Canadians conceded they had a very poor trade because Lisa's people paid a higher price than the Canadians could afford. As early as 1811 a Hudson's Bay Company factor recommended discontinuing the Mandan trade because it was no longer profitable. The number of parties from Canada going to the Missouri declined over the next few years and may have stopped near the end of 1818. When the Americans returned in force in the early 1820s, they found no traders from the north.[45]

British trade east of the Missouri River was also in retreat. Joseph Renville, an American citizen, nearly had a monopoly on the trade from his post on the shores of Lake Traverse. He advertised himself as an independent trader, but all of his business ties were with Hudson's Bay until 1822, when he allied himself with the Columbia Fur Company.[46] Most of the employees and the partners were expatriates from Canada, including Kenneth McKenzie, the true head of the company. The president of Columbia was William P. Tilton, a U.S. citizen in whose name the trade licenses were issued, thus complying with the letter of the law. It is not surprising that many Americans were convinced the Columbia Company was only a front for traders in Canada.[47] The acerbic Benjamin O'Fallon

45. Wood and Thiessen, *Early Fur Trade on the Northern Plains*, 18, 32–34, 39, table 1. Other historians have come to similar conclusions. John A. Alwin, "Pelts, Provisions, and Perceptions: The Hudson's Bay Company Mandan Indian Trade, 1795–1812," *Montana The Magazine of Western History* 29 (1979): 16–27.

46. John C. Jackson, "Old Traders in a New Corporation: The Hudson's Bay Company Retreats North in 1822," *North Dakota History* 55 (1988): 27.

hear. Pilcher's testimony, based upon first-hand experience, reflected the situation in the latter part of 1823. He described several attacks on trading parties by Indians and suggested British traders were at the root of the trouble. He felt military protection was the only solution to the predicament, and offered his advice concerning the deployment of soldiers. It was his opinion that a large post was unnecessary at the Council Bluffs. Instead, a small garrison should be maintained there, as well as one in the vicinity of the Great Bend of the Missouri and one at the Mandan villages. He recommended the principal fort be near the mouth of the Yellowstone River. Pilcher maintained that these forts were "so indispensably necessary for the preservation of the fur trade on the upper Missouri, that, without them, the most valuable part of that trade may be considered as lost to American citizens, and surrendered to the British."[42]

Agent Benjamin O'Fallon added to the anti-British sentiment when he wrote a scathing report for Atkinson, blaming the Hudson's Bay Company for encouraging Indians to attack U.S. citizens in the upper Missouri.[43] O'Fallon's commentary found its way into the hands of the British ambassador, who passed it on to an official of the Hudson's Bay Company. The firm denied any culpability, but did admit it knew of an attack on the Missouri Fur Company party in which seven lives had been lost. The company also admitted purchasing beaver skins carrying the Missouri company's markings from a Blackfeet party at Edmonton House, the Hudson's Bay Company post on the Saskatchewan River. Hudson's Bay executives promised to reimburse the Missouri company despite a considerable financial loss, and ordered their clerks to refuse to make similar purchases in the future. The British, who also complained about the perfidy of the Blackfeet, attempted to show the charges leveled against them by O'Fallon were false, but western Americans continued to see Canadians in league with Blackfeet hiding behind every tree, ready to pounce on Americans and their property.[44]

42. "Pilcher's Answers to Questions," *American State Papers: Indian Affairs*, 2:455–57.

43. *American State Papers: Military Affairs*, 2:579–80.

44. Abraham P. Nasatir, "The International Significance of the Jones and Immell Massacre and the Aricara Outbreak of 1823," *Pacific Northwest Quarterly* 30 (1939): 77–108; Frederick Merk, *Fur Trade and Empire, George Simpson's Journal* (Cambridge: Harvard University Press, 1931), 4, 282.

that the Arikaras were the perpetrators. Experienced westerners were not surprised by these events, which they recognized as acts of revenge resulting from the losses the Arikaras had suffered during the army's attack on their village.[57] The Arikaras were still in a vengeful mood a decade later when George Catlin traveled up the Missouri. He noted, "They have recently sworn death and destruction to every white man who comes in their way; and there is no doubt, that they are ready to execute their threats."[58]

Early in 1824 there were disturbing reports of hostilities by the Tetons, who had been on friendly terms with the whites. Atkinson feared they might prevent traders from crossing their territory, thus halting travel on the river above the Great Bend.[59] Some years later Edwin Denig was trading with the Teton and discovered the genesis of the tribe's militant attitude. The Tetons who had been present during Leavenworth's attack on the Arikaras thought they were going to witness a show of U.S. military power. Instead, they saw some ineffective artillery fire and then what appeared to be a retreat by the soldiers. The Tetons concluded that the Americans were cowards. According to Denig, "The result of the expedition ruined the reputation of all whites in the eyes of the Indians."[60]

The losses suffered in 1823–24 forced most white Americans to abandon the upper Missouri and contributed to some permanent changes in the fur trade. Pilcher's company would never fully recover from its rout by the Blackfeet in 1822. Pilcher's men left the mountains and in the summer of 1824 even abandoned Cedar Fort near the Great Bend.[61] After the Arikara attack, Ashley avoided the tribe by sending his parties overland due west from the Great Bend of the Missouri to the Rocky Mountains. In the spring of

---

57. Morgan, *The West of William H. Ashley*, 73–76.

58. George Catlin, *Letters and Notes on the Manners, Customs, and Condition of the North American Indians*, 2 vols. (New York: Wiley and Putman, 1841), 1:204.

59. Atkinson to Winfield Scott, Mar. 30, 1824, quoted in Morgan, *The West of William H. Ashley*, 76.

60. Edwin Thompson Denig, *Five Indian Tribes of the Upper Missouri*, ed. John C. Ewers (Norman: University of Oklahoma Press, 1961), 57.

61. The Missouri Fur Company's fort established in 1821 was sometimes called Fort Recovery. Sunder, *Joshua Pilcher*, 29. These may have been the ruins Kearny noted in his diary on June 16, 1825.

and his band, who would meet the soldiers again in 1825 and sign a peace treaty.

When the brigade reached the village, Leavenworth placed cannons on the surrounding hills and shelled the town until the ammunition was nearly gone. Although the bombardment had little effect on the earthlodges, the Arikaras sued for peace. The negotiations proceeded slowly and the Indians took advantage of the armistice to slip away during the night and were out of sight when reveille was sounded in the morning. Leavenworth felt the Arikaras had been punished sufficiently and that a peace treaty had been effected. Rather than pursue the Indians, he ordered his troops to board their boats and return to Fort Atkinson. His Indian allies scattered, but not before taking a dozen of the army's horses and mules and a significant quantity of roasting ears from the Arikara cornfields. The fur traders, who did not think the Arikaras had suffered enough, set fire to the earthlodges. Leavenworth reported, "There is no doubt that they have been consumed to ashes. Nor is there any doubt but that they were set on fire by one M'Donald, a partner, and one Gordon, a clerk of the Missouri Fur Company." Angus McDonald would later admit to setting the fire in a letter to the *Washington Gazette*.[56]

Sporadic violence continued during the winter. One trader was killed in the doorway of the Columbia Fur Company post, and five men of B. Pratte and Company were killed on the Missouri near their post. When the first reports began to filter in, the identity of the attackers was uncertain, but after a time there was general agreement

---

55. Doane Robinson, "Official Correspondence Pertaining to the Leavenworth Expedition into South Dakota in 1823," *South Dakota Historical Collections* 1 (1902): 181–88; Dale L. Morgan, *The West of William H. Ashley* (Denver: Old West Publishing Co., 1964), 52–53.

56. Robinson, "Official Correspondence," 186–99; John E. Sunder, *Joshua Pilcher, Fur Trader and Indian Agent* (Norman: University of Oklahoma Press, 1968), 48, n.23. Agent Benjamin O'Fallon greatly overestimated the power of the army to intimidate the Arikara, but he was correct in his prediction that the Lakota would "get some plunder, prisoners &c. and the Villages will be burnt." Pilcher's orders are in O'Fallon to William Clark, Jan. 14, 1824, O'Fallon Letterbook.

At least one of the six-pounder cannon balls fired by Leavenworth's troops is purported to have turned up at Pipestone Quarry in Minnesota. It was used to break rocks in quarrying for Catlinite. Donald Dean Parker, ed., *The Recollections of Philander Prescott* (Lincoln: University of Nebraska Press, 1966), 139.

their land. Rich specifically cited the Arikara attack on Ashley as an example of this kind of retaliation. For good measure Rich blamed the British for instigating some of the trouble. Fortunately for Benton, Rich was unaware of a speech made in 1815 by the Omaha chief Big Elk. Big Elk considered trappers to be poachers and complained to William Clark about the whites who "kill those animals the great spirit gave us to subsist on. I wish to preserve these animals for food for my people."[68]

Senator Mahlon Dickerson, who had no love for the military, was also critical of Benton's bill. In attacking the provision for a fort, Dickerson reminded his colleagues of the cost overruns that had plagued the Yellowstone Expedition, noting that transportation costs alone exceeded a quarter of a million dollars. He then speculated on what it might cost to send troops twice that distance up the Missouri. He assured his fellow senators that once built, the price of maintaining a fort high on the upper river would be enormous. He then questioned the legality of building forts on land that belonged to Indians without first gaining their permission. Dickerson also brought up the hunting issue, declaring that the only purpose of the forts was to protect trappers from the Indians' revenge for the destruction of their means of livelihood.[69]

David Barton, Missouri's other senator, seemed to be joining ranks with Benton's opponents. Barton agreed with Dickerson that the recent troubles stemmed from whites trapping on Indian land. He believed illegal trapping must be stopped, and the only way to accomplish it was to have a strong military presence on the Missouri.[70] In the end Barton voted for the bill, but Missourians were not happy with his reasoning and the senator was soundly condemned in the press.[71]

Benton had many supporters among the westerners, who complained bitterly about the stance taken by Rich and his compatriots.

---

68. *Annals of the Congress, 18th Cong., 1st Sess.*, 896–97. Rich's comments also appeared in the *St. Louis Enquirer*, Jan. 27, 1824. Rich may have applied a liberal interpretation of the law. It did outlaw hunting, but may have been meant to apply only to Indian lands secured by treaty east of the Missouri. Peters, *Public Statutes at Large*, 2:139–46; Oglesby, *Manuel Lisa*, 158.

69. *Annals of the Congress, 18th Cong., 1st Sess.*, 449–62.

70. *St. Louis Enquirer*, May 10, 1824.

71. *Missouri Advocate*, June 17, 1825.

The editor of the *St. Louis Enquirer* remarked angrily that Congress first refused to protect citizens in the upper Missouri by limiting funds for the military and then proposed ways to deny trappers and hunters their livelihood.[72] Support for Benton's bill also came from within the government. Indian Agent Benjamin O'Fallon admitted that some settlers along the border did at times cross the line into Indian territory to hunt. O'Fallon minimized the impact of this kind of subsistence hunting and also pointed out that the Indians had never complained about it. He went on to say that intensive trapping on the upper Missouri was an entirely different situation because there were no white hunters on "lands to which any tribe or tribes of Indians have an *exclusive* claim." Instead, the area was "held in common like the high seas" and therefore there was no violation of the law. Finally, O'Fallon warned that if Americans were not allowed to trap, the upper Missouri country would fall into the hands of the Hudson's Bay Company and the Blackfeet and Assiniboin, whom he labeled as the company's "subsidiaries." O'Fallon also argued that the company had already derived a substantial profit in the upper Missouri country, which rightfully belonged to the Americans.[73]

Benton also tried to explain the issue of hunting and trapping, but his argument lacked O'Fallon's creative reasoning. Benton said when Meriwether Lewis was governor of the territory Lewis had approved trapping to prevent the furs from falling into British hands, and the trappers believed they still had lawful permission.[74] If Benton's explanation of fur hunting lacked his usual confident rhetoric, he more than made up for it by playing upon anti-British sentiment. Benton claimed British agents were telling Indians they both were

---

72. *St. Louis Enquirer*, Feb. 9, 1824. The *Louisville Public Advertiser* was another proponent of forts at the Mandan villages and at the mouth of the Yellowstone, claiming they were necessary to counteract British influence and to safeguard the Americans. The paper's editor concluded that "the wisdom and policy of this plan, will be acknowledged by every citizen of candor." *Missouri Intelligencer*, Dec. 9, 1823, quoting the *Louisville Public Advertiser*.

73. *St. Louis Enquirer*, Feb. 9, 1824. Earlier, O'Fallon expressed the opinion that hunting and trapping were acceptable in areas inhabited by tribes unfriendly to the U.S. and under presumed British influence. Hemphill, *Papers of John C. Calhoun*, 7:23.

74. *Annals of the Congress, 18th Cong., 1st Sess.*, 438.

children of the Great Spirit. Americans, however, "grew from the scum of the great waters when it was troubled by the Wicked Spirit, and the froth was driven into the woods by a strong East wind."[75] Whether or not the British told the story or whether or not the Indians believed it was of no concern to Benton. He was counting on support from stoutly ethnocentric Americans, who were certain to be offended.

When William Ashley's plan to ascend the Missouri became known early in 1822, Gen. Henry Atkinson passed the information along to Secretary of War Calhoun. Atkinson did not mention trapping, but said the company intended to send one hundred traders to the Yellowstone country and did not foresee any problems with such an expedition. Accordingly, Calhoun gave Ashley and his partner, Andrew Henry, permission to trade with Indians on the upper Missouri.[76] William Clark, now superintendent of Indian affairs at St. Louis, also wrote to Calhoun in August 1822 to voice his approval because he believed Ashley would "cultivate the friendship" of the tribes and thereby "strengthen the confidence those Tribes have in our government."[77] Although the act banning trapping was passed three months prior to Clark's letter, he seems to have been unaware of it or interpreted it differently than did Congressman Rich and his supporters. There can be no doubt Clark knew the real purpose of Ashley's expedition long before it was made public in mid-April, when the *St. Louis Enquirer* specifically reported "the object of this company is to trap and hunt." The account was copied in a Washington paper in late May, which Rich may have seen.[78]

Ashley and others like him continued to ascend the river even after it was known they were primarily interested in trapping. Colonel Leavenworth wrote to Atkinson late in 1823 complaining that "this

---

75. Ibid., 433. Lavender attributed nearly identical words to Tenskwatawa, the Shawnee prophet, uttered prior to the War of 1812. David Lavender, *The Fist in the Wilderness* (reprint, Lincoln: University of Nebraska Press, Bison Book, 1998), 95.

76. Hemphill, *Papers of John C. Calhoun*, 6:633; 7:28.

77. Clark to Calhoun, Aug. 9, 1822, Letters Received by the Office of the Secretary of War (Registered Series), 1801–70 (National Archives Microfilm Publication M221, roll 95), Records of the Office of the Secretary of War, Record Group 107, NARA (hereafter cited as Letters Received, M221, and the roll number).

78. *St. Louis Enquirer*, Apr. 13, 1822. A similar article appeared in the *Daily National Intelligencer*, May 27, 1822.

trapping business is carried on under a license to *trade*." He pointed out that the practice was not only "a palpable and plain violation of the letter, spirit and meaning of the law," but was also "a violation of the rights of a poor miserable set of savages whose only means of support is thus destroyed contrary to the benign policy of our Government." Leavenworth warned if trapping were not stopped, the Indians would increase attacks on the trappers at a great loss of life. He recommended establishing a fort with a "respectable force" on the upper river, but when he spoke of this plan he seemed more concerned about curbing the liquor trade than stopping whites from hunting, or even evicting the British.[79]

A ban on the importation of "ardent spirits" was imposed in May 1822, and the army was given the difficult task of enforcement with the right to search traders' goods, even if there was only a suspicion that contraband was being carried. Flagrant violations of the law continued for years because the army did not have the manpower to enforce it. Just one of many infractions took place in the fall of 1836, when John Cabanné successfully smuggled 363 gallons of whiskey, valued in St. Louis at $454.69, to his post a few miles south of the Council Bluffs. A year later there were 1,050 gallons of alcohol, worth $1,260, on hand at the post.[80] Apparently the army was exempt from the law because General Atkinson gave liberal quantities of liquor to tribal leaders who signed the treaties of 1825.

Early in 1824 military commanders and personnel in the Indian office received sternly worded orders to enforce the restrictions on hunting and trapping. The order covered people already in Indian country, as well as those who might enter in the future "no matter

79. Leavenworth to Atkinson, Nov. 22, 1823, Letters Received by the Office of the Adjutant General (Main Series), 1822–60 (National Archives Microfilm Publication M567, roll 7), Records of the Adjutant General's Office, Record Group 94, NARA (hereafter cited as Letters Received, M567, and the roll number). In his letter, Leavenworth accused the Missouri Fur Company of circumventing the law by importing wine. Angus McDonald, a partner in the company, freely admitted using wine, pointing out that the law banned only ardent spirits. McDonald to Lucien Fontenelle, Mar. 21, 1825, Marshall McDonald Papers, William R. Perkins Library, Duke University, Durham, North Carolina.

80. Peters, *Public Statutes at Large*, 3:682–83; Hemphill, *Papers of John C. Calhoun*, 7:128; Bernard Pratt and Company Ledger Invoice Blotter, Microfilm Book Z, 71, 319, American Fur Company Papers, Missouri Historical Society, St. Louis, Missouri.

by what means," a clear reference to licensed traders.[81] Atkinson was among the first to issue a directive to his officers, but the wording of his order was ambiguous. He mentioned citizens crossing the boundary into Indian land and then ordered a halt to hunting in the "contiguous sections of Country." The wording may have been simply a matter of poor composition, but it could have been interpreted to apply only to settlers who occasionally crossed the line for a few miles, while excluding the big trapping parties like Ashley's in the very heart of Indian country.[82]

Three months later, in late April, anti-trapping orders were issued to Indian agents. Secretary Calhoun said the delay resulted from his hope that Congress would provide more precise guidelines on the matter, but it had failed to do so. Nonetheless, the secretary ordered his agents to forbid hunting and trapping by private individuals, as well as by those who were licensed to trade.[83] In spite of these clear regulations, trapping continued unabated because neither the Office of Indian Affairs nor the army had the capability to enforce the anti-trapping law.

Benton began to realize his bill for a military expedition to the upper Missouri and a fort near the mouth of the Yellowstone River was in jeopardy. To salvage what he could, Benton jettisoned the fort and agreed to a single military expedition up the Missouri. The appropriation in the original bill was reduced by about 30 percent, which probably turned some nays to yeas in Congress. This compromise bill allocated $10,000 to cover the cost of the military expedition and a similar amount for gifts to the Indians and other expenses incurred in negotiating treaties of peace and friendship (see Appendix C). The bill was approved near the end of the congressional session and President James Monroe signed it into law on May 25, 1824.[84]

---

81. Scott, Order No. 18, Mar. 2, 1824, vol. 1:244, Orders by Atkinson, RG 393.

82. Atkinson, Order No. 4, Jan. 28, 1824, vol. 1:263, ibid.

83. Calhoun to superintendents of Indian affairs, Apr. 20, 1824, entry 5589, Orders and Special Orders Received from the War Department, Records of Named Departments, Records of U.S. Army Continental Commands, Record Group 393, NARA (hereafter cited as Orders and Special Orders of the War Department, RG 393).

84. Peters, *Public Statutes at Large*, 4:35–36.

BENJAMIN O'FALLON *(1793–1842), c. 1833. The Upper Missouri agent responsible for the tribes above the mouth of the Platte River, O'Fallon was appointed special commissioner in 1825 to represent, with General Atkinson, the president at the signing of fifteen treaties of peace with tribes within his jurisdiction.*

NATIONAL PORTRAIT GALLERY, SMITHSONIAN INSTITUTION, WASHINGTON, D.C.

HENRY ATKINSON *(1782–1842). A proponent of frequent military expeditions up the Missouri River, Brig. Gen. Henry Atkinson led such an expedition in 1824–26.*

PHOTOGRAPH OF THE PAINTING, NEBRASKA STATE HISTORICAL SOCIETY, LINCOLN

Benton's constituents in Missouri complimented him for his determined efforts to secure another fort, but predicted dire consequences would come from the lack of a military base on the upper river. The *Missouri Advocate* editorialized: "Let the blood of our countrymen spilt in the forest rest on those of our household who opposed so strenuously the Missouri expedition, and the establishment of another military post at the mouth of the Yellowstone."[85]

Once the Benton bill was passed, the responsibility for its execution fell to General Atkinson. As commander of the Right Wing of the Western Department of the Army his authority included the Missouri River country. In addition, the president appointed him, along with Indian Agent Benjamin O'Fallon, to be special commissioners with authority to negotiate the treaties with the Indians met during the expedition.[86] In this dual capacity the general faced a multitude of challenges. It was a chance to again command troops in the field and was also an ideal opportunity to prove the superiority of the man-powered paddle wheel boats he had designed (see Appendix B).

Atkinson began work in St. Louis in the fall of 1824 to get the expedition underway. Four conventional keelboats were equipped with wheel mechanisms and christened the *Beaver*, *Mink*, *Muskrat*, and *Raccoon*.[87] On September 17 Maj. Stephen Watts Kearny's command boarded the wheel boats for the trip to Fort Atkinson. It would be the first extensive test of the boats' capabilities, but after a few days on the river it seemed they might fail. The machinery did not work properly, and a mechanic was summoned from St. Louis to make adjustments and repairs. The corrections improved the boats' performance, but occasionally the soldiers were forced to trudge along the bank with a long tow rope or cordelle over their shoulders, pulling the boats up the river. It was this kind of drudgery that Atkinson hoped to avoid with his wheel boat design.

---

85. *Missouri Advocate*, June 17, 1825.

86. The appointments were made on June 5, 1824. Angus L. Langham, "Journal of the Commissioners under the Act of Congress Approved 25th May 1824 to Enable the President to hold Treaties," entry 106, Journals of Commissions, 1824–39, Records of the Bureau of Indian Affairs, Record Group 75, NARA (hereafter cited as Journal of the Commissioners).

87. Contemporary writers did not agree on the spelling of some of the boats' names. Some preferred *Buffaloe*, *Rackoon*, and *Muscrat*. The original spelling has been retained in the transcription of the journals.

In addition to the boats' machinery, Kearny had to contend with other problems common to moving a large number of troops. His command consisted of ten officers and about 156 non-commissioned officers, musicians, and privates of the First Infantry. There were also about sixty recruits destined for the Sixth Infantry at the fort, plus a few civilians.[88] Soldiers, especially the recruits, did not always adjust to army life on the river and desertion was common. A few escaped, but most were recaptured, including one who found army life so unendurable he committed suicide. One soldier died of natural causes, while an accident claimed the life of a third. Other events were not as sorrowful. One of the laundresses accompanying the detachment gave birth to a girl on September 24. Kearny's detachment arrived at Fort Atkinson on November 2, 1824, and was quartered with the Sixth Infantry.[89]

During the winter the officers at Fort Atkinson turned their attention to one of the recurring problems of military life. The number of troops at the fort had declined as men completed their enlistments and replacements had to be found. The recruits who came up the river with Kearny helped fill the ranks, but Atkinson estimated that three hundred more recruits would be needed for the First and Sixth Infantry. He recommended they come from western states because "men recruited in eastern cities are not well calculated for the frontier service. Very many of them desert us on the march."[90] To fill the ranks officers were sent on recruiting duty and by spring the Sixth was again near full strength, with ten companies totalling about 480 men. Additions to Kearny's command also brought it nearly to full strength.[91]

---

88. Fort Atkinson Post Returns, 1821–27, Returns from U.S. Military Posts (National Archives Microfilm Publication M617, roll 49), Records of the Adjutant General's Office, Record Group 94, NARA (hereafter cited as Fort Atkinson Post Returns, M617, and the roll number). It is difficult to determine the exact number of recruits. Kearny's journal puts the number at sixty, but the Fort Atkinson records suggest it was closer to forty-five.

89. In a letter to Atkinson, Leavenworth promised to have barracks at Fort Atkinson ready for the men of the expedition. Orderly Book 35, Sixth Infantry, in Addison E. Sheldon, "Records of Fort Atkinson" 1819–1827, 6 vols., Nebraska State Historical Society, Lincoln, 6:162. These volumes contain selected copies of the Sixth Infantry's orderly books transcribed by Sheldon in 1915–16. Most of the original records are now in the National Archives, but a few dating from 1825 were found only among Sheldon's transcriptions.

90. Atkinson to Jacob Brown, Jan. 5, 1824, Letters Received, M567, roll 19.

While the recruiting campaign was underway, Atkinson ordered his carpenters to install paddle wheel machinery in the remaining boats of the flotilla, the *Elk*, *Buffalo*, and *White Bear*.[92] These boats, along with the *Raccoon*, would carry four companies of the Sixth Infantry to the upper Missouri. The *Mink* was the command or flag boat, which carried Atkinson and members of his staff. The crew was from the Sixth's Company E. Another wheel boat, the *Otter*, had been rigged in St. Louis and did not leave until late October. It carried about sixty recruits under the command of Capt. Ephriam Shaler, but ice on the Missouri forced them into temporary winter quarters near the mouth of the Kansas River. In the spring the *Otter* reached Fort Atkinson.[93] The *Otter*, *Beaver*, and *Muskrat* would transport Kearny's four companies of the First Infantry to the upper

91. At the end of October 1824, there were only 415 soldiers in the Sixth Infantry. Recruiting brought the regiment to nearly full strength of about 480 men by the following April. In the 1820s an army company at full strength consisted of a captain, two lieutenants, two sergeants, three corporals, forty privates, and two musicians. A fifty-man company was rarely maintained because troops would be absent due to illness, furlough, desertion, and the numerous details requiring troops to be away from their company. These absences usually ran from 5 to 10 percent, but were occasionally greater. For example, approximately 15 percent of Major Kearny's command was absent at any given time while it was at Fort Atkinson during the winter of 1824–25. These temporary losses were expected and accepted. A more serious problem was the loss resulting from soldiers who left the army after fulfilling their enlistments and the difficulty in replacing them with new enlistees. Despite the isolated location of Fort Atkinson, a few civilians did enlist there. Most of the recruits were found by officers who were sent on recruiting duty in the East. Muster Rolls of the Sixth Infantry, 1824–25, Muster Rolls of Regular Army Organizations, Records of the Adjutant General's Office, Record Group 94, NARA (hereafter cited as Muster Rolls, Sixth Infantry, RG 94).

92. Atkinson to Charles Nourse, Dec. 16, 1824, Letters Received, M567, roll 9; Orderly Book 25, Sheldon, "Records of Fort Atkinson," 5:64.

93. Order issued Sept. 29, 1824, vol. 1:254, Orders by Atkinson, RG 393; Atkinson to adjutant general, Sept. 29, 1824, 80–81, entry 5568, Letters Sent, Headquarters Western Department, 1821–37, Records of Named Departments, Records of U.S. Army Continental Commands, Record Group 393, NARA (hereafter cited as Letters Sent, Western Department, RG 393). The Washington D.C. *Daily National Intelligencer*, Oct. 22, 1824, reported sixty-three recruits.

Ephriam Shalor (or Shayler) joined the army in 1812 and had risen to the rank of captain in the Sixth Infantry by 1819. He retired in 1827. Francis B. Heitman, *Historical Register and Dictionary of the United States Army,* 2 vols. (Washington, D.C.: GPO, 1903), 1:878; File S-65/2, Court Martial Case Files, Records of the Office of the Judge Advocate General (Army), Record Group 153, NARA (hereafter cited as Court Martial case files, RG 153).

river.[94] One civilian boat, the *Lafayette*, accompanied the brigade part of the way, but was not officially attached to the expedition. This conventional keelboat belonged to the Fort Atkinson post sutler and was carrying goods to restock the traders' stores on the Missouri.[95]

Tons of supplies were required for the expedition. The war department had prescribed a minimum daily ration for each soldier of twelve ounces of bacon, twelve ounces of hard bread, four ounces of whiskey, and four ounces of beans.[96] Certainly other food was provided to augment this meager diet, but if only the minimum amount were taken, twenty-six tons of bacon, twenty-six tons of hard bread, over seven tons of beans, and 1,930 gallons of whiskey would be required for 476 soldiers on a 130-day expedition. The food and whiskey alone totalled sixty-two tons. Nearly five tons of clothing, arms, and ammunition would be required for the troops, while gifts for the Indians added at least three tons. Cannons, cook stoves, tents, and spare parts were some of the other items necessary for the expedition that would have brought the total to well over seventy tons.

On May 16, 1825, eight wheel boats sailed away from Fort Atkinson on a journey that would last just over four months. The brigade consisted of 476 soldiers, including Company A of the Sixth Infantry, a temporary cavalry unit that followed the boats until they reached the vicinity of the Great Bend, where the horses were returned to the fort and most of the men joined the boats.[97]

---

94. Orderly Book 28, Sheldon, "Records of Fort Atkinson," 5:1. In early June 1824 five conventional keelboats were sent to Fort Atkinson to make up a deficiency that Atkinson felt would hamper troop movements in case of an emergency. H. Atkinson, Order issued June 5, 1824, vol. 1:254, Orders by Atkinson, RG 393.

95. Near the end of October 1824 sutler James Kennerly mentioned the *Lafayette* arriving at Fort Atkinson and unloading cargo at the store. The captain of the boat was named Buche. Edgar B. Wesley, ed., "Diary of James Kennerly," *Missouri Historical Society Collections* 6 (1928): 76.

96. Johnson, "The Sixth's Elysian Fields," 10.

97. U.S. Congress, *Expedition up the Missouri, 19th Cong., 1st Sess.*, H. Doc. 117, Serial 136 (Washington, D.C.: Gales and Seaton, 1826), 6–11. This report was also published by Roger L. Nichols, ed., "General Henry Atkinson's Report of the Yellowstone Expedition of 1825," *Nebraska History* 44 (1963): 70.

Fort Atkinson post returns indicate the total strength of the expedition to be about 465 men. The difference is probably the result of the return of a few men between the time the post returns were compiled at the end of April and the departure of the command on May 16, 1825. Fort Atkinson Post Returns, M617, roll 49.

For the soldiers on the boats a working day was divided into three nearly equal parts. At dawn the men boarded and traveled until mid-morning, when they halted for breakfast. After an hour they returned to the river until early afternoon, when they stopped again for a one-hour dinner break. The final third of a day's trip often lasted until twilight, when the boats were docked, camp was pitched, and the evening meal prepared.[98] Occasionally a mechanical failure or a windstorm made travel unsafe and provided a break in the routine. The treaty-signing ceremonies, which often lasted several days, also provided a welcome relief from the monotony and hard work of an average day.

Accidents and other mishaps were infrequent. After only a few days on the river one soldier was accidentally cut with an ax and sent back to the fort. Occasionally men went on shore to hunt and were lost or left behind. All were rescued, but some were "starving and worn out" before they were found. On the return to the fort one boat hit a snag that ripped gaping holes in the hull. Fortunately the boat sank in shallow water and was saved.

There were women on the expedition, but the journalists rarely mentioned them. A Yankton girl, who had been a prisoner of the Oto, was being returned to her tribe. Atkinson also noted that a six-month-old child on the *Buffalo* had died. It is reasonable to assume that the baby was with its mother, but there is not the slightest clue to her identity.

Twelve treaties would be signed during the expedition, and all contained nearly identical wording.[99] An introductory paragraph summarized the treaty as an affirmation of peace and friendship and mentioned the past cordial relations between the particular tribe and the government. The introduction for the Arikara treaty was rewritten to reflect the recent hostilities. This treaty was "to put an end to an unprovoked hostility on the part of the Arikara" and to "restore harmony." The Mandans and the Hidatsas were chided less severely, but their treaty contained the accusation that "acts of hostility have been committed by some restless men" of the tribe.

After the introduction each treaty had six identical articles. In the first the tribe acknowledged that they lived within the United

98. Orderly Book 26, Sheldon, "Records of Fort Atkinson," 5:9.

99. All of the treaties can be found in Kappler, *Laws and Treaties*, 2:225–46.

States and conceded the government's supremacy and its right to regulate all trade. In the second article the United States promised to protect the tribe and "to extend to them, from time to time, such benefits and acts of kindness as may be convenient." Article three stated that trade could be conducted only at specified places and with U.S. citizens. In article four the tribe promised to protect these traders and any other authorized personnel in their country and to capture foreigners and turn them over to American authorities. Article five dealt with criminal activity. The Indians promised to hand over anyone from the tribe suspected of harming a white so the suspect could be tried in U.S. courts. If a white harmed an Indian, he would also be tried in U.S. courts. Furthermore, the tribal leaders would return any property stolen from a white, and the thief would be turned over to the closest Indian agent. In article six the tribe agreed not to supply guns or ammunition to tribes hostile to the United States.

The treaties were signed by the two commissioners, representing the President of the United States. Indian signatories included at least ten leaders from each tribe or band, and at least ten whites signed as witnesses. For the most part, the witnesses were military officers, but interpreters and other civilians might also be asked to sign the document. In due time the treaties were returned to Washington, D.C., where they were signed by the president on February 6, 1826, with the advice and consent of the Senate.

Atkinson was determined to demonstrate the army's ability to punish those Indians who did not obey the letter of the agreements. A newspaper reporter in Franklin, Missouri, interviewed the general and provided a terse summary of this facet of the expedition: "We understand that a respectable military force will accompany the expedition, which will impress upon the minds of the Indians the idea of our power and ability to punish them."[100] After each treaty signing Atkinson had his troops put on a full dress military parade, followed by a demonstration of the brigade's weapons. In addition to rifles and at least one six-pounder cannon, the troops also fired "thundering bombs, fire balls" and signal rockets "to

---

100. *Missouri Intelligencer*, Apr. 5, 1825, quoted in Donald McKay Frost, *Notes on General Atkinson, the Overland Trail and South Pass*, (Barre, Mass.: Barre Gazette, 1960), 126.

create an effect on the minds of the Indians."[101] In his journal Atkinson concluded, "The Indians were struck with great awe at the display." The precision drills, the fine uniforms, and the weaponry must have presented a resplendent sight, but as later events would prove, the performance did little to impress the Indians with the army's ability to punish them.

The commissioners at these treaty councils, like at most others, were frustrated by the lack of a single leader in each tribe who had authority to negotiate. The commissioners thought in terms of presidents and kings who could speak for the whole society, but among Indian tribes such a figurehead was extremely rare. In a largely unworkable attempt to vest authority in an individual, the commissioners appointed a chief or sometimes two. At the Ponca council, Young Smoke and one other Indian were named chiefs by the whites and given large medallions embossed with a likeness of the President of the United States. The commissioners also "made" soldiers or assistant chiefs, who were given smaller medals.[102] In the eyes of the tribe these were only honorary degrees and probably had little effect on the individual's status.

At the conclusion of the ceremonies surrounding the treaty signing, the commissioners distributed presents, including guns, gun-

---

101. On August 1, 1824, Colonel Henry Leavenworth, commander of Fort Atkinson, wrote to Atkinson with his recommendations for ordnance for the expedition:

> Presuming that the ordnance that may be taken up the river will be used principally to create an effect upon the minds of Indians & as the transportation will be arduous—I would respectfully suggest that one six pounder—one 5 1/2 inch Howitzer & one 10 inch mortar & 300 rounds for each should be taken. This would also be sufficient for any emergency. It is well known that the effect of the fire works upon the minds of the savages is great. It would therefore probably be well to have a good supply of compositions for the construction of thundering bombs, fire balls, carcasses & also a good supply of signal Rockets—500 hand grenades would be useful not only in this expedition but at this post or perhaps a less quantity may answer. . . . If you should think it advisable to take a 10 inch mortar it would be necessary that it be sent up as we have none here.

Orderly Book 35, Sheldon, "Records of Fort Atkinson," 6:161–62.

102. Atkinson was unable to purchase the medals in time and had to borrow them from the superintendent of Indian affairs. Atkinson to Calhoun, Feb. 16, 1825, Letters Received by the Office of Indian Affairs, 1824–81 (National Archives Microfilm Publication M234, roll 429), Records of the Bureau of Indian Affairs, Record Group 75, NARA (hereafter cited as Letters Received, M234, and the roll number).

powder, lead, chief's coats, strouding, blankets, knives, tobacco, and whiskey by the glass, bottle, or barrel. Nearly three tons of gifts for the Indians were purchased from the American Fur Company.[103]

The last treaty was signed on August 4 with a band of the Crow tribe then visiting the Mandans. The commissioners still had hopes of meeting the Blackfeet or the Assiniboin, so the expedition continued up the Missouri past the Yellowstone River, but the two tribes were still far away. By this time supplies for the soldiers were running low; on August 24 near present Poplar, Montana, Atkinson issued the order to turn the boats around and begin a dash for home.

While the expedition was in progress, the issue of a fort on the upper Missouri continued to stalk Atkinson. In mid-July Gen. Jacob Brown, commander of the army, wrote giving Atkinson discretionary authority to establish a fort at a site he might select.[104] The letter would not have reached Atkinson until near the end of the expedition, but it probably made little difference. Atkinson had never expressed wholehearted support for an upriver post and his experience on the expedition did nothing to change his mind.

After arriving at Fort Atkinson it seems the commissioners had a homecoming celebration. One purchase charged to the expedition's allocation was forty-five pounds of cheese, six kegs of crackers, five gallons of cherry bounce, and eighteen wine glasses (see Appendix C).

Atkinson and O'Fallon stayed at the fort for just over two weeks before boarding the wheel boat *Antelope* for the trip to St. Louis. They arrived at the city on October 20, where their return was celebrated at a banquet attended by most of the town's elite.[105] Kearny and his men remained behind at the fort. Because the barracks were full, Kearny's troops went downstream about six miles to the vicinity of Lisa's old post and built winter quarters christened Cantonment Barbour. Nearby was a harbor, where the boats

---

103. Voucher 1, Atkinson-O'Fallon Commission Accounts, 9534/1824–25, Records of the Accounting Officers of the Department of the Treasury, Record Group 217, NARA (hereafter cited as Commission Accounts, RG 217). See Appendix C.

104. Brown to Atkinson, July 21, 1825, Letters Sent by the Office of the Adjutant General (Main Series), 1800–90 (National Archives Microfilm Publication M565, roll 7), Records of the Adjutant General's Office, Record Group 94, NARA (hereafter cited as Letters Sent, M565, and the roll number).

105. *Missouri Advocate*, Oct. 29, 1825.

were moored for the winter.[106] On May 2, 1826, the First Infantry contingent sailed down the Missouri bound for Belle Fontaine.

After the conclusion of the expedition Atkinson submitted a report of his observations on the upper Missouri. The threat of British intrusions into the area had been a major factor in the expedition's authorization, and the general discussed this point carefully:

> Notwithstanding the many rumors that the Northwest traders are holding intercourse and exercising an injurious influence over the Indians on the Missouri, no such fact appears to exist, nor is it believed that any of their traders have been across to the Missouri below Milk River for several years. . . . If the British have traded and trapped within our limits East of the Rocky Mountains latterly, it has been above the Falls of the Missouri, among the Blackfeet Indians, which we understand has [been], and probably is now, the case. They can have no possible interest in coming to the Missouri lower than the Milk River, to trade, as the Indians below that point have little or nothing to barter but Buffalo robes, an article not trafficked in by them. . . . It is, moreover, believed, and the fact is not doubted, that none of the Indians residing on the Missouri River visit the Northwest establishments on Red River.[107]

Although not everyone agreed entirely, most people accepted Atkinson's appraisal.[108] Even Joshua Pilcher, who had once complained so bitterly about the British, reversed his stance and wrote a letter to the secretary of war corroborating Atkinson's appraisal. Pilcher had visited trading posts north of the Columbia River and found no evidence the British were inciting the Indians against U.S. trappers and, presumably, were not trapping in American territory. Perhaps Pilcher's comments were viewed with some caution because he had attempted to find employment with the Hudson's

---

106. MacRee, Order issued Oct. 7, 1825, vol. 1:312, Orders by Atkinson, RG 393.

107. U.S. Congress, *Expedition up the Missouri*, 6–11. Atkinson expressed similar conclusions in a letter to the commander-in-chief of the army. Lowrie, *American State Papers: Indian Affairs*, 2:655–57.

108. In 1829 Jedediah Smith, head of the fur trapping company of Smith, Jackson, and Sublette, complained to the secretary of war that the British were still trapping and trading for beaver above the Milk River and warned that unless they were stopped, the supply would be soon exhausted. Cooling, *New American State Papers: Military Affairs*, 1:160.

Bay Company, but he assured the secretary he had no ax to grind and had retired from the trade.[109]

Military leaders wholeheartedly accepted Atkinson's appraisal, as well as his assurances that the tribes in the upper Missouri country, with the exception of the Blackfeet, were now friends of the Americans. As a result General Brown put to rest further consideration of new forts in the far west. He judged the garrisons already in existence adequate to protect American interests until "the march of civilization advances upon" these western outposts. If hostilities should occur in the meantime, Brown suggested a "command of well trained mounted infantry, with a few pieces of light or flying artillery, to disperse any force of savages which might be collected to oppose them."[110]

There was no need for the mounted infantry because the upper Missouri remained relatively peaceful for some time. At least there were no conflicts to match those in 1822 and 1823, although it was not long before war clouds began to gather again. When George Catlin toured the Missouri in 1832, traders told him the Arikaras had sworn to kill every white person they could find, and a year later the tribe was blamed for the death of three whites. The tribe's downfall did not come at the hands of the military or the traders, however, but from disease and increasingly fierce attacks by their Indian enemies. Late in 1833 the Arikaras abandoned their village and moved north into the shadow of the Mandan villages for protection. By this time neither the Arikaras nor their hosts were sufficiently strong to merit serious consideration by the whites.[111]

The Blackfeet were accused of killing thirteen whites by 1833. They would escape white pressure because, as General Brown put it, they were so far distant from "the march of civilization." Traders did get a foothold in Blackfeet country in 1832, but the tribe's

---

109. Ibid., 1:155. In 1829 Pilcher offered to be a front for the Hudson's Bay Company and lead one of its trapping parties into American territory at the headwaters of the Missouri River. The head of the company refused the offer because it would be unethical. Sunder, *Joshua Pilcher*, 40–41.

110. Cooling, *New American State Papers: Military Affairs*, 1:96. William H. Ashley recommended a mobile force of no less than 500 light cavalry. Ibid., 1:142.

111. Catlin, *Letters and Notes*, 1:204; Maximilian, Prince of Wied, *Travels in the Interior of North America*, 3 vols. (Cleveland: Arthur H. Clark Co., 1905), 1:336.

reputation for hostility prevailed for many more years. It was not until 1855 that tribal leaders signed a peace treaty with the United States.[112]

In the years following the Atkinson-O'Fallon expedition the problems in the upper Missouri began to be resolved not by armed force, but by political and economic changes. The number of trappers passing up the river dwindled rapidly as they opted for the easier route up the Platte River and through South Pass to streams in the Rocky Mountains. The emerging American Fur Company and a few struggling competitors began opening permanent trading posts at key points along the Missouri. These posts, and the increased demand by whites for buffalo robes, gave the Plains tribes a medium of exchange and a more dependable source of trade goods.[113] These factors tended to eliminate some of the jealousy and suspicion that had caused so much trouble in the past.

---

112. Maximilian, *Travels in the Interior of North America*, 2:96; Ewers, *The Blackfeet*, 60, 215.

113. Paul Chrisler Phillips, *The Fur Trade*, 2 vols. (Norman: University of Oklahoma Press, 1961), 2:416–17. The Columbia Fur Company focused on the Missouri River and had an annual gross income of between $150,000 and $200,000 during 1825, 1826, and 1827. Approximately one-half came from buffalo robes. In 1827 the company succumbed and became the Upper Missouri Outfit, a division of the American Fur Company.

EDITORIAL PROCEDURE AND ACKNOWLEDGMENTS

THE ORIGINAL JOURNALS of Henry Atkinson and Stephen Watts Kearny are in the archives of the Missouri Historical Society, St. Louis, Missouri. Transcribing the journals was not particularly difficult. Both men were well educated and were generally able to express their thoughts clearly and concisely. Atkinson was the better journalist, was usually careful to use proper grammar, and seemed mindful of his journal's overall appearance. This care, and his peculiar habit of referring to himself in the third person, might suggest he had thoughts of publishing the journal. Whatever his intentions, the use of the third person has led scholars to speculate that the author was someone other than the general.[1] Experts at the Federal Bureau of Investigation analyzed the handwriting of the diary and of documents known to have been written by Atkinson and concluded he was the author.[2]

Kearny gave less attention to details of grammar and syntax. He was often satisfied with penning either a series of phrases separated by dashes or one exceedingly long, complex sentence. His journal seems more hastily written and the penmanship less neat. When Kearny and Atkinson were traveling together in 1825 Kearny often penned similar entries, however, Kearny's diary is not a mere

1. Reid and Gannon, editors of the first published journal, thought the author was one of Atkinson's junior officers. Russell Reid and Clell G. Gannon, eds., "Journal of the Atkinson-O'Fallon Expedition," *North Dakota Historical Quarterly* 4 (1929): 5. Dale L. Morgan speculated the author might have been Atkinson's aide-de-camp, Samuel McRee. Morgan, *The West of William H. Ashley*, 297, n.252.

2. Federal Bureau of Investigation, Washington, D.C., to James S. Hutchins, FBI File no. 95–227302, Lab. no. 81206072.

copy. He frequently gives additional information and even when describing the same event, he provides another viewpoint.

The transcriptions presented here contain some changes from the original journals, but the changes have been kept to a minimum and were made only for the reader's convenience. For example, both men, especially Kearny, used commas excessively and for no apparent reason. Most of them have been deleted. Dashes were also frequent and often unnecessary. Some were used in place of punctuation and have been retained, but many others were extraneous and have been removed. Both authors used capital letters erratically, but the only change we have made is to capitalize the first word of each sentence. Kearny underlined most proper nouns, but he was not consistent. Because the underlining is a distraction and serves no discernable purpose, it has been deleted.

Fortunately, neither journalist made extensive use of shorthand or abbreviations. Kearny might refer to the Sixth Infantry as the "6th" but the "th" usually resembled a quotation mark. The two letters have been retained throughout. Another common abbreviation was "genl" for general, with a raised and underlined last letter. The underline has been deleted and the final letter lowered. Occasionally the authors crossed out a word or phrase. Kearny tended to obliterate such changes completely, and they have been omitted without any reference to the resulting smudges. Atkinson's deletions were a single line. When any deletions could be deciphered, they are shown as follows: <*west*>. In a few cases a gap was left where it seems the author intended to insert data at some later time, but never did so. These gaps are indicated by [. . .]. The original spelling has been retained throughout, but because of poor penmanship or deterioration of the diaries, a few words were not clear and are indicated by [?]. A few words were completely illegible and are so noted in brackets. Finally, when an editorial problem could not be resolved in the text of the journal, a footnote was inserted.

Atkinson and other officers issued written orders concerning the management of the expedition. These orders are inserted with the diaries at the appropriate date but are clearly marked as not being part of either diary. While the journals are reproduced in their entirety, the accompanying orders contained material that was not relevant to the expeditions and such material is not included.

The Atkinson journal was first published in 1929, with editorial comments by Russell Reid and Clell G. Gannon. It was a significant contribution to Plains history and has served historians well, but in the intervening sixty-plus years, a vast quantity of supporting documentation has become available. For this reason it seemed appropriate to offer the journal again with the additional data. Kearny's diary of the 1824–26 expedition is published here for the first time.[3]

The editors of the journals owe a deep debt of gratitude to a number of people:

James E. Potter, Nebraska State Historical Society, for his editorial assistance.

Thomas D. Thiessen, U.S. National Park Service, who read an early draft of the manuscript and offered many helpful suggestions and leads to additional sources.

Donald G. Shomette, Upper Marlboro, Maryland, who unselfishly passed on data from his research on the early history of wheel boats.

Curt Peacock, Nebraska State Historical Society, for his drawings of the wheel boats.

The original journals of Henry Atkinson and Stephen Watts Kearny are in the archives of the Missouri Historical Society, St. Louis. We are especially indebted to Peter Michel, former director of Library and Archives at the Missouri Historical Society, for granting permission to publish them.

---

3. Reid and Gannon, "Journal of the Atkinson-O'Fallon Expedition," 5–56. In 1964 a portion of the Atkinson journal was published in Dale L. Morgan's scholarly work on William Ashley. Morgan included the entries in Atkinson's journal from August 14 through September 19, 1825. It was during this time that Ashley joined the expedition near the Yellowstone River and returned with the soldiers to Fort Atkinson. Because the journal was intended only to support the story of Ashley, Morgan chose to delete portions of the entries. A brief summary of the expedition was also published by William J. Peterson, "Up the Missouri with Atkinson," *Palimpsest* 12 (1931): 315–25. In 1969 Roger L. Nichols published a more detailed synopsis in which he described the boats and discussed their effectiveness. Roger L. Nichols, "Army Contributions to River Transportation, 1818–25," *Military Affairs* 33 (1965): 242–49. Kearny's 1820 journal of his trip from Fort Atkinson to Fort Snelling has been published by V. Mott Porter, ed., "Journal of Stephen Watts Kearny," *Missouri Historical Society Collections* 3 (1908): 8–29.

STEPHEN WATTS KEARNY *enlisted in the army and saw action in the War of 1812. After the 1824–25 expeditions up the Missouri River, he commanded other exploring missions and army posts in the West. Brigadier General Kearny led troops in the Mexican War and was the first American military governor of California. He died at Jefferson Barracks, St. Louis, on October 31, 1848.*

PHOTOGRAPH OF THE PAINTING, NEBRASKA STATE HISTORICAL SOCIETY

THE ATKINSON-KEARNY JOURNAL, 1824–26

In mid-September 1824 General Atkinson ordered Major Kearny to take a detachment of the First Infantry to Fort Atkinson at the Council Bluffs. The order marked the commencement of the preliminary stage of the Atkinson-O'Fallon expedition.

147
No. Head Qrs. West. Dept.
Special Order. St. Louis Sept. 16, 1824

The detachment of the first Regt. Infy and the Recruits of the 6th Regt. will proceed to Council Bluffs under the immediate orders of Major Kearny. Keel Boats Beaver, Muskrat, Rackoon and Mink comprise his transportation. He will commence his movement from this place as soon as the weather will permit. On his arrival at Belle Fontaine he will receive special instructions.

H. Atkinson
B. Gen. U.S. Army[1]

The next day Kearny and his troops departed for the Bluffs. For the next two years the major kept a journal during the time he was traveling. The first two pages of his diary contain notes added after the expedition was completed. Across the top of the first page is the heading, "Sept 17 -1824 to May 10 1826." Below this heading and at right angles to it is:

Price for plank & cartage	$5.75
wrenches, spikes & screws	— 11
Sockets for poles	— 11

1. Vol. 1:296, Orders by Atkinson, RG 393.

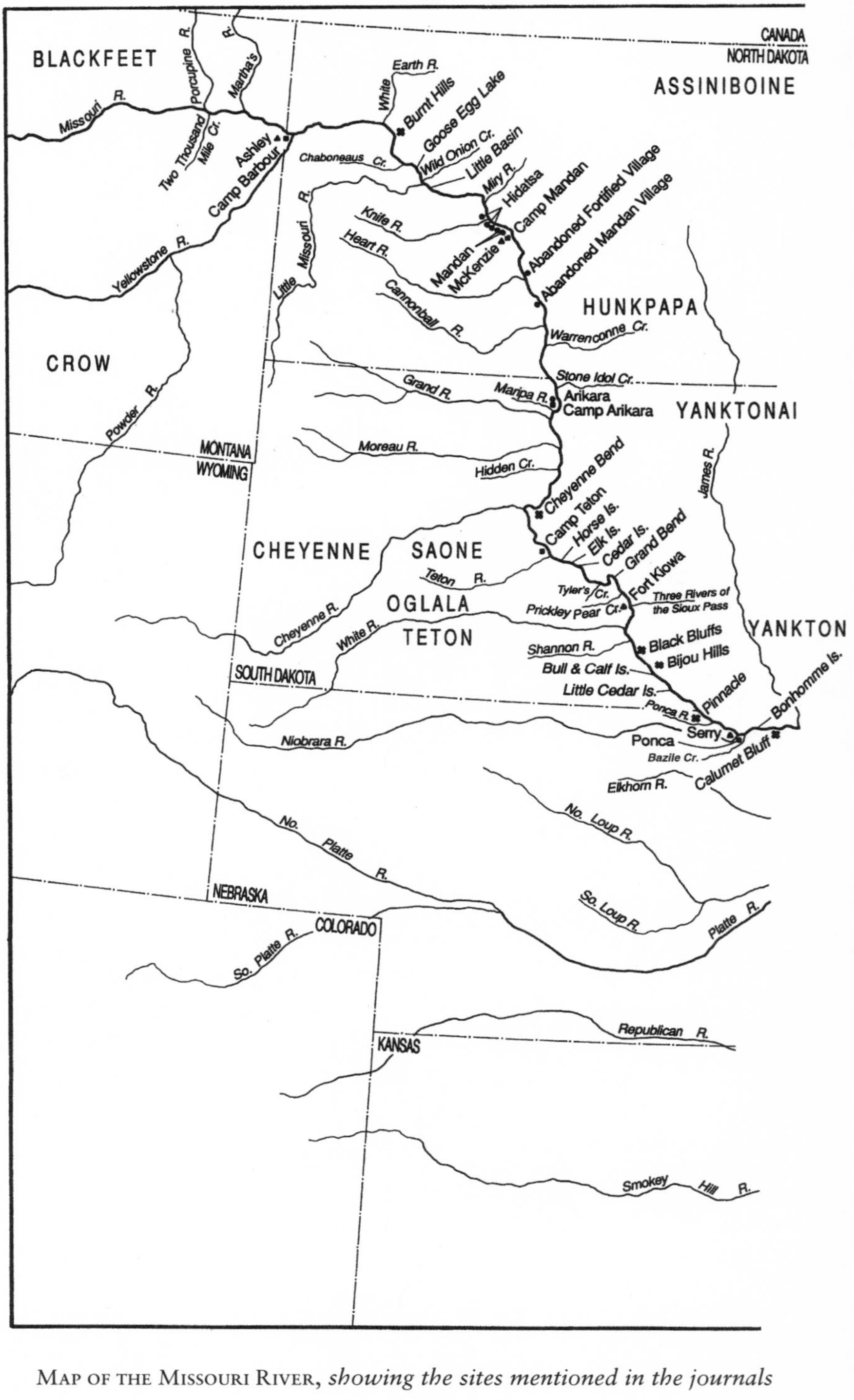

Map of the Missouri River, *showing the sites mentioned in the journals*

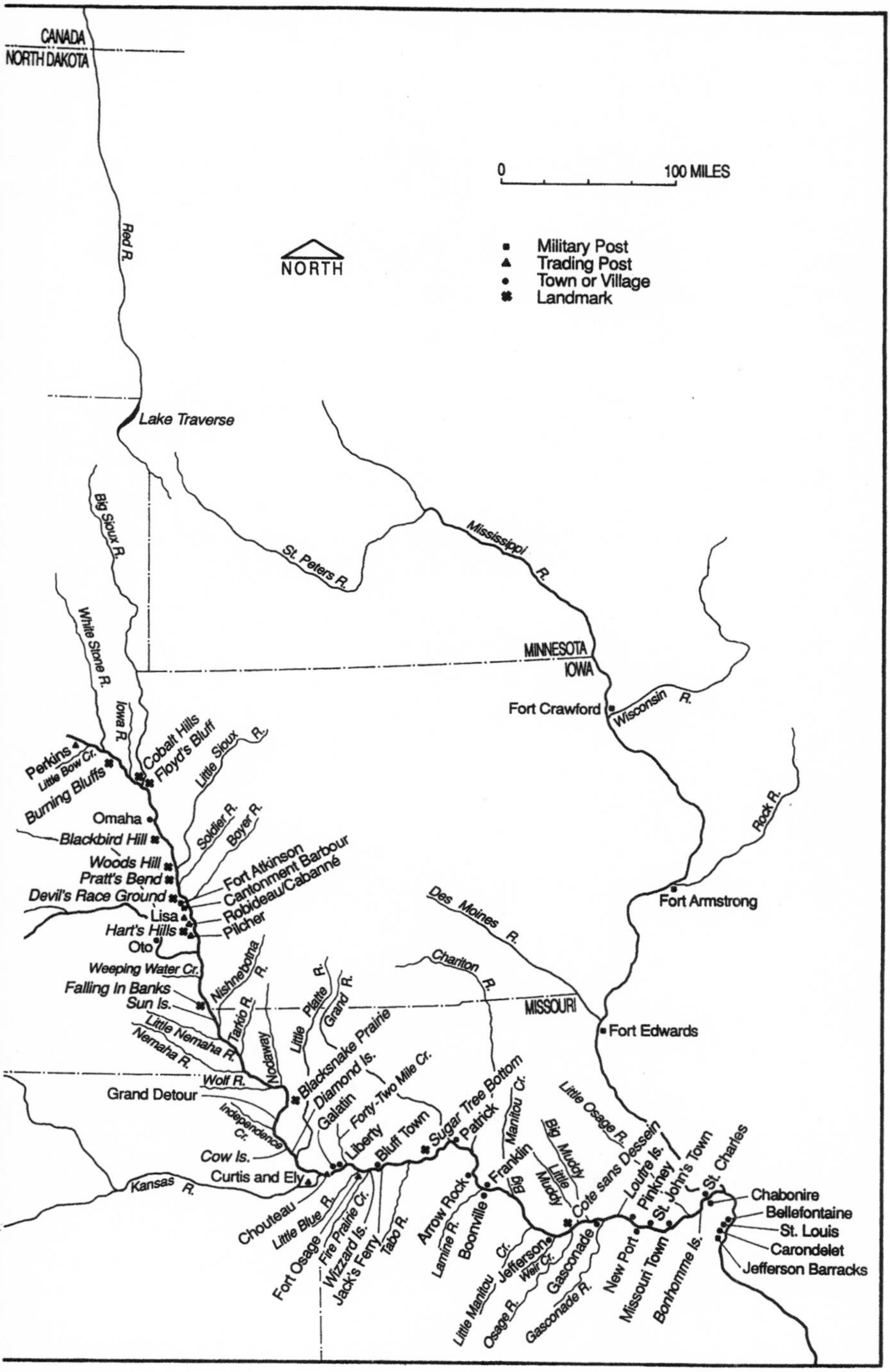
CANADA
NORTH DAKOTA
0
100 MILES
NORTH
Military Post
Trading Post
Town or Village
Landmark
Red R.
Lake Traverse
Big Sioux R.
St. Peters R.
Mississippi R.
White Stone R.
MINNESOTA
IOWA
Fort Crawford
Wisconsin R.
Iowa R.
Perkins
Little Bow Cr.
Burning Bluffs
Cobalt Hills
Floyd's Bluff
Little Sioux R.
Rock R.
Omaha
Blackbird Hill
Soldier R.
Boyer R.
Woods Hill
Pratt's Bend
Devil's Race Ground
Fort Atkinson
Cantonment Barbour
Robideau/Cabanné
Lisa
Hart's Hills
Pilcher
Oto
Fort Armstrong
Des Moines R.
Weeping Water Cr.
Nishnebotna R.
Charlton R.
Falling In Banks
Sun Is.
Tarkio R.
Little Platte R.
Grand R.
MISSOURI
Fort Edwards
Little Nemaha R.
Nemaha R.
Nodaway
Blacksnake Prairie
Wolf R.
Grand Detour
Diamond Is.
Gallatin
Forty-Two Mile Cr.
Sugar Tree Bottom
Independence Cr.
Liberty
Bluff Town
Patrick
Manitou Cr.
Little Osage R.
Cow Is.
Big Muddy
Little Muddy
Cote sans Dessein
Loutre Is.
St. John's Town
St. Charles
Curtis and Ely
Kansas R.
Franklin
Big
Chabonire
Bellefontaine
St. Louis
Carondelet
Jefferson Barracks
Arrow Rock
Pinkney
Chouteau
Little Blue R.
Fire Prairie Cr.
Fort Osage
Wizzard Is.
Jack's Ferry
Tabo R.
Lamine R.
Boonville
Little Manitou Cr.
Jefferson
Weir Cr.
Osage R.
Gasconade
Gasconade R.
New Port
Missouri Town
Bonhomme Is.

Nebraska State Historical Society, Lincoln

Pvt Kennerly[2] May 16 $22
from note 4.00 Aug 2
Sept & Octob.

Page two of the journal has a list of miles traveled per day and a running total:

16	17 = 353
6 = 22	9 = 362
8 = 30	16 = 378
13 = 43	14 = 392
15 = 58	20 = 412
18 = 76	18 = 430
16 = 92	20 = 450
16 = 108	16 = 466
16 = 124	20 = 486
17 = 141	8 1/2 = 494 1/2
16 = 157	14 1/2 = 509
15 = 172	16 = 525
15 = 187	17 = 542
15 = 202	20 = 562
13 = 215	17 = 579
20 = 235	1/2 = 579 1/2
6 = 241	8 1/2 = 588
18 = 259	10 = 598
19 = 278	4 = 602
16 = 294	8 = 620
16 = 310	16 = 636
12 = 322	16 = 652
14 = 336	16 = 668
	12 = 680

On page three Kearny commences his record of the trip to Fort Atkinson.

Friday Sept 17th 1824

Four Comps of the 1st Infy, A. B. H. & I commanded by Lieut Harney, Capt Spencer, Lieut Gwynn, & Capt Mason, having been

---

2. Although the handwriting seems legible, there is no record of a Private Kennerly. It is possible Kearny was referring to one of the Kennerlys who served as sutler for the Sixth Infantry.

assigned to Keel Boats Muskrat, Mink, Racoon & Beaver, the whole under direction of Major Kearny, left Saint Louis on the morning of the 17th destined for Council Bluff.[3] The shore was lined with spectators to witness our departure, most, if not all of whom take considerable interest in the success of the expedition, & as we are to attempt to navigate the Missouri differently from which it has hither to been, many remarks & observations were made respecting the feasibility of our plan. Genl. Atkinson is with us.

We ran up to within two miles of the mouth of the Missouri & halted for the night. 16 miles

Sept 18th

At day break, the bugle sounded to rise, & shortly after we started & reached the Missouri about sunrise & advanced up it to Belle Fontaine where we arrived at 1/2 past 9. 6 miles

---

3. Lt. William Selby Harney was the company commander of Light Company A, First Infantry. Fort Atkinson Post Returns, M617, roll 49. He was transferred to the First Infantry on December 21, 1822, and was promoted to captain on May 14, 1825. During the Mexican War he was court-martialed for disobeying orders, but President James Polk reversed the verdict. Harney earned the rank of brevet brigadier general for his service in Mexico. Later he was given command of the Department of the Platte, which encompassed some of the area he first saw during the 1824–25 expeditions. Harney died in 1889. Dumas Malone, ed., "William Selby Harney," *Dictionary of American Biography* (New York: Charles Scribner's Sons, 1943), 13:280; Richmond L. Clow, "General William S. Harney on the Northern Plains," *South Dakota History* 16 (1986): 229–48.

George C. Spencer joined the First Infantry in 1818, was promoted to captain on June 1, 1822, and resigned from the service in 1831. Heitman, *Historical Register*, 1:910. In 1824–25 he commanded Company B of the First Infantry. Fort Atkinson Post Returns, M617, roll 49.

Thomas Page Gwynn entered the First Infantry from the military academy in 1818. In 1824 he was promoted to first lieutenant. Heitman, *Historical Register*, 1:485. In 1824 Gwynn was moved from B Company of the First Infantry to command H Company. Fort Atkinson Post Returns, M617, roll 49.

Richard Barnes Mason enlisted in 1817 and in July 1819 was made a captain in the First Infantry. He served under Stephen Watts Kearny during the Mexican War. They occupied San Francisco in 1847 and when Kearny left, Mason became the acting governor of California until he was replaced by Bennet Riley. "Richard Barnes Mason," Malone, *Dictionary* 12:373. Mason commanded Company I of the First Infantry in 1824–25. Fort Atkinson Post Returns, M617, roll 49.

The *Missouri Advocate*, May 27, 1825, listed the officers who left Fort Atkinson for the upper river. All are mentioned in the journals except Henry R. Stewart, a West Point graduate who was a second lieutenant in the First Infantry. Heitman, *Historical Register*, 1:924.

We now commenced taking out part of the freight of the Boats, they already being deeply loaded, & we having considerable Pork, whiskey, company baggage &c. to put on board of them.

Sept 19. Sunday

Genl Atkinson left Belle Fontaine about 10 to meet us again to morrow. Our Boats being loaded, we got off at 2 P.M., & ran up to & halted before dark at Mr. Quarles Plantation.[4] 8 miles

About 60 Recruits for the 6th Infy were distributed at Belle Fontaine amongst the 4 Boats.

Sept 20th Monday

Started at 1/2 past 5 & 3 miles above stopped to breakfast, during which we altered the buckets of the Beaver, they dipping too deep in the water. Passed Chabonaire, & reached Saint Charles at 1/2 past 3. There met Genl. Atkinson & Mr. Benton (Senator from Missouri) & received from the former my final instructions.[5]

We were detained here 'til 6 P.M in repairing some Iron work for the Beaver & as constant complaints are made by the officers respecting the machinery of the Boats I determined upon taking along with me, Mr. MacDonald the Head Carpenter, who had been engaged in constructing it.[6] Halted 3 miles above Saint Charles. 13 miles

---

4. The *Missouri Republican*, Aug. 30, 1827, published a brief obituary of a Maj. Robert Quarles, a veteran of the Revolutionary War, who came to Missouri in 1819 and died on August 23, 1827. The rank of major must have been honorary because he is not listed in Heitman, *Historical Register*.

5. Edwin James visited Chabonire in 1819 and was told the village was named by the earliest settlers because several narrow beds of coal were found at the base of a high sandstone cliff near the river. Edwin James, *Account of an Expedition from Pittsburgh to the Rocky Mountains*, vol. 1 of *Early Western Travels, 1748–1846*, ed. Reuben Gold Thwaites (Cleveland: Arthur H. Clark Co, 1905), 125–26.

St. Charles was founded in 1769 by Louis Blanchette. It was a fur trading post, but by the 1820s had grown to a small town. Louis Houck, *A History of Missouri from the Earliest Explorations and Settlements until the Admission of the State into the Union*, 3 vols. (Chicago: R. R. Donnelley and Sons, 1908), 2:79.

In 1819 Edwin James commented, "within two or three years, many substantial brick buildings had been added, and several were now in progress: we could enumerate, however, only about one hundred houses. There are two brick kilns, a tanyard, and several stores." James, *Account of an Expedition*, 126.

Sept 21st Tuesday

Started at 1/2 past 5 & advanced 3 miles to breakfast. Repaired the slides of the Mink. Met with a strong current. Passed what we consider to be Dr Littlejohns grave on the Beach. Stopped at the foot of Bonhomme Island for dinner. After which when again underway; running up on the <*left*> right bank of the river, found current very strong. Put out the cordell. On a falling in bank, a large tree inclined over very much & threatened the destruction of our boat to the considerable alarm of some on board. Halted 2 miles below Lewis ferry, having made 15 miles[7]

Sept 22. Wednesday

Got underway shortly after 5. Passed the Little Osage River. Sent the skiff for a firkin of butter to Mr. Pitmans at Lewis Ferry. Stopt at 12 at Missouri Town (9 miles) & took in 19 barrels Pork for the command. Got off again at 1 P.M. & continued 'til 6. Passed by a small settlement called St Johns Town, & halted a few miles above on the right bank, having made 18 miles[8]
This day saw several flocks of pigeons, & had a strong favorable wind.

Sept 23d Thursday

Started at 1/2 past 5, & with a great deal of difficulty made one mile by 9 o'clock. A very strong current against us & the sand bar

---

6. Gregg McDanel was the head carpenter. He had worked for Atkinson on experimental wheel boats in 1823. Atkinson to McDanel, Aug. 12, 1823, Commission Accounts, 3020/1824, RG 217.

7. The grave of U.S. Army Asst. Surg. Samuel H. Littlejohn would have been about eight miles south of St. Charles on the right bank of the Missouri River. He died on September 8, 1824, while on his way to Fort Atkinson. Atkinson to Charles Nourse, Oct. 20, 1824, Letters Received, M567, roll 9. Lewis Ferry was at or very near the Little Osage River.

8. Missouri Town was probably the "flourishing American settlement" mentioned by Dr. John Gale in 1818. Roger L. Nichols, *The Missouri Expedition 1818–1820: The Journal of Surgeon John Gale with Related Documents* (Norman: University of Oklahoma Press, 1969), 10.

St. Johns Town, or La Charette, was a French outpost founded about 1796. It had been swept away by the Missouri by 1900. John Bradbury, *Travels in the Interior of America*, vol. 8 of *Early Western Travels, 1748–1846*, ed. Reuben Gold Thwaites (Cleveland: Arthur H. Clark Co., 1904), 42, n.15.

difficult to cross. Proceeded at 10, passed by New Port, a small place on the right bank, & stopt at dark having made 16 miles[9] The Rackoon this morning was in some danger of being lost in consequence of her men on the cordell, not hearing the Command given them from the Boat. Stubbs and McBride of the Recruits deserted from the Muskrat.[10]

Sept 24. Friday

Started at 1/2 past 5, soon after which it commenced raining. Made 4 miles by 8 o'clock & stopt, to breakfast, on the right bank. Passed Pinkney, a small Town on the Left, after which met with much difficulty in stemming strong currents & getting on Sand Bars. The Beaver swung twice this afternoon. Hamondine fell over board but saved himself by swimming! Mrs Hill, one of the Camp women, was delivered of a daughter.[11] Was not able to reach shore 'til an hour after dark, at which time we had made 16 miles Allison one of the Recruits deserted to day from the Muscrat. Very stormy day but wind favorable.[12]

---

9. New Port may be the "few poor cabins" mentioned by Paul Wilhelm in 1823. Paul Wilhelm, *Travels in North America*, ed. Savoie Lottinville, trans. W. Robert Nitske (Norman: University of Oklahoma Press, 1973), 215.

10. Desertion was a common and serious problem among recruits who may have expected more of army life than cordelling a boat up the Missouri. Only a month earlier Colonel Leavenworth, commander at Fort Atkinson, issued a lengthy order in an attempt of curb the practice. Leavenworth said he felt deserters should be executed. Leavenworth, Order issued Aug. 28, 1824, 212–13, Orders Issued, Sixth Infantry, RG 391.

Westley Stubbs began his second enlistment in 1824, but after his desertion in September he disappears from army records. Presumably he was successful in escaping from the military. Register of Enlistments in the U.S. Army, 1789–1914 (National Archives Microfilm Publication M233, roll 18), Records of the Adjutant General's Office, Record Group 94, NARA (hereafter cited as Register of Enlistments, M233, and the roll number). William McBride enlisted in 1824 and also disappears. Ibid.

11. Pinkney, or Pinckney, was founded in 1819. Harold L. Conrad, ed., *Encyclopedia of the History of Missouri*, 6 vols. (New York: Southern History Co., 1901), 5:141. Lancelotte John Hamondine concluded one five-year enlistment when he reenlisted in August 1824 and was assigned to Company I, First Infantry. Register of Enlistments, M233, rolls 15, 18. Mrs. Hill was probably an enlisted man's wife, who went along as a laundress for one of the companies.

12. Joseph Allison enlisted in the Sixth Infantry in May 1824. He deserted in August, in September, and again in November, but was quickly captured each time. Although he enlisted for five years, he was discharged after only seventeen

Sept 25th Saturday

The Muskrat & Mink lay on a Sand bar all night & were not able to get off 'til near 8 this morning. The other two Boats lay at the <*head of*> Loutre Island. We all started about 9. It again commenced raining, the wind blowing from the N. W — ahead. Passed the Gasconade & halted about 4 miles above it having made, 16 miles[13] Campbell, of the Recruits, deserted this morning from the Beaver.[14] Mr. O'Fallon, Indian agent from the Bluffs, met us this afternoon at the Gasconade.

Sept 26th Sunday

Started at 1/2 past 5. Run up 3 miles to breakfast. Stopt to dinner at 1 P.M opposite to Big Muddy, after which passed Little Muddy & encamped on the Left bank having made 18 miles

Sept 27th Monday

Started about 1/2 past 5. Breakfasted opposite to Cote Sans Dessein. Passed the Osage river & a little after sun down halted at the Town of Jefferson, at the mouth of Weir creek. This morning the Comy Lieut Day went ahead to procure some fresh beef.[15] He joined

---

months. Allison enlisted again in 1826, only to desert again. He enlisted for the third time in 1828 and deserted a year later, which seems to have been the end of his military career. Register of Enlistments, M233, roll 18.

13. In 1819 Loutre or Otter Island was about nine miles long and one mile wide. Several families lived there and the settlement dated to about 1798. James, *Account of an Expedition*, 129, 134.

Paul Wilhelm noted the settlement of Gasconade, where "a few water mills make their somewhat rare appearances in the state." Wilhelm, *Travels in North America*, 224.

14. Thomas Campbell enlisted in the Sixth Infantry on May 20, 1824. Since there is no further military record for him, it is likely he successfully escaped the military. Register of Enlistments, M233, roll 18.

15. Edwin James called Cote sans Dessein "an isolated round-topped hill." In 1819 a community there consisted of about thirty French families, a tavern, store, and smith shop. James, *Account of an Expedition*, 137, 140. By 1823 a number of Americans had settled in the vicinity. Wilhelm, *Travels in North America*, 232, 237.

Jefferson struggled to survive, although it had been designated the capital of Missouri in 1821. Two years later it was described as "a so-called town, consisting of three wretched cabins." Wilhelm, *Travels in North America*, 240. By 1826 it was the home of only thirty-one families. Conrad, *Encyclopedia*, 3:127.

William Day of the First Infantry became a first lieutenant on December 25, 1823. He was promoted to captain nine years later and died in 1840. He was

us after dark, having made a contract with a man on the opposite shore to supply us before day break. Made 16 miles
Having no further use for Mr McDonald [McDanel], I told him, this evening, he could return to Saint Louis. He will do so in the morning together with Col. Nash, a gentleman who has accompanied us from Belle Fontaine.[16]

Sept 28th Tuesday

In consequence of the fresh beef not arriving 'til near 7 A.M, we breakfasted at our encampment of last night, & at 8 we put off, & passing thro' a strong current for a short distance, made 10 miles when we stopt for dinner at 1 P.M. A part of the machinery of the Rackoon, gave way. Killed a few Quails, & put off at 2. In the afternoon, the Beaver & Muskrat ran against each other, when all the buckets of one wheel of the former were broken! They were replaced in 40 minutes, after which there was a long & well contested race between the Beaver & the Mink — as well as between the Racoon & the Muskrat. Made at Sundown 16 miles

Sept 29th Wednesday

Started as usual — passed the Little Manitou having made 3 miles.[17] Stopped to breakfast — met two men in a canoe from the Bluffs — proceeded 5 miles & stopt for dinner after which continued 'til near Sun down passing thro' some strong currents & halted on the Right bank. 15 miles

---

transferred from Company G to take command of Company H from Capt. Garston Powell, who went on furlough prior to resigning on December 31, 1824. Fort Atkinson Post Returns, M617, roll 49; Heitman, *Historical Register*, 1:362, 802.

16. This may have been Ira P. Nash, a doctor and wealthy eccentric, who was in the real estate business. Angus L. Langham, secretary to Atkinson and O'Fallon, was in his employ at this time. Nash came to Missouri from Virginia in 1819 and died in 1844. Walter Williams, ed., *History of Northeast Missouri*, 3 vols. (Chicago: Lewis Publishing Co., 1911), 1:262–65.

17. Little Manitou was Moniteau Creek, which Paul Wilhelm called "an unimportant creek." He mentioned a more noticeable landmark called "Little Manitou, a rock of more than one hundred feet in height and fifty feet in width whose smooth steep walls were decorated with Indian paintings and pictures of idols." Wilhelm, *Travels in North America*, 245.

Sept 30th Thursday

Started at day break & breakfasted at the Manitou Bluffs. Afterwards passed the Big Manitou & halted at dark opposite Franklin at Boonvill, having made 16 miles[18]
After dark, went over in a skiff to Franklin & set a blacksmith at work to make spikes, screws, wrenches &c.
Whitaker of the Recruits was caught steeling cabbages & put in Jail by the civil authority.[19]

October 1st Friday

The Boats came over to Franklin at day break. Took in 150 empty pork barrels. We drew fresh beef & were detained til 10 A.M in getting plank for buckets & the things from the blacksmith. Left a man behind to obtain sockets for Poles, & put off, the shore lined with spectators to witness the operation of the machinery of the Boats. Passed the La Mine River & stopt on the Right bank 13 miles

---

18. James described Manitou Bluff: "The Missouri again washes the base of the rocky hills, which bound its immediate valley. The rocks advance boldly to the brink of the river, exhibiting a perpendicular front, variegated with several colours arranged in broad stripes. Here is a fine spring of water gushing out at the base of the precipice; over it are several rude paintings executed by the Indians. These cliffs are called Big Manito rocks." James, *Account of an Expedition*, 147. Bradbury noticed, "On these rocks several rude figures have been drawn by the Indians with red paint: they are chiefly in imitation of buffaloe, deer, &c." Bradbury, *Travels in the Interior of America*, 51.

In 1819 Edwin James described Franklin as a rapidly growing community consisting of "about one hundred and twenty log houses of one story, several framed dwellings of two stories, and two of brick, thirteen shops for the sale of merchandize, four taverns, two smiths' shops, two large team-mills, two billiard-rooms, a court-house, a log prison of two stories, a post-office, and a printing-press issuing a weekly paper." James, *Account of an Expedition*, 148. Prince Paul perceived Franklin very differently, describing it as "a small but not entirely unimportant town where I noticed only two well-built houses at the time. All the rest were merely wooden shacks." Wilhelm, *Travels in North America*, 255. By 1825 the town had a population of about 1,600, but the Missouri had begun to erode the site and it had to be moved. Conrad, *Encyclopedia*, 5:9–10.

At Booneville, Prince Paul mentioned only "a few scattered cabins." Wilhelm, *Travels in North America*, 255. The *Missouri Intelligencer*, December 31, 1822, claimed it had forty-one dwellings and a brick county courthouse.

19. Jesse Whitaker joined the First Infantry on May 24, 1824. Register of Enlistments, M233, roll 18. No record of a punishment for the theft could be found.

Octob. 2d Saturday

Started at day break. Passed the Arrow Rock. Made 4 miles & breakfasted on the Right bank. Sergt Shuffield & Privs Cotnam of Compy H. & Brown of the Recruits were reported as Deserters. Lieuts Miller & Kingsbury were sent in persuit of them.[20] Continued on our journey, passed the Chanton & halted about dark 3 miles above it. 20 miles

Stratton the man left behind at Franklin for the Sockets joined us near the Arrow Rock with 10 of them.[21]

Octob. 3d Sunday

Put off at day break & run up 3 1/2 miles to breakfast, which we took on the Left bank. Bachelor & Harrison were reported as Deserted last night from Compy. B.[22] Advanced up 2 1/2 miles further & halted for the remainder of the Day! The Boats here were all unloaded & cleaned out, after which they were again loaded & much better arrangements made of their cargos. 6 miles

---

20. Arrow Rock was a sparsely settled area. A ferry was established there in 1811. Conrad, *Encyclopedia*, 1:63.

Robert Brown enlisted in June 1824 and was assigned to the Sixth Infantry. Register of Enlistments, M233, roll 18. The lack of additional records suggests his desertion was successful. John M. Cotnam, a blacksmith, enlisted in 1824. He was apprehended on October 8 and had to forfeit thirty dollars from his pay. He would serve sixteen years in the army before being discharged due to ill health. Ibid., rolls 18, 20. George Shuffield enlisted in 1812. He was apprehended on October 7 and continued to serve until receiving a medical discharge in 1827. Ibid., rolls 11, 18. Albert S. Miller graduated from the military academy in 1818. He became a second lieutenant in the First Infantry on July 1, 1823. He went on to serve in the Mexican War and died in 1852. Heitman, *Historical Register*, 1:709. He was assigned to Company B and went to the upper Missouri. Fort Atkinson Post Returns, M617, roll 49. James Wilkinson Kingsbury entered the First Infantry on August 19, 1823, from the military academy. Heitman, *Historical Register*, 1:601. He was a second lieutenant in Company I, but was sent east before the expedition went upriver in 1825. Fort Atkinson Post Returns, M617, roll 49.

21. John Stratton enlisted in 1814 and was with the Rifle Regiment during the founding of Fort Atkinson. Later he reenlisted and was assigned to the First Infantry. He died at Jefferson Barracks in 1830. Register of Enlistments, M233, rolls 11, 18.

22. James G. Harrison was captured on October 7 and committed suicide three days later. Harrison joined the army in 1823 and had deserted on two previous occasions. Ibid., roll 18. John Bachelor, Company B, First Infantry, enlisted in 1823. He deserted and was apprehended four times before his death in a military prison in 1827. Ibid.

Octob 4th Monday

Started at day break. Halted to dinner where Mr Culbertson it appear'd had slept the night previous.[23] Continued on meeting with some very strong water: The afternoon rainy & wind ahead. Stopped a little after dark, having made 18 miles
Capt Spencer having complained that he had not men enough for the Mink, sent him 3 from the Beaver & 2 from the Muskrat.

Octob 5th Tuesday

Started at 6. Passed the Grand River & then a pass where we found many snags. Made 12 to dinner, which we took at a Point nearly opposite McNarrans Mountain, at which place the Pilot saw Mr Culbertsons Boat 1 1/2 miles ahead.[24] Stopped as usual one hour for dinner after which we put off, determined to over take Mr C-s Boats which we effected about 1/2 past 7, the moon shining perfectly clear, & halted, having made 19 miles
This morng at breakfast, we sent out one hunter from each boat. That from the Mink is the only one that has returned. D. Coleman went out & we took him up, near dark, he bringing a turkey with him.[25] He reports having seen much game. This is the first clear day we have had since the 24th Ult'o.

Octob 6th Wednesday

Started at day break & ran up 3 miles for breakfast. Four men, Hagerman of the Recruits & Deode of Compy B — Vilneuf & Bartlett

---

23. Capt. John Culbertson was honorably discharged from the army in 1821 after nine years of service. Heitman, *Historical Register*, 1:343. He was appointed sutler for the First Infantry in August 1821, when the regiment was stationed in Louisiana. In 1823, when plans were underway to take part of the First Infantry to the upper Missouri, Culbertson feared he would not be allowed to accompany the troops and thereby lose most of his business. He successfully petitioned the commanding officer to accompany the troops. Entry 333, Register of Post Traders, Records of the Adjutant General's Office, Record Group 94, NARA.

24. The pilot was Jean Mousette. Henry Atkinson, Voucher 21, Commission Accounts, 10987/1824–25, RG 217. He probably also served as the pilot of the *Antelope* in 1825, although Langham renders the pilot's name as Moset. Journal of the Commissioners, 1.

Kearny's script could be interpreted as McHanans Mountain. Its exact location is uncertain.

25. Dr. Richard H. Coleman entered the service in 1818. In 1824 he was an assistant surgeon of the First Infantry. Fort Atkinson Post Returns, M617, roll 49.

of Compy H, were reported as Deserted. The two former from the Mink, the two latter from the Racoon. Came 10 miles to dinner & at the expiration of the hour, it being 3 P.M as we put off, Mr. C-s Boats came up. Proceded to the Sugar Tree Bottom & halted.[26]

16 miles

In the evening walked up with the Comy & others about a mile & contracted for fresh beef to be delivered at sunrise. Mr. C-s boats stopped about 2 miles in rear of us.

Octob 7 Thursday

The Boats started a little after day break & I walked up a mile & had the fresh beef ready for delivery at Sunrise! About 10 A.M. took up Lt Kingsbury, who brought Sergt Shuffield & Cotnam of Compy H, Bachelor & Harrison of Compy B. deserters. In the afternoon, the Racoon took up the two hunters from the Beaver & Racoon who brings with them Hagerman of the Recruits who had been reported as Deserter. Passed the Tabo, & halted 3 miles above it.

16 miles

Octob 8th Friday

Started at day break and ran up 3 1/2 miles to breakfast & just before landing, while in a strong current, the main cross piece of the Rear slide to which the Piston is attached, (of the Beaver) broke in two, directly in the center! Remained 'til near 12 in putting in the new one, when we proceded, & ran up, passing the Big dry Bar & the Beaver & Racoon. Stopt on one side of a Willow Island, the other two Boats passed on the other, & went to the main shore.

12 miles

---

26. There was no record of a Hagerman in the Sixth Infantry, but there was a William Hageman and an Ares Hageman. Register of Enlistments, M233, rolls 15, 18. Joseph Vilneuf enlisted in the First Infantry on August 10, 1824, and deserted two days later. He was apprehended only to desert again as recorded by Kearny. This time it seems he was successful. Ibid., roll 18. Joseph Diode enlisted in the First Infantry on August 10, 1824. His desertion was apparently successful for no further military records exist for him. Ibid., roll 19. Constantine Bartlett enlisted on August 21, 1824, and was assigned to Company H of the First Infantry. He was apprehended and discharged from service, but reenlisted in 1829 at Fort Snelling. He also deserted there, but was apprehended and completed his enlistment. Ibid., rolls 18, 19.

Sugar Tree Bottom was about thirty miles long and up to ten miles wide. *Missouri Intelligencer*, December 3, 1822.

Octob 9th Saturday

Got off at day break. About 10 A.M passed Bluff Town on the Left bank.[27] Strong head wind & current. In the afternoon the Muskrat took in the hunter who went from her on the 5th. Ran on 'til 6 P.M, passing Fire Prairie Creek & halted on the Right Bank, having made 14 miles

Passed this afternoon Le isle du Sorceir (Wizzards Island) of which a curious story is extant among the French Boatmen vis — that about 11 years since, as a Boat was ascending, one of the hunters saw on the Island an Elk rode by a man without a head. He fired all his ammunition (27 shot) at him without effect, when he returned to the Boat, procured more, & 11 men to accompany him, all of whom saw & repeatedly fired at this monster without success.[28]

Octob 10th Sunday

Started shortly after day break & in 2 1/2 hours ran up to Fort Osage distance 5 miles. Halted for breakfast during which I walked up to see Mr & Mrs Sibley.[29] When I returned found that Harrison

---

27. Bluff Town or Bluffton was described by Prince Paul as "a group of cabins" with "a pretty good tavern." Wilhelm, *Travels in North America*, 255.

28. Wizzard Island was near the south shore, but has been washed away. According to Brackenridge, "The superstitious boatmen believe that a wizzard inhabits this island; they declare that a man has been frequently seen on the sand beach, at the point, but suddenly disappears, on the approach of any one." H. M. Brackenridge, *Journal of a Voyage up the Missouri, Performed in 1811*, vol. 6 of *Early Western Travels 1748–1846*, ed. Reuben Gold Thwaites (Cleveland: Arthur H. Clark Co., 1904), 54–55.

29. Fort Osage was founded in 1808 to protect the neighboring government-owned factory or trading post. Kate L. Gregg, "History of Fort Osage," *Missouri Historical Review* 34 (1940): 439–42.

In 1819 Edwin James described the fort "on an elevated bluff, commanding a beautiful view of the river, both above and below. The works are a stockade, of an irregular pentagonal form, with strong log pickets perforated with loop-holes; two block houses are placed at opposite angles; one of them, however, flanks one of its curtains too obliquely to be of much service in defending it. There is also a small bastion at a third angle. Within are two series of buildings for quarters, store-houses &c." James, *Account of an Expedition*, 168.

George C. Sibley began his western career as a clerk in the Office of Indian Affairs in 1808 when he went up the Missouri River with a military detachment to build Fort Osage, then called Fort Clark. He was appointed factor at the nearby government trading house. In 1815 Sibley married Mary Easton and in 1825 they left the fort. Sibley accompanied a commission to mark the Santa Fe Trail and soon after retired from the Indian service. The Sibleys moved to St. Charles, where

of Compy B had cut his throat. He was buried & we proceded. Halted about dark on the Left Bank having made 17 miles

During the afternoon had some rain & near eveng it lightened. We passed to day the Little Blue & found many sand bars.

Octob 11th Monday

Started as usual — morning cloudy, cool, & wind strong ahead. At about 11 A.M the Beaver's rudder was unshipped (in a very strong current) by striking on a sawyer, ran her on a Sand Bar, & fixed it! Were obliged to put to at 12, & in consequence of a very strong head wind, the Boats were detained here 'til 3 P.M. Came up opposite to Liberty & stopped an hour before Sun down to obtain fresh beef, but in this was disappointed.[30] 9 miles

Octob 12 Tuesday

Started at day break; morning cool, frosty, & a heavy fog on the water. Made 3 1/2 to breakfast. Came up to Mr Choteaus Trading House to dinner, where we found the Kickapoos & the Kansas were expected to morrow. Made some purchases. In the afternoon passed the Kansas River & halted one mile above it on the Left Bank opposite the Curtis & Ely's Trading house having made 16 miles[31]

---

they opened a girl's school that later became Lindenwood College. "George C. Sibley," Malone, *Dictionary* 17:144.

30. Liberty was settled in 1821. John Barber White, "The Missouri Merchant One Hundred Years Ago," *Missouri Historical Review* 13 (1910): 109–10. Prince Paul expressed his usual disdain for frontier settlements saying, "Liberty consists of a few poor log cabins put up for temporary use. The tavern where I spent the night was crowded with people." Wilhelm, *Travels in North America*, 266.

31. The main Kansa village was on the Kansas River near present Manhattan, Kansas. William E. Unrau, *The Kansa Indians: A History of the Wind People* (Norman: University of Oklahoma Press, 1971).

Some of the Kickapoos had lived in southwestern Missouri since 1800 and many more joined them in the 1819–20 removal from their Illinois homeland. George R. Nielson, *The Kickapoo People* (Phoenix: Indian Tribal Series, 1975), 32–33.

About 1821 Francis G. Chouteau opened a trading post on the left bank or possibly on an island below present Kansas City, Missouri. Louise Barry, *The Beginning of the West: Annals of the Kansas Gateway to the American West, 1540–1854* (Topeka: Kansas State Historical Society, 1972), 102.

Curtis and Ely's trading house was just above the mouth of the Kansas River. When Prince Paul visited the post in 1823, it was merely "two large dwellings" and "the entire population of this little settlement consisted of only a few persons,

Octob 13th Wednesday

Started at day break, which as the days are becoming shorter, is now at about 1/4 before 6. About 11 A.M the Beaver got on a log, which with much difficulty, she was removed from; at noon, the main cross Piece of the after Slide of the Racoon broke in two, similar to that of the Beaver on the 8th. In the afternoon passed the Little Platte coming in on the Left Side, & passed by the Missouri State Line. Came up to Diamond Island & halted on it at Sunset 14 miles

Octob 14th Thursday

Started shortly after day break. Went up 3 1/2 to breakfast. Made 6 more to dinner & halted at 7 P.M on the Left Bank, having made 20 miles

Octob 15th Friday

Started at day break. Came to 4 miles & breakfast. After which, reached Cow Island. Passed the old Cant of the Rifle Regt on it, but few vestages remaining.[32] Dined at the upper end of the Island & proceded 'til about Sun set when we halted on the right bank having made 18 miles

Octob 16th Saturday

Came 6 miles to breakfast after which we passed Independence creek. Met with considerable difficulty & detention on account of Sand bars & stopt at dark on the right bank, at the lower end of the Grand Detour[33] 20 miles

---

Creoles and half-bloods, whose occupation is trade with the Kansa Indians, some hunting, and agriculture." Wilhelm, *Travels in North America*, 270.

Michael Ely and Cyrus Curtis were partners from about 1822 through 1826. The next year Ely entered the Santa Fe trade. His name was frequently spelled Eley. Charbonneau Family Papers, Missouri Historical Society, St. Louis.

32. Cantonment Martin was built on Cow Island in 1818 as winter quarters for the soldiers of the Rifle Regiment, who were the advance troops of the Yellowstone Expedition. Nichols, *The Missouri Expedition*, 28.

33. According to Prince Paul, "At the mouth of the channel Grand Detour, great masses of driftwood had been piled up. . . . Travel along this pile of timber was most difficult and dangerous." Wilhelm, *Travels in North America*, 292.

Octob 17th Sunday

Morning very foggy. Started at day break & came thro' a difficult 4 miles to breakfast. Stopped at night on the Right bank at the head of the Grand Detour 16 miles
The Mink remained a mile in the Rear & in the evening took in Drum Major Rogers & his Son who started on the 11th for a few hours hunt.[34]

Kittler of Compy B. was reported to day to have been left behind this morning.[35]

Octob 18th Monday

Waited 'til Sunrise for the Mink to come up when we started. Passed on, & about noon, passed the Black Snake Prairie & the Yellow Banks.[36] About dark, stopped on the Right bank on a Sand bar having made 20 miles

Octob 19th Tuesday

Started at half past 6. The morning being overcast run up to the lower slough of the Nodowa 5 miles to breakfast. After which moved up 3 1/2 miles, & on account of a very strong head wind & current, found it impossible to make any head way &
Stopped under a point on Nodowa Island at 1 P.M having made 8 1/2 miles
About 3 P.M, about 60 or 70 men turned out in order to drive the upper end of the Island (it being not more than a mile wide) which was effected, tho' without success.[37]

---

34. John Rogers, a thirty-two-year-old musician, joined the First Infantry on August 7, 1824. On the same day, Samuel Rogers also enlisted in the First. He was listed as a fifteen-year-old musician. The elder Rogers was assigned to the noncommissioned staff, but was discharged in 1827. The younger Rogers completed his five-year enlistment despite two desertions. Register of Enlistments, M233, roll 18.

35. Bous Kittler enlisted in August 1824 and served in the First Infantry for five years. Ibid.

36. "Black Snake Prairie & the yellow banks" refers to what was more commonly called the Blacksnake Hills. Joseph Robidoux established a trading house there and a settlement grew up around it and became St. Joseph, Missouri. Merrill J. Mattes, "Joseph Robidoux," *Mountain Men and the Fur Trade* 8:287–314. Paul Wilhelm mentioned the trading post only in passing. Wilhelm, *Travels in North America*, 294.

37. The sixty men were attempting to drive game to the head of the island, where they could be more easily killed.

Octob 20th Wednesday

Pushed off at day break. Wind yet strong ahead, moved up above the head of the Island for breakfast. Strong current. At Sunset reached Wolf river & stopped. 14 miles

Shortly before stopping, passed a Keel Boat 5 days from C. B. [Council Bluffs]. Sent a skiff to her to obtain news.

Octob 21th Thursday

Started at day break & reached the Nemaha (coming in on the right bank) at Sunset & stopped on the opposite side of the River, having made 16 miles

Octob. 22d Friday

Started at day break. Made 4 1/2 to breakfast. At this time, Stansbery of the 6th was reported absent from the Mink.[38] Sent two men in a skiff after him. Passed the Tarkio coming in on the Left Bank. Had much difficulty with Sand bars & strong currents, & stopped at Sunset on a bar on the Left shore, having made 17 miles

About noon passed a Keel Boat from the Bluffs, but at too great a distance to hail them.

Octob 23d Saturday

Put off at day break & ran up to the Nishnebotona, 10 miles to breakfast. The Boats stopped, seperate from each other, & we came up passed the Little Nemaha on the Right bank & encamped or halted after dark two miles above it, at a small willow bar 20 miles

This day at dinner, Thomas of the Recruits attached to the Mink, was found Dead & buried with the honors of War.[39]

Octob 24th Sunday

Started at day break. Made 4 miles to breakfast. Passed Sun Island & stopped on a Sand bar at Sundown on the right bank, having made 17 miles

---

38. Joseph Sandsberrie enlisted in June 1824 and his military career ended with a medical discharge seven months later. Register of Enlistments, M233, roll 18.

39. Elisha Thomas joined the Sixth Infantry on June 4, 1824. Ibid.

Nearly opposite to us is the place where the Nishnebotona approaches within 150 yards of the Missouri, & we are now 37 miles from the mouth of the former.

The Prairie we find this evening to be on fire.

Octob 25th Monday

The Mink, about day break, was blown off from the shore, and in regaining her position, broke the main cross piece of the forward slide. She remained here during the remainder of the day. The other Boats moved up with much difficulty 1/2 a mile & stopped under a willow point. The wind very fresh from the N.W. so as to prevent our moving further. 1/2 mile

Octob 26th Tuesday

Very cold morning, clear & still. Started at day break & made 5 miles to breakfast, shortly after which it again commenced blowing very hard from the N.W. & we were obliged to lay bye 'til near 5 P.M. when we put off & made by 7 P.M 8 1/2 miles
Passed this morning a small keel Boat 3 days from the Bluffs, who informed us of Genl A's arrival there.[40]
At 8 P.M. Brown & Fields, who had been sent after Stansbery on the 22d came up, leaving the man behind, he not being able to travel with them. Sent them back to find him with orders to await the arrival of Mr Culbertsons Boats & to come up in them.
Corpl Jolley of the Recruits is missing, but it is supposed he will go by Land to C. B.[41]

Octob 27th Wednesday

Started shortly after day break & came up to Le Grand eboulment or falling in banks to breakfast 3 miles.[42] At this time we had a little snow — after which it cleared away & the wind again commenced

40. Atkinson arrived at Fort Atkinson on the Council Bluffs on October 31, and began his return trip to St. Louis ten days later. Atkinson to Nourse, Dec. 16, 1824, Letters Received, M567, roll 9.

41. Philip L. Brown joined the Sixth Infantry in 1824 and served one enlistment. Register of Enlistments, M233, roll 18. Willis Fields was assigned to Company A, Sixth Infantry, after his enlistment in June 1824 and would serve five years. Ibid. George Jolly first enlisted in 1819. He apparently rejoined the unit as Kearny suspected, because there is nothing to suggest he deserted. Ibid., roll 16.

blowing from the N. W. Moved on with considerable difficulty & stopped on a Sand bar on the Right bank about 5 P.M. 10 miles

Octob 28th Thursday

The wind at day break abated a little & we put off about 6 A.M. Made 3 miles to breakfast & stopped on a bar on the Right bank, the wind blowing very hard & directly ahead. In the afternoon moved up, overtook, & stopped along side of J. Consols Boat[43] 4. miles

In Consols Boat found Burrows, who had been lost whilst hunting on the 25th & met by one of the hunters on the 26th starving & warn out. 7 Lodges of the Ottoes are 4 miles from this, & Dr Coleman engaged some of them to go in pursuit of his man George who has been missing since the 24th.[44]

Octob 29th Friday

Last night was very cold and this morning we had a great deal of ice. Got off at 6 A.M (the wind having ceased) in front of Consols Boat & came up 5 miles to Weeping Water creek to breakfast. The wind commenced blowing from the S. E & we stopped at dark on the right bank, along side of the Sail Boat, having made 18 miles

Octob 30th Saturday

Started at 6 A.M with a strong favorable wind. The Sail Boat soon ran by us. At 1 P.M, having made 9 miles passed the Platte and

---

42. Wilhelm called the eroding bank the Grand Debouli. It extended for two miles along the right shore and consisted of friable limestone and sandstone. Wilhelm, *Travels in North America*, 308.

In approximately this same location, Lewis and Clark noted on the left bank, "the hills come to the river. This Hill has Sliped into the river for about 3/4 of a mile, and leaves a Bluff of considerable hight back of it." Moulton, *The Journals of the Lewis and Clark Expedition*, 2:391.

43. The *Missouri Republican*, June 14, 1851, carried a brief obituary: "Captain James Consol, an old Missouri River pilot, died in this city yesterday, after only a short illness."

44. Ezra Hull Burrows enlisted in 1824 in Company H of the First Infantry. Register of Enlistments, M233, roll 19. The Ottoes or Oto Indians had an earthlodge village on the right bank of the Platte River east of present Wahoo, Nebraska. The seven lodges Kearny mentions were a hunting camp. George was probably Coleman's slave.

stopped about 7 on the right bank, 2 miles below Pilchers Trading house having made 16 miles[45]

Octob 31st Sunday

Started at 6 A.M. the wind ahead. Passed by Pilchers Trading house where we saw many of the Ottoes. The Mink having for the last week or two, kept so far in the Rear, we, after breakfast sent her 24 Men, 8 from each of the other Boats, & sent as many of hers to them in order to ascertain whither her slow proceeding was caused from the laziness of her crew, or the Boats fault. About 1 P.M passed Consols Boat, & about this time Wells of Compy B fell overboard from the Muskrat (where he had been sent) & was immediately drowned.[46] Stopped after dark on the Right bank having made 16 miles

<*Octob 3*> Nov 1st Monday

Started at 6 A.M. Came 4 miles to breakfast. In the afternoon passed Robideous Trading house where we saw many of the Ottoes.[47] About Sunset passed the Bouyer & stopped on a Sand bar on the Left having made 16 miles
This morng at day break we heard several cannon from the Bluffs & during the day we understood that Genl A. arrived there last night.

---

45. The Platte River usually elicits more enthusiasm than Kearny's terse record. In 1811 Brackenridge explained, "The Platte is regarded by the navigators of the Missouri as a point of as much importance, as the equinoctial line amongst mariners. All those who had not passed it before, were required to be shaved, unless they could compromise the matter by a treat. . . . From this we enter what is called the Upper Missouri." Brackenridge, *Journal of a Voyage*, 77.

Pilcher's trading house was also called Bellevue and its founding marks the beginning of the present town of Bellevue, Nebraska. The trading post was founded by Joshua Pilcher of the Missouri Fur Company about two years prior to Kearny's visit. In 1832 Bellevue was sold to the Office of Indian Affairs and became the agency for the upper Missouri Indians. Richard E. Jensen, "Bellevue: The First Twenty Years," *Nebraska History* 56 (1975): 339–74.

46. John Wells, a shoemaker, enlisted in 1823. Register of Enlistments, M233, roll 18.

47. The trading house was probably founded in the latter part of 1822. Jensen, *Fontenelle and Cabanné*. It seems Cabanné and Robidoux alternated duties at the post. Kennerly mentions first one and then the other as being in charge. Wesley, "Diary of James Kennerly," 54ff. Prince Paul visited the post and described it: "The building of the French Company, to which they apply the name fort, is set near a small creek. . . . The house is rather firmly put together and has chimneys of brick." Wilhelm, *Travels in North America*, 315.

Nov 2d Thursday

Started at day break. The Mink was left last night as we suppose 2 miles in rear of us; passed by Lisas old Trading Establishment & the old Engineer Cantt & breakfasted on the right bank having made 4 miles.[48] Waited here a considerable time for the Mink. She not coming up, the other Boats moved off & arrived about 1 P.M. at C. B. The Mink came up in the afternoon having been retarded by having her Rudder carried away. 12 miles

---

Kearny ended this portion of his journal with his arrival at Fort Atkinson. A few days later General Atkinson issued the following congratulatory communication on the success of Kearny's trip.

Head Quarters Western Dept.
Orders No. 65 Fort Atkinson 8 Nov. 1824

The Commanding General takes this occasion to express his thanks to Maj. Kearney & the officers & men under his Command for the zeal & promptitude manifested by them in performing their late voyage from the Mississippi to this post.

The detachment consisting of four Companies of the 1st Regt. of Inf. & sixty recruits of the 6 Inf. moved from Bellefontaine in the afternoon of the 19 September, in four Keel boats, propelled by machinery on a new plan & arrived at this post after several days delay by head winds, at noon on the 2 Instant performing the trip in one third less time than is common to the most experienced Voyagers with select French crews.

Signed H. Atkinson
Br. Gen. U.S.A.[49]

---

48. Lisa's post was located a short distance south of Fort Atkinson. It was built about 1813 by the Missouri Fur Company and abandoned after Joshua Pilcher built the new headquarters at Bellevue. Jensen, *Fontenelle and Cabanné*.

Engineers Cantonment was occupied only during the winter of 1819–20 by Maj. Stephen Long and the party of scientists who came up the Missouri on the steamboat *Western Engineer*. In the spring they left on an exploring tour up the Platte River. Roger L. Nichols, *General Henry Atkinson, A Western Military Career* (Norman: University of Oklahoma Press, 1965).

49. Vol. 2:174, entry 5579, Orders and Special Orders Issued, 1820–53, Western Department, Records of Named Departments, Records of U.S. Army Continental Commands, Record Group 393, NARA.

Kearny's First Infantry was billeted with the Sixth Infantry at the fort during the winter. With the approach of spring, Atkinson and other officers began issuing orders in preparation for the trip to the upper Missouri.

Head Qrs. 6th Regt. Fort Atkinson 7th March 1825. Orders.

Capt. Riley, Lts. Nute & Batman & 60 men (including six good boatmen to be selected, will be detained to go to the Boyer [River] & bring up the three boats which have not been furnished with wheels. . . . Signed. H. Leavenworth. Col. Commdg.[50]

Hd Qs Right Wing West. Dept

Orders No 2 Ft Atkinson 23 April, 1825

The troops that will compose the contemplated expedition up the Missouri will consist of the detachment of the 1st Infantry at this post under Major Kearney [and] a detachment from the 6th Infy to consist of Captns Riley's, Gray's, Gantt's, Pentland's and late Larrabee's companies under Col. Leavenworth and Capt. Armstrong's company the latter mounted.[51]

---

50. Bennet Riley enlisted in the Rifle Regiment in January 1813, received his captaincy on August 6, 1818, and was with the Yellowstone Expedition in 1819. On October 3, 1821, he transferred to the Sixth Infantry. In the Mexican War he attained the rank of brevet major general and replaced Richard B. Mason as the provisional governor of California. "Bennet Riley," Malone, *Dictionary*, 16:608–9. In 1824–25 Riley commanded Company B of the Sixth Infantry. Muster Rolls, Sixth Infantry, RG 94.

Levi M. Nute graduated from the military academy in 1823 and resigned from the army in 1838 as a captain. Heitman, *Historical Register*, 1:754. During the expedition he was a second lieutenant in Company G, Sixth Infantry. Muster Rolls, Sixth Infantry, RG 94.

Mark W. Batman graduated from the military academy in 1823. He attained the rank of captain in 1836 but died the following year. Heitman, *Historical Register*, 1:199. Second Lieutenant Batman was in Company I of the Sixth Infantry during the expedition. Muster Rolls, Sixth Infantry, RG 94.

51. The First Infantry detachment under Kearny included Lieutenant Harney's Company A of forty-seven men, Captain Spencer's Company B with forty-one, Lieutenant Day's Company H of forty-seven, and Captain Mason's Company I with forty-four. Fort Atkinson Post Returns, M617, roll 49.

Atkinson ordered six companies of the Sixth Infantry to take part in the expedition. James S. Gray commanded Company I. Muster Rolls, Sixth Infantry, RG 94. He joined the army in 1813 and was transferred to the Sixth Infantry as a captain in 1821. He resigned in 1826. Heitman, *Historical Register*, 1:472.

To Major Kearney's command is assigned transport boats Beaver, Otter and Muskrat.

To Col. Leavenworth's command transport boats Buffaloe, Elk, White Bear and Raccoon. The transport Mink will be used for the Commissioners and manned by the hands of both corps and a detachment to be specified in subsequent orders. Capt Armstrong's command is to consist of 40 men. Crews of the largest class of Boats from 58 to 60 men and the smaller from 48 to 50. If the companies named in this detail after leaving at this post from 4 to 6 men (to attend to Company gardening) should be found insufficient to man the transports and mount the party as above specified, the deficiency will be made up by detail from the companies to be left at the post. Orders more in detail will be given before the movement takes place.

By order of Brigr Genl Atkinson
Signed S. MacRee Lt & A.D.C.[52]

John Gantt or Gant from Virginia enlisted in the Rifle Regiment in 1817. He transferred to the Sixth Infantry in 1821, made captain in 1823, and was dismissed from the service in 1829. Heitman, *Historical Register*, 1:444. He commanded Company G. Muster Rolls, Sixth Infantry, RG 94. After leaving the army, Gantt entered the fur trade and then served as Indian agent to the Pottawatomie opposite the Council Bluffs in the late 1830s. Janet Lecompte, "Gantt's Fort and Bent's Picket Post," *Colorado Magazine* 41 (1964): 111–25.

Charles Pentland joined the army in 1814 and transferred to the Sixth Infantry in 1821, where he made captain in 1823. He was dismissed from the service in February 1826. Heitman, *Historical Register*, 1:783. During the expedition he commanded Company F. Muster Rolls, Sixth Infantry, RG 94. He was regimental adjutant from 1821 until July 17, 1825. Orderly Book 25, Sheldon, "Records of Fort Atkinson," 5:111.

Charles Larrabee entered the army in 1808. During the War of 1812 he lost his left arm and was promoted to brevet major. Larrabee resigned from the Sixth Infantry on April 7, 1825. Heitman, *Historical Register*, 1:616. Prior to his retirement he commanded Company E. Muster Rolls, Sixth Infantry, RG 94.

William Armstrong enlisted in the Rifle Regiment in 1813. He was promoted to captain on July 31, 1818, and transferred to the Sixth Infantry on June 1, 1821. He died on February 11, 1827. Heitman, *Historical Register*, 1:170. He commanded Company A of the Sixth Infantry. Muster Rolls, Sixth Infantry, RG 94. His company was mounted infantry, but all but ten of the horses were sent back when they reached Camp Teton.

52. Samuel McRee entered the military academy in 1815. Upon graduation he was assigned to the Eighth Infantry and in 1821 he transferred to the First Infantry. In 1823 he was promoted to first lieutenant. Heitman, *Historical Register*, 1:682. During the expedition he was Atkinson's aide-de-camp. In the journals his name is rendered as MacRee. Vol. 1:18–19, entry 1210, Orders Received, Sixth Infantry,

---

Hd Qrs Right Wing
Western Department
Orders No 3 Ft. Atkinson 29th Apr 1825

Brevet Major Ketchum is appointed to the duties of Act. Ass. Insp. Genl (to the Missouri expedition) which he will enter upon as soon as the Brigade is organized.[53]

Lt Holmes 6th Infty will in addition to his Regimental duties act as Conductor of Ordnance to the expedition, and will at once enter upon the arrangements & receipts of the requisite ordnance & ordnance Stores.[54]

By order of Brigr Genl Atkinson
Signed S. MacRee Lt. & Aid de Camp[55]

Hd Qrs Right Wing, West. Dept.
Orders No 4 Fort Atkinson, 5th May 1825

Col. Leavenworth will at once make the detail to complete his command for the Missouri expedition, agreeably to the wing order of the 23rd Ult. observing that the crews of the largest class of boats amount only to 58 Non Commissd Officers, Musicians & privates and of the smallest to 48.

He will also fill by detail Capt. Armstrong's command which is to be immediately organized under the direction of the General.

Records of the Infantry, 1815–1942, Records of United States Regular Army Mobile Units, Record Group 391, NARA (hereafter cited as Orders Received, Sixth Infantry, RG 391).

53. Daniel Ketchum of Connecticut entered the military in 1812 and was promoted to captain a year later. He served in the Sixth Infantry from 1815 until his death in 1828. Heitman, *Historical Register*, 1:595. He commanded Company D and served as the acting assistant inspector general. Muster Rolls, Sixth Infantry, RG 94.

54. Reuben Holmes was a military academy graduate who attained the rank of captain before he died in 1833. He was a second lieutenant in the Sixth Infantry at the time of the expedition. Heitman, *Historical Register*, 1:538.

On August 21, 1824, Colonel Leavenworth replied to a letter from Atkinson suggesting the ordnance should include "one six pounder — one 5 1/2 inch Howitzer & one 10 inch mortar & 300 rounds for each should be taken. This would also be sufficient for any emergency." Orderly Book 35, Sheldon, "Records of Fort Atkinson," 6:161–62.

55. Vol. 1:22, Orders Received, Sixth Infantry, RG 391.

Major Kearney will also organize his command according to the above standard with respect to the crews of his boats leaving out the band of the corps as indicated in the order of the 23rd Ult.

These details completed Colonel Leavenworth's and Major Kearney's Battallions and Capt. Armstrong's mounted company will form as a Brigade under the immediate order of the General.

The company women left behind by the companies forming the Brigade, are to be quartered in the Fort and protected by the commandant of the Post, in their allowances and priviledges agreeably to Army regulations, and that no mistake may arise in the absence of the Company Officers they will respectively make out monthly returns for their company women entitled to rations, and deposit them with the Ass. Commy of Subsce who will issue upon them respectively.[56]

The Adjts of Corps will also make out similar returns for the women of the respective bands who are entitled to rations.

In computing the crews of the Mink, the detail will be made exclusively from late Larrabee's company 6th Infy.

By order of Brigr Genl Atkinson
Signed S. MacRee Lt Aid de Camp[57]

Head Qrs. 6th Regt. Fort Atkinson. 6th May 1825.

The following detail from the 6th Regt. is made in compliance with the wing order of 5th May, 1825 to complete the crews of the transport boats Elk, Buffalo, White Bear, Rackoon, Viz. For the Elk, Command of Capt. Gray Comp. J. For the Buffalo under the command of Capt. Riley. For the White Bear under the command of Capt. Pentland. For the Rackoon, Under the command of Capt. Gantt . . . and the Comg. Officer will see that they prepare themselves to move at any moment. By Order of Col. Leavenworth, Signed J. Pentland. Adj. 6th Regt.[58]

---

56. The order refers to the laundresses who lived at the fort. Many of them were wives of enlisted men.

57. Vol. 1:28–29, Orders Received, Sixth Infantry, RG 391.

58. Orderly Book 25, Sheldon, "Records of Fort Atkinson," 5:83. Joseph Pentland graduated from the military academy in 1818. He was named the Sixth Infantry's regimental adjutant on July 17, 1825, to replace Charles Pentland. Two years later he was promoted to captain. Heitman, *Historical Register*, 1:783. First Lieutenant Pentland was assigned to Company D during the expedition. Muster Rolls, Sixth Infantry, RG 94.

Council Bluffs
Dear Sir, 9th May 1825

I send you herewith enclosed my accounts. . . . [There follows a lengthy report concerning expenses in the Office of Indian Affairs] Although my health has improved, I am still much afflicted and restless to set out with the expedition, which has been, and is still delayed by a Boat with Clothing, Shoes &c. of which the Troops are all most destitute. The boat is hourly expected. Immediately after our arrival at this post Capt. Riley, whom you know to be an Officer of great energy & experience in navigation, was dispatched with eight men to meet and assist the Antalope, which I am afraid cannot reach this before our departure. Fortunately, we can dispence with most of the articles on board. Such articles [as] are indispensable Capt. Riley will bring up by land in time to overtake us a short distance above this place. Taking all things into consideration, under existing circumstances, I have every reason to believe that we will make our final departure from this place, on the 12th or 13th inst. We are loosing precious time, but our mission must and will be effectual. Our return must be later in the fall than was anticipated. The Military Escort has been organized and consists of about five hundred rank & file to assend in eight Boats except 50 men who form a mounted core by land. A number of Ottoes & Ioways have expressed such anxiety to accompany me that I have been compelled to permit a few of each Tribe to accompany me.

Yours affectionately
To Gen. Wm. Clark Benjn. O'Fallon
St. Louis Missouri U. S. Agt. Indn. Affs.[59]

Head Qrs Right Wing W. Dept
Orders No 5 Fort Atkinson, 11th May 1825

The troops detailed for the Missouri expedition are to be completed pr man, under the direction of Commts of Corps with the following articles of Clothing to wit: One uniform Coat and Cap complete, one Stock, two pr of Cotton Pantaloons, two pr Stock-

59. O'Fallon concludes this long letter with a general discussion of Indian affairs. O'Fallon Letterbook. Atkinson mentions an Oto being with the expedition on August 15.

ings, one grey jacket, one pr Grey Pantaloons, two flannel Shirts, two pr Socks, one pr Shoes, one pr boots, one great coat, one blanket, and forage cap. Many of the above articles of clothing that are in use & partly worn will answer.

Such articles of clothing of Capt. Armstrong's mounted men as they cannot conveniently carry with them are to be packed up and put on board one of the boats of the 6th Regt.

The men of the Battalions of the 1st & 6th Regts are to be supplied with twenty four rounds of Musket Cartridges and three spare flints each, and the mounted men with a convenient quantity of loose powder & Ball and spare flints also a convenient quantity of Pistol Cartridges.

As it is expected the expedition will move on the morning of the 14th or 15th Inst Commandants of Battalions will commence loading their transport boats tomorrow morning, first by taking in their respective proportion of Subsistence stores, after which a due porportion of Ordnance & ordnance Stores. The Subsistence Stores will be equalized and delivered by Ass. Commy of Subce (Lieut. Palmer) to the Actg Ass. Commy of Subce of Battalions, who will receipt for the articles received by them, and be held responsible that they are issued upon none but proper returns, signed by Commdts of Corps, or the Commanding General.[60]

The troops will not be allowed to take any thing on board of the transports but their arms, accoutrements and effects. The Actg Ass. Insp. Genl Major Ketchum will enter upon his duties.

By order of Br. Genl Atkinson
Signed S. MacRee Lt & A. D. Camp[61]

Head Qrs. 6th Regt. Fort Atkinson 11th May 1825. Orders

Comgs. of Companies belonging to the escort Brigade will immediately make requisitions for the several articles necessary to furnish their men agreeably to wing orders of 11th May, and also requisitions on the Ordinance Department for the supply required of Cartriges and flints. The boat assigned to the 6th Regt. will be

---

60. The assistant commissary of subsistence, Zalmon C. Palmer, joined the army in 1812 and worked through the ranks. He received his captaincy in February 1826 and resigned in 1836. Heitman, *Historical Register*, 1:768.

61. Vol. 1:29–30, Orders Received, Sixth Infantry, RG 391.

laden in rotation, commencing tomorrow morning as follows: The Elk, Rackoon, White Bear, and Buffalo. This will be strictly attended to by Commanders of boats. They will be held responsible that the boats are laden agreeably to the wing order before moving. Lt. Noel is charged with the command of the Buffalo when Capt. Riley returns. . . . By Order of Col. Leavenworth. Signed. J. Pentland. Adj. 6th Regt.[62]

Head Qrs. 6th Regt. Fort Atkinson 15th May 1825 Orders. The boats of the 6th Regt. will move this 18th May as follows. The Buffalo, White Bear, Elk and Rackoon in the order in which they are named. The commanding officer of the Regt. will be on board the Elk with the head Qr. of the Regt. That boat, will therefore take such position in the line of the Batta. as the commander may direct. The movement on the succeeding days will be regulated according to circumstances. The regulated order of movement will be adhered to as far as possible. There must be strong necessity for so doing to justify departure from it. By Order of Col. Leavenworth. Signed J. Pentland. Adj. 6th Regt.[63]

Hd Qrs Right Wing West. Dept
Orders No Fort Atkinson, 15th May 1825

All preparations having been completed for the movement of the Military escort, the Battalions of Inf. under Colo Leavenworth & Major Kearney will embark as soon as the weather will permit, at an hour that will be fixed upon in subsequent orders.

On embarking the Flotilla will commence its ascent of the River at the Signal to advance, that will be given on the Bugle from the Commandants boat.

The 1st Inf. succeeded by the Flag or commandants boat and followed by the 6th Infy, this will be the habitual order of move-

---

62. Thomas Noel of Maryland graduated from the military academy in 1820 and attained the rank of brevet major in 1846 during the war against the Florida Indians. First Lieutenant Noel was the Sixth Infantry's regimental adjutant from July 17, 1825, until May 1, 1827. Heitman, *Historical Register*, 1:749. He was in Company B and before the end of the expedition was transferred to Company G. Muster Rolls, Sixth Infantry, RG 94; Orderly Book 25, Sheldon, "Records of Fort Atkinson," 5:84–85.

63. Orderly Book 25, Sheldon, "Records of Fort Atkinson," 5:89.

ment, each Battalion leading alternately, every other day. The flag boat however taking her position in the fleet in advancing & coming to, as the commandant may direct.

The following signals on the Bugle from the Flag boat will regulate the movement of the Flotilla viz. The Assembly twenty minutes preparatory to embarking — the signal termed embark for embarking — signal to advance for advancing, Signal to halt for halting which being given or the discharge of two swivels in quick succession, the fleet will immediately halt at all hours of the day and come to in regular succession, observing a space between each, of from ten to thirty feet according to the nature of the ground. The bugle signals will be taken and repeated by the Battalion bugles.

Should a boat fall in distress, the commandant thereof will cause two Muskets to be fired in quick succession and others at intervals 'till relieved. Upon these signals of distress the nearest boats will proceed with the least possible delay to the succor of the distressed boat.

The habitual order of encamping will be in line, parallel to the river facing outwards with one Company on each flank thrown perpendicular to the line & facing also outwards.

The detail for guard duty 'til further orders will be Subalterns command and a Captain as Officer of the day. The guard to consist of one Subaltern, one Sergeant, two Corporals and twenty one Privates.

As soon as the movement of the troops takes place, the orders will assume the character of Brigade orders, which will emanate from Brigade Head Quarters for Details & other purposes.

Orderly hours when the troops are stationary will be at 12 Oclock, when advancing at the hour of halt for dinner.

Capt Armstrong will receive Special orders in reference to the movement of his mounted party.

By order of Brigr Genl Atkinson
Signed S. MacRee Lt & A. D. Camp[64]

Brigade Head Qrs. Fort Atkinson May 15th 1825 Orders.

The Brigade of Infantry composing the Artillery escort will embark tomorrow morning at 7 o'clock and commence the ascent of the river as directed by orders. The troops will breakfast previous to embarking and take with them the residue of this days provisions

64. Vol. 1:30–31, Orders Received, Sixth Infantry, RG 391.

ready cooked. By Order of Brigr. Gen. Atkinson. Signed S. MacRee Lt. & A.D. Camp.[65]

Orders Hd. Qrs. 6th Regt. Transport Boat The Elk, 16th May, 1825.

As soon as the first call for embarking has been sounded the field music or such of them as the Adj. shall direct will repair to the Adjt's. tent and immediately beat the "Generale." Every tent will fall at a signal tap to be given after that beat. The tents of the flank will fall from the river. Those in front the line, up the river. The splash boards will be constantly kept in their proper places when the boats are under way — Comdr. of boats will see to this. Morning reports of the respective boats will be handed to the Adj. every morning at the call for breakfast. Every Sunday Morning a report will be handed to the Adj. by the Comdr. of each boat embarking a state of his crew and showing the company to which each man properly belongs. There will be consolidated and entered by the Adj. in a book for that purpose. Similar reports will be made at the end of each month, on which the monthly returns will be forwarded. By Order of Col. Leavenworth, Col. Comg. Signed J. Pentland. Adj. 6th Regt.[66]

On May 16 the expedition left Fort Atkinson for the upper Missouri. General Atkinson began his journal and Major Kearny resumed his.

[Atkinson]

Fort Atkinson, Monday May 16th 1825

Set out at 7 oc this morning on the Missouri expedition with 8 keel boats & 435 men leaving Capt. Armstrong to follow by land with 40 mounted men. Run under our wheels generally till 11. o.c. & came to above the devils race ground one mile.[67] The wind freshing up, remained in this position 'till 5 o.c. Got under way & proceeded

---

65. Orderly Book 25, Sheldon, "Records of Fort Atkinson," 5:90.

66. Ibid, 120–21.

67. Maximilian said the Devil's Race Ground was so named because it had so many snags. Maximilian, *Travels in the Interior of North America*, 1:276. When Lewis and Clark passed this place, Clark described it as a "projecting Rock of 1/2 a mile in extent which the Current runs." Moulton, *Journals of the Lewis and Clark Expedition*, 2:249.

4 miles & encamped on the right bank of the river on a prairie. Before halting at 11. o.c. Middleton, a soldier of the 6th Rgt. got badly wounded by an axe striking his leg that was thrown to him on shore. He was sent back to the Fort and Madden, a soldier of the 6th Rgt., was sent up to supply his place.[68] Made 12 miles this day.

May 16th 1825 — Monday [Kearny]

Left Council Bluffs at 7 this morning with 3 Boats, the Beaver, Otter & Muskrat assigned to the 1st Infy. 4 more, the Elk, Buffalo, White Bear & Racoon being assigned to the 6th Infy & the Mink on board of which is Genl. A. who commands the Brigade, & is one of the commissioners. Made today about 11 miles & stopt on the Left bank 11 miles

---

Brigade Hd Quarters

Orders Flag Boat Mink 16th May 1825

Several accidents having already happened by the irregularity of the running and position of the boats of the Flotilla, the General directs that no boat shall be permitted to run so near a boat preseeding her as to strike or endanger her or injure herself. Boats using the Cordelle will not run so far near the presceeding boat as to throw her men in the advance of her. Boats crossing the river will not land above a boat on the Cordell, if by so doing she stops the progress of such boat.

The boats after setting out in the order prescribed in the order of the 15th inst will make the best progress they can, under the special instructions of the respective Commandants of Battalions.

The ration of hard bread will be sixteen ounces, the other parts of the ration as prescribed by regulations. A gill of Extra Whiskey will be issued by the Commissaries daily to the men, on requisitions countersigned by commandants of battalions 'till further orders. No greater supply of extra whiskey will be allowed from the public supplies.

By order of Brigr Genl Atkinson
Signed. S. MacRee Lt ADCamp A. A. A. Genl[69]

---

68. Thomas Middleton served in the army from 1818 until his death in 1831 at age thirty-two. Register of Enlistments, M233, rolls 16, 19. Daniel Madden enlisted in 1817 and apparently deserted after twelve years of service. Ibid.

69. Vol. 1:56–57, Orders Received, Sixth Infantry, RG 391.

[Atkinson]

Tuesday 17th May. Set out at half past 4. Ran 6 miles & halted for breakfast at 1/2 past 8. Set out at 10 & proceed till one & halted for dinner making 6 miles. Set out at 1/2 past 2 & proceed 6 1/2 miles & halted for the night on the right bank of the river, making 18 1/2 miles.

May 17th Tuesday [Kearny]

Put off shortly after day break & after meeting, during the day, with very strong currents & several of the Boats in the fleet swinging, & meeting with much danger, we stopt about 6 P.M having made about 17 miles

[Atkinson]

Wednesday 18. Set out 1/2 past 4. Cloudy & light winds, proceed 6 miles & halted at 8 for breakfast. Proceeded at 10 passed soldier river at 12 & halted at 1 after making 5 1/2 miles for dinner. At 1/2 past 2 set out and proceed 6 1/2 miles & halted on a sand point on the <*right*> left bank of the river for the night. Here is an eddy & rapid current. Capt. Mason & Capt. Riley encamped on the opposite side of the river. Making 18 1/2 miles.

May 18th Wednesday [Kearny]

Started shortly after day break. Crossed the River & had difficulty getting round a Bar. At noon, a very strong head wind. After an hours detention moved on & stopt about 6 P. M, the Beaver & Buffalo on the Right bank, the remainder of the fleet on the opposite side, & a short distance above. Made about [. . .] About Sun down Capt Mason killed two geese. We this morning passed Soldier River, coming in on the left.

[Atkinson]

Thursday 19. Set out at half past 4. Drift running rapidly in great quantity & the river rising rapidly. Proceeded 5 1/2 miles & halted for breakfast. Here Capt. Spencers boat, the Otter, injured her machinery in coming to in crossing the river & Maj. Kearny with the three boats of the 1 Rgt. were left behind to repair the boat, which was done in an hour, & in attempting to bring the Otter round the point her cordel broke & the mast gave way & again detained her. Maj. Kearny sent an express with this news stating that the boat would be repaired by the morning. After leaving Maj. Kearny we came 7 miles with the other 5 Boats & halted at 1 oclock for dinner. Heavy squalls coming up & the other boats being behind we lay out [at] the head of a slue all night. Here the sutlers boat came up at 1/2 past 5 in the afternoon.[70] Making 12 1/2 miles today.

May 19th Thursday [Kearny]

Put off at day break. Crossed the River & overtook the other Boats. Met with much strong water, & drift wood. Stopt on the left bank for breakfast. The Otter, after having crossed, swung & instead of the 2d boat in advance, became the last. On her next attempt she struck so hard against the bank as to move for four inches, the shafts & to shake her machinery. After being repared, she started about 12 & after doubling a difficult point, the men being on the cordell, her bridle broke & her mast snapt in two near the deck. The Boats of the 6th Infy with the Genl. had left us whilst we were reparing Otters machinery. Wrote to the Genl. informing him of our accident & the Carpenters went into the woods, cut down a Cotton tree, & commensed a new mast. About 4 P. M, Mr. Kennerlys boat, which left C. B. the afternoon of the same day that we did, passed us.[71]

Brigade Hd Qrs

Orders Flag Boat Mink 19th May 1825

The General deems it necessary to call the attention of commandants of Transport boats to the exercise of the greatest care and attention to the safety & preservation of their respective boats. Boats after crossing the river should come to shore with such caution as not to endanger the machinery, and in running, the banks of the river and drifts should be avoided, if possible, that the wheels of the boats may not be injured. The General has great confidence in the discretion of his Officers, but his solicitude for the safety of

70. Later, Atkinson identified the sutler's boat as the *Lafayette*. It carried oars, which the *Raccoon* borrowed when its machinery malfunctioned.

71. George H. Kennerly received his appointment as the sutler for the Sixth Infantry in 1823. Kennerly to Calhoun, June 27, 1823, Letters Received, M567, roll 7. He had served in the army but resigned in 1819 with the rank of lieutenant. Heitman, *Historical Register*, 1:592. After O'Fallon resigned, Kennerly served briefly in 1827 as Upper Missouri agent. Clark to Eaton, Sept. 15, 1829, Letters Received, M234, roll 883.

the transports on which the result of the expedition materially depends, urges him to this admonition.

By order of Brigr Genl Atkinson
Signed S. MacRee Lt. A.D. Camp & A. A. A. Genl[72]

[Atkinson]

Friday 20. Set out at 1/2 past 4. Proceeded till 1/2 past 7 & halted for breakfast having made 8 miles. Proceeded at 40 minutes after nine & run till 11 when we came to in consequence of the Rackoon having lost her mast in passing a sand barr (below the little Sioux river) on the right bank of this river. At 2 o.c. the Rackoon being repaired got under way and passed the little Sioux at 1/2 past 2. o.c. Proceeded till 1/2 past six o.c & came to on the right bank of the river near the upper end of the long reach above the little Sioux. Making 21 miles this day.

At 7 A.M. recd. a note from Maj. Kearny (who was left behind the day before yesterday to repair the Otter) stating that in addition to the injuries the Otter had before recd. the iron box, or journal, on which the shaft of the upper cogwheel runs was broken, but that he would notwithstanding be able to proceed with his detachment of boats.

May 20th Friday [Kearny]

The new mast of the Otter being completed, we got off at 1/2 past 5 A.M. Ran up about 6 miles & breakfasted on the right bank. Overtook the Boats of the 6th Infy at noon. Found them reparing the mast of the Racoon, which had broken a short time previous. At this time, the box of the shaft of the Otter broke, which detained us 2 hours. Proceded & in the afternoon came to the longest stretch which we have yet seen in the Missouri. Stopt at Sun down 1 1/2 miles in rear of the Genl.

[Atkinson]

Saturday 21. Ordered Col Leavenworth to proceeded with the 4 transports of the 6 Rgt. that the Flag boat would wait for Maj. Kearny to come up. The Col. got under way at 1/2 past 4, having left the Blacksmiths tools for Maj. Kearny to repair the Otter. The Beaver & Musk-

---

72. Vol. 1:57, Orders Received, Sixth Infantry, RG 391.

rat came up at 1/2 past 5 & proceed on (the Otter a mile behind). The flag boat Mink followed. The Beaver & <*Otter*> Muskrat proceeded 6 miles & halted on the left Bank <*of the*> for breakfast at 8 oclock. The wind began to blow which detained us till 1/2 past 2 when we got under way. Doubled a sand point encountering a strong current. Proceeded 6 miles & came to on the left bank of the river at 1/2 past 4 for the night. Run from the sand point under sail. The Otter was left below the sand point repairing her machinery. One of the journals on which the upper shaft run having broken. The Bever & Muskrat waited above the point for the Otter. Making 12 miles today.

May 21st [Kearny]

Started at day break, overtook & passed the Genl. & 6th Infy & stopt at 9 A. M to breakft. The Otters machinery was again repared, which detained us the rest of the day. 6 miles

[Atkinson]

Sunday 22 May. Proceeded this morning at 10 minutes before 5 & ran 5 miles to breakfast — left bank. Here Maj. Kearny came up with the Beaver Muskrat & Otter at 8. o.c. Proceeded at 15 minutes past 9 & run till 1 o.c. & came to on the left Bank for dinner, 5 miles. Proceeded at 2 o.c. and run near Woods' Hills making 10 miles. All together 20 miles today.

May 22d Sunday [Kearny]

Started at day break. Rainy morng, overtook the remainder of the fleet at breakfast. From here entered on Pratt's bend — 15 miles around — 500 yards across. Got some coal which 2 men of the Otter's crew (who went ahead, on the 20th) had burned. Encamped on the right bank 20 miles

An Express, which left C. B yesterday morng at 10, overtook us at noon.

[Atkinson]

Monday 23. Very Boisterous & cloudy. Waited till 1/4 past 5 & set out on the cordels. Proceeded some 400 yards & came to the wind being too high to proceed & the Otter having again broke her mast. The Muskrat swung in coming around a point of drift. Came to below on her wheels. The wind having lulled we proceeded at 1/4 past 10. Passed the upper point of Woods' hills at 1 oc. Cross the river, recross & came to 1/2 mile above the hills & halted on the right bank for dinner at 1/4 past 1. Proceeded at 1/4 past 2 and run till 7. o.c. & came to for the night on the right bank of the river: making twelve miles today. Lt. Harris went on shore at 4 o.c. & has not come in.[73] The White Bear & Rackoon did not come up. They stopped for the night at a point two & half miles below.

May 23d Monday [Kearny]

Started early. The wind strong & ahead. After proceeding about 200 yards, the new mast of the Otter broke in two. The rest of the fleet proceded after breakfast; those of the 1st Infy remained behind. Got another mast & started at 1/2 past 12. Passed Woods Hill which comes to the river on Right hand in a high bluff of yellow clay. In the afternoon, passed the 6th Infy & stopt on the Right bank about Sun down. 12 miles

[Atkinson]

Tuesday 24th. The White Bear & Rackoon came in view this morning & we proceeded at 5 o.c. Run 3 miles & came to on the right bank on acct. of strong north winds. Breakfasted here & the White Bear & Rackoon came up. The wind lulling a little — proceeded at 9 o.c & run 5 miles & came to for dinner at 1 o.c. The boats not being able to get thro' the nearest slue at the great cut off a short distance above Black-Birds Hills.[74] Proceeded at two the Boats turning back into the main channel & passing round an island. Some of the Boats had great difficulty in passing the lower end of the island in consequence of counter eddies & currents. The Buffalo &

73. William L. Harris was a military academy graduate assigned to the First Infantry on July 1, 1824. He was promoted to first lieutenant in 1830, dismissed from service in 1836, and died in 1837. He was in Company A. Heitman, *Historical Register*, 1:504; Fort Atkinson Post Returns, M617, roll 49.

74. Blackbird Hill was a conspicuous landmark described by nearly every passerby including Brackenridge: "It rises on the common range to the height of four or five hundred feet. The Missouri at its base, begins a strange winding course, several times returning upon its steps, and at length coming within nine hundred yards of where the hills first approach; so that in a course of thirty miles the Black-bird hill is still near us. It takes its name from a celebrated chief of the Mahas, who caused himself to be interred on the top: a mound has been erected on the pinnacle, with a branch stuck in it, a flag was formerly attached to it. He was buried, sitting erect on horse back; the reason which he gave for choosing this spot, was that he might see the traders as they ascended." Brackenridge, *Journal of a Voyage*, 81–82. Blackbird died in a smallpox epidemic during the winter of 1799–1800.

White Bear fell back several times. Run 9 miles & halted on the right bank for the night. The White Bear did not get up to us. Passed Black-Birds Hills at 10 o.c. The Hunters from the Elk bro't in a fine Buck. This & two others are all the deer yet taken & no other game but a few geese & ducks. Some Elk were seen today. 14 miles today. Lt. Harris still absent. Hunters were sent out in the morning to look for him, cannot find & the Muskrat left behind for him. This boat came without him after night.

May 24th Tuesday [Kearny]

Our Boats got off at day break & ran up 3 miles to breakfast. Lieut Harris of the 1st Infy having been missing since yesterday & fearing that he is lost in the woods, sent 2 hunters in pursuit of him. Left the Muskrat, hoping he may see her from the opposite shore, with directions to fire her Swivel occasionally. Set off & passed Black birds Hills so called from a celebrated Maha chief buried on the top of it. At this place, a bear crossed the river a short distance in front of us. Some fired at it but without success.

[Atkinson]

Wednesday 25 May. Proceeded at 1/2 past 4 passed Yellow Bluffs on the right Bank some ceader on their crowns at 1/2 past 5. Halted at 6 miles on the right bank 1/2 past 8. for breakfast. Proceeded at 1/2 past 10. (Here sent Maj. Ketchum back by land to bring up the White Bear which has not been seen since yesterday.) Halted for dinner at 1/2 past 1 on the left bank having run 6 miles since breakfast. Proceeded at 3. o.c. & run 7 miles & encamped for the night on an island near the right bank at 1/2 past 6. The White Bear still behind. We are about opposite the Maha Village.[75] The men returning from looking for Lt. Harris without having seen him.

May 25th Wednesday [Kearny]

Started early. The water is falling & the river much more easy to navigate. At noon, some of the Parties who had been in search of Lieut Harris, returned without success. Sent out another party. Stopt at night near the old Maha village. 15 miles

75. The Maha or Omaha Indian village was north of present Homer, Nebraska.

[Atkinson]

Thursday 26th. Proceeded at 1/4 before 5. Run three miles on the wheels. The wind springing up hoisted sail & run three miles further & halted at 1/2 past 8 on the left Bank for Breakfast. The bend of the river making the wind ahead. 4 men were dispatched this morning to find Lt. Harris if possible. Proceeded at 1/2 past 11. & run <*2 1/2*> 3 miles under sail. Came to in consequence of high winds on the left bank. Proceeded at 4 & run under a heavy press of sail till 1/2 past 7 & came to a mile above Floyds Bluffs making 20 miles today.[76] The Buffaloe, Beaver, Otter & Muskrat encamped a mile above us. Recd. a note at 8. o.c. from Maj. Ketchum stating that the White Bear was lying 15 miles below us not being able to turn a sand bar after the wind came up fresh at 11. o.c. this morning. He requests that the fleet should halt for him as the boat should be lightened. Lt. Harris joined the Boats this morning. He had been lost for 4 days.

May 26th Thursday [Kearny]

Sent a party of 5 good hunters in search of Lieut Harris with directions to return to the place where he left the Boats & to use all possible endeavors to find him. Started at day break. In the afternoon had a strong and fair wind. Passed Floyds Bluffs & River & stopt in the evening 2 miles above it on the Right bank. 20 miles

After dark, we were hailed from the opposite shore. Sent a small boat over & found Lieut Harris nearly worn out.

[Atkinson]

Friday 27. Sent Lt. Nute & two men back this morning to the White Bear with instructions that she should be pushed forward with speed & that the fleet would halt for her. Proceed at 6 this morning and run to the mouth of the Big Sioux river & halted for the White Bear to come up. At 1/2 past 2 the sutlers Boat came up. At 6 the White Bear arrived. Her machinery out of order. Commenced reparing it. Capt. Riley here erected a saw pit sawed plank & made a new rudder to his boat before night. Sign of Buffalo on the Sioux. 3 miles made.

---

76. Sgt. Charles Floyd was the only fatality on the Lewis and Clark expedition. He died, probably of a ruptured appendix, and was buried on a bluff at present Sioux City, Iowa. Moulton, *Journals of the Lewis and Clark Expedition*, 2:495.

May 27th Friday [Kearny]

Remained 'til about 6 A.M waiting for the Genl. & the boats of the 6th Infy to come up. Then started & ran up to the mouth of the Sioux River coming in on the left side & remained here the rest of the day, waiting for the White Bear which has been in the rear for 2 days past.

[Atkinson]

Saturday 28th. Waited till 7 this morning for the machinery of the White Bear to be repaired. Proceeded at that Hour and run 2 1/2 miles & halted in consequence of strong head winds. Lay to all day.

May 28th Saturday [Kearny]

Started about 6 A.M. Ran up one mile with considerable difficulty & on account of strong head winds & currents, were obliged to lay by the rest of the day.

[Atkinson]

Sunday 29th. Started at 4 this morning. Light Breeze and ran 11 miles & came to on the left bank of the river at 9 o.c for breakfast. The boats all up. The sutlers boat which is in compy. proceed under sail. Got under way at 1/2 past 10 & run 10 miles & came to at 1/2 past 3. o.c. on the right Bank for dinner. We waited here with the 6 Rgt. transports till 1/4 past 6 that the Elk might repair her machinery. One of the boxes under the shaft of the fly wheel having given way. The three transports of the 1st Rgt. proceeded an hour before us. We run till dusk & came to on an island on the right shore & encamped for the night having run 3 miles farther. Making 24 miles today. The Boats of the 1st Rgt. camped a mile above us.

May 29th Sunday [Kearny]

Got off at day break. Fair wind. Took in (in the afternoon) the party which had been sent out on the 26th in search of Lieut Harris. Ran up near the Iowa River & halted at dark on the right hand side.

22 miles

[Atkinson]

Monday 30 May. Proceed at 1/2 past 4 & run 4 miles (bad navigation) & came to the Cobalt Hills & halted at 3/4 past 7 on the right bank for Breakfast. Proceeded 1/2 past 1. o.c & run 5 miles & came to on the left Bank of the river at 6 o.c. Heavy rain & wind since 6 o.c this morning. We were put to much trouble to pass the sand bars between this & the Cobalt Hills.

May 30th Monday [Kearny]

Started at day break. Got up opposite to the Iowa River & had some difficulty in getting up on account of sand bars. Was overtaken here by the Genl. & 6th Infy whom we left behind yesterday. It commenced raining very hard which lasted til 1 P.M when it abated a little & we moved on. Stopt at about 6 P.M on the left hand shore, a very large sand bar opposite to us & extending for several miles.

[Atkinson]

Tuesday 31. The wind being fresh from the north and directly ahead we waited till 1/4 past 8 & proceeded against a head wind. The wind seems to lull a little. A very large Black Bear was killed by one of Capt. Gantts men last evening.[77] Run 4 miles and came to at 12 o.c in consequence of head winds. The transports Otter, Buffalo, White Bear & Elk were detained below us 2 miles at the point of a sand bar till evening by the wind. They came up at 1/2 past 6 & encamped with us for the night. The River began to rise today at 12 o.c. It had risen 14 inches by night.

May 31th Tuesday [Kearny]

The wind being strong & ahead detained us 'til 8 A.M. Then started & ran up about 4 miles where we remained the rest of the day waiting for the rear Boats, which in consequence of head winds, lay for several hours on a Sand bar & would not move.

4 miles

[Atkinson]

Wednesday 1 June 1825. The river has risen since yesterday 12 o.c, two feet. Proceeded at 1/2 past 4 & ran 7 miles. Came to on the right bank for breakfast at 8. o.c. Passed a range of clifts on the right Bank this morning. They appear to be of sand stone in horizontal strata. Proceeded at 1/2 past nine & ran <*6*> 8 miles & came to at 1 o.c on the left Bank (opposite the Blue Hill) for dinner. Got under way at 1/4 before 3. o.c. Here a skiff was sent across the river to bring in an Elk which was killed by one of Capt. Pentland's men, the Boats proceeded leaving the skiff & men to bring on the game.

This morning a dead Buffalo floated by us. Came to (after run-

77. Later they would encounter the white or grizzly bear, *Ursus horribilis*, which they did not consider to be as tasty as the black bear, *Ursus americanus*.

ning 6 miles) on the right bank of the river, making 21 miles. It was after dark before the Buffalo, Elk, Rackoon & White Bear came up, having been detained by the latter running on a snag, no injury to the Boat from it.

The Buffalo had a new Box put under the shaft of her fly wheel. It was done <*during the*> at night.

June 1st Wednesday [Kearny]

The River rose since yesterday noon nearly three feet. Started at day break. Fine morning. No wind. Run up & stopt at Sun down on the right bank having made about 20 miles

[Atkinson]

Thursday 2nd June. Proceeded at 1/4 before five, hoisting sail under a light wind & ran 8 miles and came to on the right Bank at 1/4 past 8 for breakfast. The Mink, Buffalo & Rackoon were detained by running on sand bars. The first did not get up till 1/4 before 10. The latter not till 1/4 past 11.

Passed the Ioway river and hills this morning. The Hills present a smooth & uniform range. Their elevation appear to be at 180 feet. Above the middle of the ridge that approaches the river the nearest there is an Indian grave of pretty large size. The Boats with the exception of the Buffalo and Rackoon got under way at 1/2 past 11. These Boats were directed to wait & let their men Breakfast & in the mean time repair the Machinery of the Buffalo. The wind blew in heavy squalls from the so. east & rendered our navigation of the river difficult & dangerous.

The Otter had her yard arm broken by the wind after running two miles from our last halt. The Beaver & Muskrat ran ahead and encamped on the right Bank of the river after making ten miles. The Mink, Buffalo, W. Bear & Rackoon encamped on the same side of the river two miles below. The Sutlers Boat passed by to the camp of the Beaver & Muskrat. She had been behind since the day before yesterday. The Otter came up after dark & encamped on an island a mile Below us. The Elk remained three miles below.

June 2d Thursday [Kearny]

Started early. Good wind. Run about 8 miles passed the White Stone [Vermillion] River & stopt for breakfast after which, put off, the wind very strong & proceded about 10 miles further, and stopt at 4 P.M (the Beaver & Muscrat) to await the arrival of the other boats. 18 miles

[Atkinson]

Friday 3 June. The Elk & Otter came up at 6 o.c. The men took Breakfast & we got under way at 20 minutes past 7. Wind fresh from the south. We run under the cordels, the wind at this point being adverse & the river snaggy & rapid. Came up with the Beaver & Otter at 1/4 past 8 who got under way & proceeded us. Ran under the oars past a sand island & hoisted sail. Ran two miles & took in sail near the little Bow crke [creek], below & above which are beautiful bottoms clothed with ash, Elm, oak, cottonwood &c. Made sail at the point above the Bluff and ran 4 miles to an island. Cordelled a short distance around it & again made sail & ran 7 miles to the chalk Bluffs & encamped one mile above on the left bank with the Beaver, Elk & White Bear & Mink. The Buffalo & Muskrat encamped 1 1/2 miles above on the opposite side of the river. The Otter & Rackoon did not come up. Rain wind & thunder this night. Came 18 miles.

Two Elk were killed by Lt. Van Swearingen & a man of the Muskrats crew.[78]

June 3d Friday [Kearny]

Put off at 8 A.M. The river being much more straight. Fair wind. About 3 P. M. passed the Chalk Bluffs & Perkin's old Trading House opposite to it.[79] Stopt 2 miles above here at 4 P.M, having much injured the rudder of the Beaver whilst running thru some very strong water. 15 miles

78. Joseph VanSwearingen was a military academy graduate assigned to the First Infantry and then transferred to the Sixth in 1824. Heitman, *Historical Register*, 1:939. Kappler, *Laws and Treaties*, 2:230, lists a witness to one of the treaties as Lt. H. Swearingen, but he died in 1819. It is probable the witness was VanSwearingen.

79. Brackenridge also noted "bluffs of a chalky appearance, perhaps limestone" in this vicinity. Brackenridge, *Journal of a Voyage*, 89. Perkins's old trading house may have belonged to Joseph Perkins, who became a partner in the Missouri Fur Company in 1819. Sunder, *Joshua Pilcher*, 29. In August 1821 he was taking a keelboat to the company's Fort Lisa, but the boat sank near St. Louis. Dale L. Morgan and Eleanor Towles Harris, *The Rocky Mountain Journals of William Marshall Anderson* (San Marino, Calif.: Huntington Library, 1967), 308.

Orders, Hd. Qrs. 6th Regt. Transport Elk June 3rd, 1825.

When there are two or more officers for duty to a boat one of them will always be on the shore with the Cordell men when the boats are cordelling. The Col. Comg. deems this essentially necessary to equalize the labor of the men. He has observed that the good men exert themselves constantly while others avoid labor when not under the eye of an Officer.[80]

Corpl King of Comp. J is hereby detailed as orderly for the Col. Comg. and will be respected accordingly until further orders. He will be excused from guard duty, but no other. Signed H. Leavenworth. Col. Comg.[81]

[Atkinson]

Saturday 4 June. Rain & thunder this morning. Proceeded at 1/4 past 7 & ran to the encampment of the Buffalo & Muskrat who proceeded on. At 4 miles we halted on the right Bank at 11 o.c for dinner & to await the coming up of the otter & Rackoon who arrived at 3. o.c. Proceeded at 1/4 past 4 & ran 6 miles & came to on the right Bank for the night. The Buffalo & Otter encamped opposite on the other bank. Passed the River Jack [James] this morning. The appearance of the country about it similar to the discription given by Lewis & Clark.[82] The river for several miles above and below the mouth of the river Jack appears to have changed its bed repeatedly since Lewis & Clark ascended, turning greatly to the right & leaving several islands & many sand bars in the neighborhood. At the mouth of the Jack a skin was found flying on a pole as a flag with the figure of a man drawn upon it pointing down the Missouri, which is supposed to indicate the descent of some trader & intended

---

80. Apparently the men on the cordelles began to share the work more equitably because the order was revoked on July 13, 1825. Orderly Book 25, Sheldon, "Records of Fort Atkinson," 5:124.

81. Matthew W. King joined the Sixth Infantry in 1820. He reenlisted five years later and in 1829 was killed by Indians on the Santa Fe Trail. Register of Enlistments, M233, rolls 16, 18; Orderly Book 25, Sheldon, "Records of Fort Atkinson," 5:121.

82. William Clark's description is not very specific, but he does mention passing a long line of white, chalky bluffs "incrusted with a Substanc like Glas which I take to be Cabolt." Moulton, *Journals of the Lewis and Clark Expedition*, 3:16.

for the information of the companies men who may have been left behind on employment in other places. It continued to rain 'till near night. 6 miles above the river Jack we came to a beautiful plain on the left bank elevated an 100 feet stretching east & west. Opposite is a rich cotton wood bottom.

June 4th Saturday [Kearny]

During last night, a severe storm of rain & hail, thunder & lightening & hard winds. Put off about 5 A.M. Ran up thru a slough for 2 miles & stopt for breakfast a mile above the River Jaque coming in on the left side. Proceeded at 12. & come up about

16 miles

[Atkinson]

Sunday 5 June. Proceeded at 1/4 before five & with great difficulty made 2 1/2 miles by 8 o.c the river being filled with sand bars over which the water flows with great rapidity. Halted on the right bank for breakfast at 8 o.c. Rich cotton wood bottom. Proceeded at 9 o.c. Passed the Calumnet Bluffs at 11 o.c. They appear to be 180 feet high — clothed with grass — cut down perpendicular when they touch the river & present a face of mineral stone: color of sand stone. Beautiful prairie on the opposite shore. Came to 4 miles above the Bluffs on the right bank for dinner at 1/2 past 1 o.c. Proceeded at 4 (having waited for the Elk & Otter to come up) & ran 7 miles & halted on the right bank for the night, making 18 1/2 miles today. Here Rose, the interpreter, & a corporal & one private of Capt. Armstrongs Commd. came to us & informed us that the Capt. had been ten days at the punca's [Ponca Indians] waiting for us, & that he had killed little or no game.[83] Sent him some pork & Bread by the corporal.

June 5th Sunday [Kearny]

Started early. Passed the Calumet Bluffs. Handsome & extensive Praires. Hills approaching very near the river in the evening

83. Edwin Rose lived for many years on the upper Missouri, usually with the Crows or the Arikaras, but he remains a shadowy historical figure. Willis Blenkenson, "Edwin Rose," *Mountain Men and the Fur Trade*, 4:335–49.

On June 8 the battalion reached the Ponca village located on present Bazile Creek. Lewis and Clark noted a large abandoned village there in 1804 when the Poncas were living near present Verdel, Nebraska. Moulton, *Journals of the Lewis and Clark Expedition*, 3:46, 48.

when we halted. Rose a half Indian, came to us from the Poncas. He states the whole Nation is there waiting for us & that Capt Armstrong, with his party, (the horse) have been there 11 days.

[Atkinson]

Monday 6th June. Proceeded at 1/2 past 4 & run 7 miles & halted on an Island for Breakfast at 1/2 past 8. Proceeded at 10 o.c. & ran 7 miles and came to for dinner on the right bank at 1/2 past 2 for dinner.[84] Proceeded at 4 & ran 4 miles & came to on the right bank at 9 o.c. for the night. We were much perplexed with sand bars for two miles below our camp. The Beaver swung on a sand bar & after encountering much danger she was got off by the assistance of the crew of the Rackoon.

The Elk, Otter & White Bear encamped opposite to us on the left bank.

June 6th Monday [Kearny]

Rain again last night. Proceded at day break. Ran up about 4 miles & stopt for breakfast on Bon Homme Island on the left side, when we saw what is called by some, the remains of an ancient fortification which, (as is evident, that this Island was commenced by the collection of sand around a Snag & formed from that) 'tis most probable that it is nothing more than what once was a Sand-bar when this Island was inundated.[85] In the afternoon passing up the River, a young Elk ran by us within a few yards. Got on a bar about 6 P.M & were two hours in getting off, during which the Beaver was in much danger of being lost. Slept near Plumb creek.

[Atkinson]

Tuesday <*8*> 7. June. Proceeded at 6 o.c & ran 2 miles & came to at 1/2 past 9 the wind being ahead & the Beaver having swung on a

84. This is near the end of a page in Atkinson's journal. Below it and written upside down is the following in Atkinson's hand: "Passed the little Sioux at 1/2 past 2 o.c. & encamped at 1/2 past 6 near the head of the straight making since Breakfast 13 miles. 21 miles today." The entry was crossed with diagonal lines. The same information is given in the entry for May 20, thirteen pages before the lined entry.

85. Lewis and Clark were convinced this natural feature on Bon Homme Island was an elaborate prehistoric fortification. Moulton, *Journals of the Lewis and Clark Expedition*, 3:44. Brackenridge called it L'isle a bon homme and noted the presence of fortifications. Brackenridge, *Journal of a Voyage*, 91.

sand bar. The wind increased to a gale & the boats lay to till the ensuing morning except the Muskrat & Rackoon who proceed 3 miles farther. Capt. Armstrong came to us today & remained all night.

June 7th Tuesday [Kearny]

Put of at 6 A.M at which time the wind commenced blowing strong ahead. Having made a mile the Beavers cordel broke. Threw over the anchor which she dragged for a Quarter of a mile. She was got to shore safely, tho with much difficulty & exposed to great danger. Were detained the rest of the day in consequence of the wind.

Hd. Qrs. 6th Regt. Transport Boat Elk 8th June 1825.

The Order in relation to the striking of tents by the beat of drum is hereby revoked. . . .[86]

[Atkinson]

Wednesday <9> 8. Proceeded at 1/2 past 4 & ran 4 miles to the Puncar village at 8 o.c. Here we found Capt. Armstrongs party who had been waiting 13 days. On our arrival the ground was immediately cleared off below the mouth of paint creek & our camp pitched.[87] At 2 Maj. O Fallon & myself recd. the chiefs & head men of the Tribe & explained to them thro' Genl. A. the object of our visit & appointed the next day at 11 o.c to hold a council with the Tribe for the purpose of forming a treaty.

June 8th Wednesday [Kearny]

Started at day break & having made about 5 miles, stopt at the mouth of White Paint Creek, within a few hundred yards of the Puncah village.

After clearing away ground for an encampment, our Boats were unloaded, cleaned & the cargoes put back, which employed us the remainder of the day. In the evening an express came up from C. Bluffs bringing our letters & papers.

---

86. Leavenworth gave the order to strike the tents on May 16. Orderly Book 25, Sheldon, "Records of Fort Atkinson," 5:121.

87. Paint Creek, or White Paint Creek as Kearny calls it, is present Bazile Creek.

Head Quarters Ponca Village
Orders 8th June 1825

The troops will appear tomorrow morning at 9 Oclock under arms and in uniform for review. Knapsacks will be dispensed with. Signed H. Atkinson Brigr Genl U S Army[88]

[Atkinson]

Thursday <*10*> 9th June. The troops were paraded in Brigade in uniform at 9 this morning & was reviewed by Genl. A. in rear of the Puncar Village. They appeared extreemly well & excited great curiosity in the Indians[,] the whole Tribe, men, women & children leaving the Village to witness the scene. The troops returned at 10 o.c. & we opened a council with the Indians at 12 o.c. Almost the whole Tribe were present. Maj. O Fallon first spoke on the subjects relating to his agency & appointed the Young Smoke & one another, chiefs, & gave medals to them, made seven soldiers & gave them gargets.[89]

Genl. A. then addressed the Indians on the subject of the Mission and explained a Treaty that was previously drawn up which was unanimously agreed to and signed by the chiefs & 14 Braves and ourselves. Presents were then distributed, consisting of 4 guns, strouding, Blankets, Knives, Tobaco &c. &c. The Indians retired at 5 o.c.

June 9th Thursday [Kearny]

The two Battalions paraded at 9. A.M near the Village & were reviewed by the Genl. Morning exceedingly hot & oppressive. After which the Indians came into our camp & the Commissioners held a Council and made a Treaty with them. They count about 150 Warriors & about 450 souls. They have 60 lodges & are about 350 miles, by water, from C. Bluffs.[90]

88. Vol. 1:58, Orders Received, Sixth Infantry, RG 391.

89. The agent and the army appointed men as chiefs who may or may not have had any authority within the tribe, but who seemed amenable to the wishes of the Americans. They also "made" chiefs of some of the Indians they met on July 21. The name of the first Ponca to sign the treaty was translated as "He Who Makes Smoke." Kappler, *Laws and Treaties*, 2:227.

90. Atkinson arrived at very different figures for the Ponca. He estimated the population as no more than 1,000, with 180 "warriors." They were armed with

[Atkinson]

Friday 10th. We were engaged the two preceeding days in repairing the machinery of our Boats and till 1/2 past 12 today. At 1/2 past one o.clock we got under way and ran above the mouth of the Eau de coure [Niobrara River], & halted for the night on the right Bank of the river, making 6 miles & a half today. The weather being fine today except head wind in the morning. This morning the warriors assembled in front of our Boat & performed a war dance. They were dressed in various fancies - some in leggins and breech clout & painted, with dresses of eagles feathers, or the skins of animals. Some were entirely naked except a small piece of fur around the waist, their privates exposed, the prepos or fore skin being pulled forward & lifted up with a string pressing the penis back. The whole body & limbs of these men were painted, as also the testicales & penis.[91]

June 10th Friday [Kearny]

The Indians came into our Camp this morning & entertained us with a dance. We departed at 1 P.M. Ran up about 5 miles & stopt a half mile above the Leau qui coure [Niobrara River], an important stream, & from which 'tis said the Missouri receives much of its character. At the mouth of this River saw an old Trading House formerly occupied by Mr Paschal Cerry.[92]

Poncar Village, Missouri
River — 10th June 1825

Sir I have the honor to report that we arrived at this place on the morning of the 8th inst. and yesterday concluded a treaty with the Poncar Tribe of Indians.

---

inferior trade guns, but were well supplied with horses and mules. They hunted buffalo and raised corn and a few other crops. For years they had been at war with the Sioux, but recently had made peace with the Yankton, their nearest neighbors. U.S. Congress, *Expedition up the Missouri*, 8.

91. The bull dance of the Mandan is quite similar. George Catlin, *O-kee-pa, A Religious Ceremony and other Customs of the Mandans*, ed. John C. Ewers (New Haven, Conn.: Yale University Press, 1967), 58.

92. Paschal Cerry operated a trading post for the company of Berthold and Chouteau as late as 1823. Lecompte, "Pierre Chouteau, Junior," *Mountain Men and the Fur Trade*, 9:98.

We have met with no accident since we left out and have every prospect of succeeding prosperously in our Mission

With very great respect Sir

I have the honor to be Your Mo. ob. Servt

H. Atkinson Br Genl U.S. Army[93]

[Atkinson]

Saturday 11 June. Proceeded at 1/4 past 4 & ran 4 miles to Breakfast & halted at 1/2 past 8 on the right bank above the mouth of Poncar River. Proceeded at 1/2 past 9 & ran 6 miles & halted on the right bank for dinner. An antelope was killed this morning (the first) by a hunter from the transport Elk. Proceeded at 4 & ran till 1/2 past seven & halted on the right bank making 25 miles today. The Pinicle is seen five miles ahead.[94] The Bluffs on the right bank have been straight for 12 miles — elevated 150 to 200 feet — containing rotten slate & chalk. 4 burrowing squrrels [prairie dogs] were killed by one of Capt. Rileys hunters on the Bluffs at dinner time. 2 were sent to us.

June 11th Saturday [Kearny]

Got off at day break. Wind fair passed the Puncah creek on which that Tribe formerly resided.[95] Dined at what is called the Grand Tower & after making about 23 miles, stopt on the Right bank nearly opposite to a creek on which are found some boiling springs.

The River to day much straighter & the current less rapid than we have found it for the same distance since leaving Saint Louis.

[Atkinson]

Sunday <*13*> 12th June. Proceeded at 1/4 past 4 & ran 6 miles to Breakfast on the left Bank, a mile above the Pinacle on the opposite side. Halt at 8. Proceeded at 1/4 after nine & hoisted sail with a light wind. Signs of Buffalo was seen coming into the water this morning quite fresh. We ran 12 miles & halted at 2 o.c <*halted*> on the right bank for dinner. Proceeded at 3 o.c & ran till 7 & came to on the left

93. Atkinson to "sir," June 10, 1825, Letters Received, M567, roll 13.

94. The pinnacle, or grand tower as Kearny calls it, was a prominent landmark on the Missouri River.

95. Brackenridge noted a Ponca Indian village on Ponca Creek in 1811. Brackenridge, *Journal of a Voyage*, 94.

bank for the night, making 30 miles today. We are troubled with sand bars & islands. Timber becomes scarce & the hills approach the river nearer than at points below. The country becomes more rugged.

June 12th Sunday [Kearny]

Fine morning. Fair wind. Started at day break. Passed up on the Left side under the Cordele. A large portion of the bank falling in directly along side of the Otter put her in much danger. Another injured the Mink by springing her mast. Handsome ridges of hills on both sides & they approach much nearer the River than below, leaving the Bottoms much narrower. Many signs of Buffaloe, both on the Praires & on the banks. None of them yet seen from the Boats. Stopt at dark on the left bank near an old village (deserted) of burrowing squirrels.

[Atkinson]

Monday <*14*> 13 June. Proceeded at 1/4 before 5 & ran 7 miles to breakfast on the point of an island. The Rackoon was left at our last nights encampment to fix the crank of her fly wheel which has been occasionally loose for several days. She is expected to overtake us today. Fresh sign of Buffalo & Elk coming to the river for water. We have seen none of either these three days & none at all yet of Buffalo. Ran 6 miles to breakfast & halted at 8 o.c. Proceeded at 9 & ran 12 miles under sail & came to for dinner at 1/2 past 3 on the right bank, proceeded at 5 & ran 6 miles & came to on the left bank for dinner. 24 miles today. The Rackoon did not come up.

June 13th Monday [Kearny]

Shortly after starting, the Cordell of the Beaver broke. Dropt astern a short distance & made fast to the Elk without damage. At Sun rise, the wind commenced again from the South. Continued under sail during the day, making halts for breakfast & dinner. Passed in the afternoon Little Cedar Island & stopt a short distance above it on the left bank.[96] The 1st Reg't in advance.

---

96. Brackenridge described Little Cedar Island as "a beautiful island, called Little Cedar island, on which grows fine cedar, the trees uncommonly large. This is a delightful spot, the soil of the island is rich, and it may contain about three thousand acres — the middle of the island is a beautiful prairie, but the adjacent country is bleak and barren." Ibid., 95.

Brigade Hd Quarters
Flag boat Mink 70 miles above
Orders the Poncas (Mo River)

The men in halting for breakfast, dinner or to encamp for the night, are in the habit of easing themselves on the call of nature, on the ground necessary to be occupied by the troops, this practice is forbid. In future to comply with such calls all persons must retire from the river from 60 to 100 yards as the nature of the ground may indicate.

As it is found that the boats cannot always keep together, the head boats will invariably halt as early as 8 am for breakfast, at half past one pm for dinner and in the evening, time enough for the rear boats to encamp before dark. When the wind is fair, this rule may be dispensed with and the boats may continue to progress, the crews eating on board by squads, except as to halting in the evening time enough for the rear boats to come up before dark which must be strictly attended to. The above order will be read to the respective Companies of the Brigade.

Signed H. Atkinson Brigr Genl US Army[97]

[Atkinson]

Tuesday 14th. Proceeded at 1/4 before five and ran under sail 8 miles & came to on the right bank for breakfast at 8 o.c. We have been greatly troubled with sand bars in running by an Island covered with ceder, Calf Island & Bull Island. A Buffalo Bull swam across from the left Bank just above the head Boats, but the sand bars & wind prevented his being taken. Proceeded at 9. o.c. & ran 8 miles & came to on the right bank at 1/2 past 1 o.c. for dinner. Here we collected copperas, ocre, petrified back bone of an animal & several specimens of earth containing strata of some substance like crystal, some round stones &c. Some black currents or gooseberries were found in the Bluff sides & the service berry getting ripe. Maj. Ketchum & Doct. Gale killed two antelope 3 miles below & bro't them up in the Beaver.[98] Proceeded at 1/2 past 3 o.c.

---

97. Vol. 1:58–59, Orders Received, Sixth Infantry, RG 391.

98. Dr. John Gale was the surgeon assigned to the Sixth Infantry. Muster Rolls, Sixth Infantry, RG 94. He joined the army as a surgeon's mate in 1812 and

under the cordelle — the wind not serving as the river turns here So. West. Getting to a point on running two miles hoisted sail & ran till 1/2 past 7 & came to on the left bank for the night, having made 26 miles today. Rackoon not yet come up.

June 14th Tuesday [Kearny]

The remaining boats coming up, we started at Sunrise. Fair wind. Saw a buffaloe & several antelopes. One of the party killed two of the latter.

[Atkinson]

Wednesday 15th June. Proceeded at 1/4 past 4 & ran under the cordelle 5 miles & came to on the right bank for breakfast at the upper part of the Black Bluffs. Lt. [Van] Swearingen killed 2 antelope this morning on these Bluffs. Proceeded at 1/2 past 9 & ran 8 miles to dinner at 2 o.c. on the right bank. Proceeded at 4 o.c. Passed Capt. Armstrongs party at 6 & ran 5 miles & came to on the right bank for the night. The Elk separated from us this afternoon & got among sand bars on the opposite shore & lay three miles below us. Capt. Armstrong informs us that he had killed 4 Buffalo on the Puncar creek & yesterday put part of the flesh on board of the Rackoon near the Island of cedars. The Rackoon still behind.

June 15th Wednesday [Kearny]

Wind continues fair. Started very early. The bugle sounded before day break. In the afternoon passed Capt Armstrong & his mounted party being driven in from the hills, in consequence of heat & want of water.

The Elk got on a sand bar before dark & fired signals of distress — sent to ascertain the cause of it.

[Atkinson]

Thursday 16th June. Proceeded at 6 o.c. after breakfasting. Run three miles to the mouth of White river & crossed the Missouri to the Bluffs for two Indians who made signs for us to come to them. It proved to be a Brave of the Sioux's & his son who were sent with letters to us from Mr. Wilson Sub. agent at Fort Kiaway.[99] They

---

was promoted to surgeon two years later. He was with the Yellowstone Expedition and was stationed at Fort Atkinson until its abandonment. Gale died in 1830 at the age of thirty-five. Nichols, *The Missouri Expedition*, xvii.

Bro't from Mr. Wilson 1/2 doz. Buffalo Tongues to Maj. O Fallon. Something was given to them to eat & they were sent back with letters informing Mr. W. that we would be at the Fort this evening or in the morning. The wind now, 1/4 past 11, is blowing a gale & we are lying to on the right bank to reef & repair our sail. Our sail the Mink's blue to pieces. We halted at 1/2 past 7 on the right bank for the night <*4 miles below this point Fort Kiaway*>. The Elk, Otter & Rackoon did not come up this evening. Made 17 miles today.

June 16th Thursday [Kearny]

Waited til near 7 for the rear Boats to come up — put off — the wind strong & fair. Passed Shannons River. 8 miles above it, White River. Afterwards the remains of old Cedar Fort. Nothing left of it, but the chimney & a short line of pickets. 'Twas abandoned & burned a few years ago.[100] Stopt 8 miles above it.

[Atkinson]

Friday 17th June. Proceed at 1/2 past 4 and ran to Fort Kiawa & halted at 8 o.c. Mr. Wilson came to us this morning & accompanied us back to this place. The Elk & Otter came up today at 4 o'clock. About 7 lodges of Sioux are encamped here. They are called the broken Arrows & are not well looked upon by the other bands of Sioux, being considered rather refractory & ungovernable. Today runners were sent to bring in the Tetons, Yanktons & Yanctonas. The principle men of the Broken arrows paid us a visit today.[101]

---

99. Peter Wilson was subagent for the Missouri River tribes and arrived at Fort Kiowa in October 1824. He spent the winter there and held talks with the Indian leaders in preparation for the meeting with the commissioners. Harry H. Anderson, "The Letters of Peter Wilson, First Resident Agent among the Teton Sioux," *Nebraska History* 42 (1961): 237–64. Early in 1826 Wilson fell ill at a Mandan village and was taken to Fort Atkinson, where he died and was buried on May 16. Order No. 113, May 16, 1826, 90, Orders Issued, Sixth Infantry, RG 391.

Fort Kiowa was built about 1822 by the French Company of Berthold, Chouteau and Pratte. Lecompte, "Pierre Chouteau, Junior," *Mountain Men and the Fur Trade*, 9:99.

100. Cedar Fort or Fort Recovery was built by the Missouri Fur Company during the winter of 1820–21 on an island in the river. Financial reverses forced the company to abandon and burn the fort in the summer of 1824. Sunder, *Joshua Pilcher*, 29.

101. The Sioux were a loose confederacy based upon ties of language, custom, and familiarity. Divisions included the Broken Arrow band, which is now extinct. The commissioners would meet the Teton, Yankton, and Yanktonai bands later.

June 17th Friday [Kearny]

Put off at day break, & after running about 5 miles reached Kiawas Fort where we found some Sioux. Many more are expected to morrow. This place being fixed on to hold treaties with them, we are now about 500 miles (by water) above Council Bluffs.

Brigade Hd Quarters
Fort Kiawa near the Great Bend

Orders 17th June 1825.

As soon as the troops are encamped, and the ground cleared off, they are to be employed in putting their Arms and effects in order.

No Non Commissioned Officer, Musician or Private will be permitted to pass the chain of sentinels but by the permission of his company Officer sanctioned by the Commandants of Corps and they must then pass the Main guard; and when permitted to go out they must be accompanied by a Non Commissioned Officer who shall be responsible for their conduct whilst absent. Any traffic between the men and the Indians for mockasins or meat must be done at the Main guard. The men are not to vend any articles of their clothing or whiskey to the Indians.

The Indians are not to be permitted to enter the Camp except at the main guard and then by invitation of an Officer of the Army or of the Indian Department.

The guard will mount in uniform to morrow evening & the troops will be prepared to appear in uniform as soon as the day after. Sinks are to be prepared for the men under the direction of the QrMas [as] soon as pitched.

By order of Brigr Genl Atkinson
Signed. S. MacRee Lt AdeCamp & A. A. A. Genl[102]

[Atkinson]

Saturday 18 June. Guard mounted uniform this morning, attended by the Band in full dress. Rose, Harris & Shania were dispatched this morning to look for the Chyan [Cheyenne] Indians & bring them to us at the Ricara's, or some convenient point on

102. Vol. 1:59, Orders Received, Sixth Infantry, RG 391.

the Missouri. The Rackoon still behind. A Yankton Indian came across the river this afternoon & informs us that the Yanktons are at Beasous [Bijou] Hills a days march from this & that they may be expected in a day or two.[103] They had the day previous surrounded a herd of Buffalo & killed a considerable number and were preparing the meat. The river commenced rising in the afternoon.

June 18th Saturday [Kearny]

This place is within a short distance of "the three Rivers of the Sioux pass" & 15 miles below the commencement of the Great Bend. The Band of Tetons is here, & the other Bands of the Sioux, have been sent for to come in.[104]

An express has started toward the "Black Hills" in search of the "Chayennes" [Cheyenne] to invite them to meet us near the Chayenne River.[105]

The Elk & Otter, came up to day — the first having been absent since the 15th & the latter since the 16th Inst.

---

103. In 1823 a "correct and intelligent young man" named Harris came from the mouth of the Yellowstone to Fort Atkinson, where he gave Atkinson a very unfavorable report on the fur trade and the Indians in the upper Missouri. Morgan, *Jedediah Smith*, 103. Harris was accompanied by another man, also named Harris, which further complicates the issue. Morgan is of the opinion that one of them was Moses "Black" Harris. Ibid., 393. Moses Harris was paid for his services as a guide for the expedition during the summer of 1825. Voucher 52, Commission Accounts, 10987, RG 217.

The Yankton then numbered about 3,000. They were nomadic buffalo hunters who ranged along the Missouri from the Big Bend southward to the Sioux River. U.S. Congress, *Expedition up the Missouri*, 8.

104. The expedition would pass the Great or Big Bend in a few days. This long, U-shaped bend is one of the most conspicuous landmarks on the Missouri and appears on some of the earliest maps of the river. Atkinson described it in his diary on June 24 and 25.

The Teton numbered about 3,000 and ranged along the White River, hunting buffalo. U.S. Congress, *Expedition up the Missouri*, 9. At this time Teton often referred only to the Brulés.

Kingsley M. Bray has examined early population estimates and concluded that the 1825 numbers were reasonably accurate. Kingsley M. Bray, "Teton Sioux Population History, 1655–1881," *Nebraska History* 75 (1994): 171.

105. The Black Hills refers to the general Rocky Mountain foothills, and not to those of Mount Rushmore fame.

Brigade Head Quarters
Orders Fort Kiawa 19th June 1825

The inconvenience arising to the prosecution of the duties assigned to the Commissioners from the frequent intoxication of the Interpreters and other persons employed by them, renders it necessary for the General to call upon the Officers of the Brigade to assist him in the suppression of the evil, they will not give nor allow others under their orders to give spirituous liquors to those men, nor are they to give it to the Indians here or those that may be met with thereafter.

By order of Brigr Genl Atkinson
Signed. S. MacRee Lt AD Camp & A. A. A. Genl[106]

[Atkinson]

Sunday 19th June. The river rose 2 feet last night & is rappidly swelling. Two men came up this morning from the Rackoon & informs us that she had been detained by breaking her crank but was above white river yesterday evening & will arrive today. Rose & Harris let their horses get away last night & Shania came in for them. They were sent back by Shania & one of Capt. Armstrongs party.

Capt. Gantt came up with the Rackoon at dusk & encamped on the opposite shore, he was not able to cross over having again broke the crank of his Boat a half mile below. Some 90 Yanktons & Yanktona's came to the opposite side of the river last night.[107]

June 19th Sunday [Kearny]

We are busily employed in reparing the Boats, the machinery of most of them being much worn.

The Band of Yanktons, this evening, arrived on the opposite shore & there made their camp up on a high hill.

[Atkinson]

Monday 20 June. The Rackoon crossed over at 9 o.clock having borrowed the oars of the Sutlers Boat, Lafayette. The Officers of

---

106. Orderly Book 26, Sheldon, "Records of Fort Atkinson," 5:10–11.

107. The Yanktonais were buffalo hunters in the country around the head of the James River. Their population was estimated at about 4,000. U.S. Congress, *Expedition up the Missouri*, 9.

the Brigade partook of a coallation with the commissioners at one o.clock today. At 3 o.c. the chiefs & warriors of the Yanktons & Yanktonays were bro't over preparatory to a council to be held tomorrow.

June 20th Monday [Kearny]

This morning the Rackoon (which was left behind on the 13th Inst) came up & brought from the opposite shore some of the Yankton chiefs. In the afternoon the Sutlers Boat was sent over & brought the Band.

Brigade Head Quarters
Orders Fort Kiawa 20th June 1825

Eight days rations of Flour and Pork for the Brigade will be deposited at this place under the care of Mr Sire until the return of the troops from upper country.[108] This object will be carried into effect under the directions of commandants of Corps, who will cause duplicate memorandums to be taken of the number of barrels of each article left, one to be left with Mr Sire and the other to be kept by the Quarter Master.

By order Signed. S. MacRee Lt AD Camp & A. A. A. Genl[109]

Brigade Head Quarters
Orders. Fort Kiawa 21st June 1825

The Brigade will appear in full uniform for review this morning at 9 o'clock on the ground immediately in front of the line of encampments, Capt Armstrong's troop forming on the right, every man for duty will appear under arms except the blacksmiths who may be employed at the forges. The troops will not probably be kept on the field more than an hour.

As the duties of the Commissioners with the Indians at this place will close by noon tomorrow it is desireable that the Flotilla should be ready to move soon afterwards.

---

108. Joseph A. Sire had a long career in the West. In the fall of 1823 he was employed by the French Company and had a temporary trading post near the mouth of the Teton River, so it is likely he would be at Fort Kiowa two years later to take charge of the army's rations. Philip St. George Cooke, *Scenes and Adventures in the Army* (Philadelphia: n.p., 1859), 150.

109. Vol. 1:60, Orders Received, Sixth Infantry, RG 391.

Lieut Holmes will perform the duties of Ass. Qr Master to the Brigade, and assume the incidental expenses appertaining thereto. By order of Brigr Genl Atkinson

Signed S. MacRee Lt AD Camp & A.A.A. Genl[110]

[Atkinson]

Tuesday 21. June. At 9 o.c this morning the Brigade appeared under Arms in full uniform, Capt. Armstrongs Troops forming on the right & was reviewed by the Genl. Himself & staff on horse back. The display was very fine & the Troops being in fine order. All the Indians witnessed the circumstance.

At 2 o.clock a council was opened with the Tetons, Yanktons & Yanktonays, nothing more was done in council today but organizing the Bands by Maj. O Fallon by appointing & recognizing chiefs & warriors, and giving up a Yankton girl that was a prisoner with the Otos who was bro't up with us for the purpose. The Indians were dismissed at 1/2 past 5 o.c with instructions to meet us in council tomorrow morning when the business of the treaty would be entered upon.

At night some 12 or 15 rockets were thrown up to amuse the Indians. The river has risen about 4 feet since we arrived on the 17th inst.

June 21d Tuesday [Kearny]

The Genl reviewed the Troops, including Capt Armstrongs party of horse, this morning at 9. After which a Council was held with the Indians, consisting of the Tetons, Yanktons & Yanktonans of the Sioux Nation, numbering (those present) about 250 warriors. Some chiefs were recognized — others made.

Grand Bend on Missouri

Dear Sir, 21st June 1825

After a fatieguing and laborious trip without any serious difficulty we reached this place on the 17th instt and are at this time setting out on our Journey up with flattering prospects of succeeding to the full extent of our wishes. We have met with the Poncas Yankton, Teton, and Yanktonon Tribes of Indians. Every thing was

---

110. Vol. 1:60–61, ibid.

succeeded and equaled our most sanguine expectations. I have been constantly engaged, not a moment to spare. Although I wish to say a great deal my situation is unfortunately such that I cant write but briefly. . . . The Sowomem [Saone?] and Ogalalas will meet us in a few days hence at the mouth of the little Missouri. The Chyenne Nation to whom we have sent runners, we expect to meet at the A'rickaras Towns. We have just received an express from the A'rickaras which will return tomorrow to announce to them our near approach and the probable time of our arrival at their villages. It has just been reported to us that Charbonoe and three men of Tilton & McKinseys Company were robbd of their goods by the Assineboins between Lake de travers and the Mandans.

With great respect & Esteem
I have the honor to be
Your Mo. Obt. Servt.
Benjn. O'Fallon
U.S. Agt. Indn. Affs

To
Genl. Wm. Clark
Supt. Indn. Affs. & Commissioner
Prarie du Chein Upper Mississippi[111]

[Atkinson]

Wednesday 22 June. We met in council with the Tetons Yankton & Yanktona's, concluded a treaty signed by us & the Chiefs & warriors of these Bands. Gave presents to the Tetons — 5 guns & various other

---

111. O' Fallon Letterbook. O'Fallon used the old fur trader's name, Little Missouri, for what is today called the Bad River. Atkinson did the same in his letter of June 23 to Colonel Jones. In his journal Atkinson called it the Teton River, a name coined by Lewis and Clark. On August 9, when the expedition was in northwestern North Dakota, they passed another Little Missouri, which has retained its name. Melburn D. Thurman, "The Little Missouri River: A Source of Confusion for Plains Ethnohistory," *Plains Anthropologist* 33 (1988): 429–77.

Toussaint Charbonneau left the North West Company in Canada and in 1796 came to a Hidatsa village near the mouth of the Knife River. About 1801 he married a captive Shoshoni teenager, Sacagawea, and together they traveled with Lewis and Clark as interpreters. He was with Leavenworth when the Arikaras were punished in 1823 and served as the interpreter while Atkinson and O'Fallon were at the Mandan villages. Dennis R. Ottoson, "Toussaint Charbonneau, A Most Durable Man," *South Dakota History* 6 (1976): 152–85.

William P. Tilton and Kenneth McKenzie were leaders of the Columbia Fur Company. It was dominated by British citizens, but because Tilton was an American citizen he was able to obtain a license to trade in American territory. The company built a trading post at the Mandan villages in 1823. Mattison, "Kenneth McKenzie," *Mountain Men and the Fur Trade*, 2:217–24.

goods. To the Yanktons the same & to the Yanktonas 2 guns & other goods, the latter tribe being represented by only 2 chiefs & a few warriors whilst the other tribes were fully represented. These Tribes deport themselves with gravity & dignity. They dress well in long leggins of dressed skin, shirts, or rather a close hunting shirt with sleeves & highly ornamented with fringe & porcupine quills. Robes of Dressed Buffalo Skins & coverings of various sorts for the head, such as skins of fured animals &c, some curiously formed with ears of animals attached in an erect manner. These Tribes presented the commissioners with a few dresses of dressed leather — a few dressed robes, 2 eagle feather caps & some 1/2 doz. pipes.

June 22d Wednesday [Kearny]

The Commissioners again met the Indians at 12. Rain for some time prevented them from proceeding, after which a Treaty was made with them, & being signed & witnessed, one was left with each Band. Presents of Robes, Pipes, Leggens &c were made by the Indians, to the Commissioners — who received from them, guns, blankets, lead, powder &c. &c.

Head Qr. Right Wing West. dept.
Fort Kiawa, at the foot of the Great Bend,
June 23rd 1825

Sir, I have the honor to inform you, for the information of the dept. of war, that the troops under my command reached this place on the morning of the 17th inst. after a very quick passage from the Poncar's. We have been detained here three or four days longer than we could have wished, to collect the Indians together, who were compelled, altho' they expected us, to go out into the Prairies to obtain a subsistence. Yesterday we concluded treaties with the Teton, Yankton and Yanktonay Tribes of the sioux Nation; and this morning at 10. o.c we shall move forward with a view of meeting the Scion [Saone] & Ogalalla Tribes, at the mouth of the little Missouri river, an hundred miles above this place. We shall next halt at the Aricara Village where together with the Aricaras, we expect to meet the Schyans, [Cheyennes] to whom we have sent an express with an invitation to that effect. From thence we shall proceed to the Mandans, the Yellow-Stone & as much further as the season will admit of.

We have not as yet lost a man or met with an accident of any sort or consequence.

With very great respect Sir
I have the honor to be
Your Mo. ob. Servt
H. Atkinson
Br. Gen. U.S. Army[112]

To
Colonel Jones
Adjt. Genl Washington City.

[Atkinson]

Thursday 23rd June. The weather being cloudy this morning & a little rain falling, together with a necessary detention to settle with the interpreters & receive a visit from their chiefs [,] the Troops did not embark till 1/4 before one o.c. when we commenced our ascent of the river & proceeded 12 miles & halted at 1/2 past 8 on the right Bank of the river for the night. We were greatly retarded & troubled today with the navigation of the river — having to cordell over banks more than 120 feet in height & thro' an excessive rapid current, the river having in the last 5 days risen more than 4 feet. Fort Kiawa consists of a range of log buildings containing 4 rooms — a log house & a store house forming a right angle leaving a space of some 30 feet <*covered by cotton wood pickets & a gate. The only entrance*>. At the south corner of the work is erected a Block House near which stands a smiths shop. At the No. corner is erected a small wooden tower, the whole work enclosed by cottonwood pickets. The sides or curtains to the works 140 feet each.

June 23d Thursday [Kearny]

A cloudy morning. Our Boats being repaired — our men recruited — the Council held & treaty made, we departed at 12 N. The wind ahead passed "the 3 Rivers of the Sioux Pass" called Pecon-la-lan-la coming in on the right side behind an Island. Cordelled this afternoon on a very high rolling bluff bank.

Stopt a little after dark, the 1st Regt in advance, about half a mile.

[Atkinson]

Friday 24th June. Proceeded at 1/2 past 4 & ran 6 miles & halted at 9 o.c <*opposite to the*> on the gorge of the grand Bend on the right

112. Col. Roger Jones filled the long-vacant position of adjutant general on March 7, 1825. Cooling, *American State Papers: Military Affairs*, 2:200; Letters Received, M567, roll 13.

bank for breakfast. Here Maj. O.Fallon, Maj. Langham & Capt. Kennerly left the Boat to proceed across the gorge to wait for the flotilla to come around. The distance across being 1 1/4 miles & 25 around. Proceeded at 1/4 past 11 o.c. & ran 6 miles and came to on the right Bank for dinner at 3 o.c. Proceeded at 1/2 past 4 and ran 7 miles & halted on the right bank for the night.

June 24th Friday [Kearny]

Started about 4 A.M & ran up to a small creek (Prickly Pear creek) to breakfast. The remainder of the Boats over took us here. We are now near the commencement of the "Great Bend" & several officers & others left us here in order to pass over it.

[Atkinson]

Saturday 25th June. Proceeded at 1/2 past 4 and ran 5 miles & came to for breakfast at 9 o.c. Proceeded at 1/2 past 10 & ran three miles by 4 o.c. having been retarded by sand bars. The Beaver stuck on a sand bar & 300 men were not able to get her off till her cargo was taken out. She was then got off by the 1st Infy. <[. . .] *at this point all night in company with the*> & came to us on the right bank 3 miles above where we had halted 1/2 past 7 for the night. The neck of land <*called*> mentioned by Lewis & Clark is as described by them an inclined plain rising as you approach the upper edge of the gorge to cliffs of 200 feet elevation. The plain is prairie entirely & its most gentle slop inclining to the northernmost part of the bend. The river around which is a continuation of sand bars on the convex shore. The river fell 2 inches last night & about 2 1/2 feet alltogether from its greatest height as yet. The rise however has not been as great by 7 or 8 feet, as yet, this season as it some times attains. It is thought now to be too late to expect a great rise this season.

June 25th Saturday [Kearny]

About noon passed some Sioux, about 40, on the left bank. At 2 P.M the Beaver struck on a bar. After considerable work, with the assistance of the crews of the other Boats & not being able to move her, she was unloaded, & got off. Her cargo being put back, she started at Sun down & over took the Boats of the 6th Infy after dark, they having proceded from when the Beaver was grounded after dining.

[Atkinson]

Sunday 26th June. Proceeded at 1/2 past 4 & ran till 7 o.c & came to at 6 miles on the right bank for breakfast. Here Garrow & a hand employed by the French traders was sent across the river & directed to proceed to the Aricaras with the news of our approach & with instructions that they should collect some Buffalo meat for us against our arrival.[113] Gen. A. sent a little Tobacco for them to smoke. Proceeded at 1/4 before 9 o.c and ran till 1/4 before 2 o.c making 8 miles & came to at the mouth of Tylers <*creek*> river for dinner, where we found Majs. O Fallon, Langham, Ketchum, Capt. Kennerly, Doctr. Gale & others who had left us at the lower end of the great bend to hunt. Tylers is a small river, or creek running but a little way back into the hills. A black tail deer was killed on this river by one of the hunters. A large rabbit, or hare similar to the English hare was killed here by Doctr. Gale. Near this place is a village of barking squirrels [prairie dogs]. Some were shot by the party. This animal is not very savory food, having a strong smell when cooked. They were ate at our table.

Proceeded at 1/2 past 3 o.c. and ran two miles. The Boats in passing a sand bar came in contact (The Beaver & White Bear) & got entangled. The Beavers rudder getting foul of the fore stay of

---

113. Joseph, Pierre, and Antoine Garreau all witnessed the treaty signing at the Arikara village. Kappler, *Laws and Treaties*, 2:239. Later, Kearny reported that Joseph Garrow had resided with the Arikaras since 1796. He had two sons, Pierre and Antoine, by his Arikara wife. Annie Heloise Abel, ed., *The Fort Clark Journal of F. A. Chardon* (Iowa City, Iowa: Athens Press, 1932), 283, n.288. Ethel A. Collins's brief biography of Pierre states he was born about 1789. She was undoubtedly misinformed when she wrote that he came to the Arikaras when he was a young man. Ethel A. Collins, "Pioneer Experiences of Horatio H. Larned," *Collections of the State Historical Society of North Dakota* 7 (1925): 39–40. A mixed blood Arikara, whose name was rendered Garrio, was killed and scalped near Bellevue in early June 1835 by some of Lucien Fontenelle's men because he was accused of killing whites in the Arikara country. Archer Butler Hulbert and Dorothy Printup Hulbert, *Marcus Whitman, Crusader*, vols. 6 and 7 of *Overland to the Pacific* (Denver: Stewart Commission of Colorado College, 1936), 84, 94–5. Francis Chardon seems to be referring to this killing when he noted the arrival at the Arikara village in 1837 of the wife and children of a man slain at Cabanne's post. Chardon also mentioned that a principal Arikara chief "swore Death and destruction" if he was not given blood money for one of his relatives killed by the whites at Cabanne's post. Abel, *The Fort Clark Journal of F. A. Chardon*, 119. Another Garreau was killed by the Blackfeet on the Yellowstone River in 1829. Morgan, *Jedediah Smith*, 428, n.29.

the Bear which was imprudently cut & the mast of the Bear gave way & fell over the side. She was bro't to shore & the damage repaired & we proceeded two miles further & came to on the right Bank for the night with the Mink, Muskrat & Bear. The other five boats encamped opposite on the other shore. The river fell 2 1/2 inches last night.

June 26th Sunday [Kearny]

Started at day break & ran up about 4 miles to the upper part of the "Great Bend" to breakfast. Stopt for dinner at Tylers creek, coming in on the right bank. The water is falling & as it leaves the Bars, they are so muddy as to make it almost impossible to pass over them. This renders the cordelling very bad. In the afternoon the White Bear ran afoul of the Beaver & in order to extricate them, the fore stay of the W. B. was cut in two, when her mast went overboard. Nothing was broken & she proceded in about an hour.

[Atkinson]

Monday 27th June. Proceeded at 1/4 past 4 o.c. & ran 6 miles & came to on the right bank for breakfast at 1/2 past 7 o.c. Proceeded at 9 o.c. & ran 7 miles & came to at 1/2 past 1. o.c on the right bank opposite Ceder Island for dinner. This island appears to be about 2 miles long containing a growth of ceader & cottonwood. The ground is high & free from inundation. Timber on the river becomes more scarce. The highlands are dry and sterile rising into sharp & high hills. Proceeded at 3 o.c & ran 7 miles & came to on the right bank at 1/2 past 7. for the night. We find here, & some 50 miles below, the black currant of large size & delicious flavor. They grow on the sandy banks & on the little ravines & points of bluffs. There seems to be little or no game in this part of the country.

June 27th Monday [Kearny]

Proceded at day break past Cedar Island where Lisa formerly had a trading establishment.[114]

[Atkinson]

Tuesday 28 June. Proceeded at 1/4 after 4 o.c. & ran 5 miles & came to at 7 o.c. on the right bank for breakfast. Here the Otter

---

114. Lisa's trading establishment was not yet built when Brackenridge went past in 1811, but he did note that Lisa promised the Indians he would build a post on the island that fall. Brackenridge, *Journal of a Voyage*, 95–96.

came up, that had been behind since yesterday morning. The Elk swung this morning at a point 2 miles below in a strong current. She was bro't to by her wheels without difficulty & again came on. Proceeded at 1/4 befor 9 o.c. The river raised 5 inches last night & is still increasing & a good deal of drift running which makes the navigation troublesome & tedious. At 12. o.c. we arrived near the head of Elk island at the upper point of which some Buffalo were discovered by Majs. O Fallon & Ketchum, who were walking on the right bank of the river. Maj. K. ran back & gave the information to Gen. A. while Maj. O.F. remained to observe their motions. The flotilla was halted at 1/2 past 12 & the men ordered to get their dinners, and a small party was formed under the direction of Maj. K. & sent over to the island to shoot the Buffalo, the troops being in want of fresh meat. The party landed & went in pursuit but their design was partly frustrated by the imprudence of Lt. Wragg who crossed over to the island shortly after the party and ran forward & fired upon the Buffalo, being three in number, who at once plunged into the river.[115] One swam across to where the Boats was lying & was shot but sank & was lost in a rapid current. The other two after swiming out returned to the island. One was killed by Capt. Mason on reaching the bank & the other ran off wounded. The one that was killed & saved weighed (the 4 quarters) 889 pounds, which afforded a seasonable issue to the men. The Boats proceeded at 1/2 past 2 o.c. & ran 7 miles & came to on the right bank for the night. At dusk Capt. Culbertson & Lt. Gwynn returned from a hunting excursion made since dinner & bro't in part of a Buffalo that they had killed out of a large herd. The residue was sent after but could not be found.

June 28th Tuesday [Kearny]

At noon whilst advancing, some of the party discovered 3 Buffalo Bulls on an Island. The Boats were halted & some men sent in persuit. Two were killed, but one only obtained which weighed upwards of 900 cwts. An issue of fresh meat was thus made to the whole command.

---

115. Samuel Wragg graduated from the military academy in 1822 and transferred from the Fourth to the First Infantry later in the year. He served as regimental adjutant from September 1823 until August 1825. Wragg died on November 27, 1828. Heitman, *Historical Register*, 1:1061.

Orders. Hd. Qrs. 6th Regt. Transport Elk, 28th June 1825.

The Col. Comg. has observed that the cooking of the rations for the men is very badly done, and he believes that much of the sickness amongst them arises from this cause. He therefore directs that in future, the rations shall be cooked together for each boat's crew. Good and sufficient cooks will be detailed for this purpose. . . . The Brigade order in relation to the navigating of the boats shall be now rigidly executed. Several accidents have already occurred in consequence of the Cordell men passing the boat in front of them. Future occurrences of this kind will be made the subject of judicial inspection. By Order of Col. Leavenworth, Signed J. Pentland. Adj. 6th Regt.[116]

[Atkinson]

Wednesday 29th June. Proceeded at 1/4 past 4. & ran till 3/4 past nine & came to on horse island with 4 boats for breakfast. The other 4 boats halted on the right bank. In this part of the river we are greatly troubled with sand bars & our progress much impeded. Proceed with 4 boats from the Island at 1/4 past 11. The other boats being already under way & ahead. The latter ran 2 1/2 miles above Teton river & came to, having been joined by the Muskrat. The Mink & the Beaver halted 2 miles below the Teton at 1/2 past 2. & sent out to bring in a Buffalo that had been killed by one of the soldiers. After getting it they proceeded to the mouth of the Teton & halted for the night. The Otter which had been thrown behind by the sand bars remained a mile or two behind for the night on the opposite side of the river.

June 29th Wednesday [Kearny]

Breakfasted at Horse Island & ran up to, & slept near the mouth of Teton, or Little Missouri River.

[Atkinson]

Thursday 30th June. The Mink & Beaver proceeded at 1/4 past 4 & joined the other Boats at their position above the Teton where we found Capt. Armstrongs mounted party. The Otter came up a few

116. Orderly Book 25, Sheldon, "Records of Fort Atkinson," 5:123.

hours after. Here we intend waiting for the Sione's [Saone], Shians [Cheyenne], & Ogelallas, the latter being encamped only 6 miles distant, the first 30 miles & the shians 80 miles, all on the Teton river.[117] For the purpose of bringing them in as early as practicable Capt. Armstrong, Capt. Kennerly 8 men & an interpreter were dispatched this morning to these tribes. Lt. Waters & a party of Capt. Armstrongs men killed today 6 Buffalo Bulls.[118] Rose, an interpreter, one of the party, we understand, covered himself with bushes & crawled into the gang of 11 Bulls & shot down the 6 on the same ground before the others ran off.

June 30th Thursday [Kearny]

Started at day break. In half a mile passed the Teton River, where we saw Capt Armstrongs horse party. Proceeded a mile above here & formed an encampment, to remain several days to council with the Indians.

Orders, Hd. Qrs. Transport Boat Elk June 30th 1825.

Commandants of Boats will with as little delay as possible see that their boats are put in as good order as possible. They will arrange to have sufficient quantity of plank saved for buckets and arms for their boats and have the men put themselves in good order for parade immediately. By Order of Col. Leavenworth Signed J. Pentland. Adj 6th Regt.[119]

---

117. The Saone numbered about 4,000 and hunted along the Missouri from the Teton or Bad River to the Cheyenne River. U.S. Congress, *Expedition up the Missouri*, 9. The Saone included the Minniconjous, Sans Arcs, Two Kettles, and Blackfeet Lakota. The term Saone disappeared about 1850. Harry H. Anderson, "Investigation of the Early Band of the Saone Group," *Journal of the Washington Academy of Sciences* 46 (1956): 87–94.

The Shians or Cheyenne hunted along the Cheyenne River to the Black Hills. Their population was about 3,000. U.S. Congress, *Expedition up the Missouri*, 10. The Oglalas were buffalo hunting nomads who ranged along the Bad River from the Missouri to the Black Hills. Ibid., 9.

118. George Washington Waters graduated from the military academy in 1823 and resigned from the army in 1837. Heitman, *Historical Register*, 1:1008. During the expedition he was a second lieutenant in Company A of the Sixth Infantry. Muster Rolls, Sixth Infantry, RG 94.

119. Orderly Book 25, Sheldon, "Records of Fort Atkinson," 5:123–24.

Orders. Hd. Qrs. Camp Teton, 1st July 1825.[120]

Commandants of Boats will immediately make out and hand to the A. Qr. Master an accurate account of the provisions on board their respective Boats. By Order of Col. Leavenworth Signed J. Pentland Adj. 6th Regt.[121]

[Atkinson]

Friday 1st July. Today the 6 Buffalo killed by Rose yesterday were bro't into camp & weighed nett 3,300. The flesh was issued to the Troops making an issue of 4 1/2 days at 1 1/2 lbs. pr. ration. Besides, the officers Messes were furnished with an abundance.

Hd Qrs Right Wing Western Department
Orders Camp near the Teton river 1st July 1825.

A General Court Martial to consist of nine members (a greater number cannot be assembled with[?] the good of the service) will convene to day at 12 Oclock at such place as the President may direct for the trial of such prisoners as may be brought before it.

Brevet Major S. Kearny 1st Infy President

Capt. B. Riley 6th Infy	Capt. R. Mason 1st Infy
Capt. G. Spencer 1st "	" J. Gantt 6th "
Capt. C. Pentland 6th "	" W. Harney 1st "
L T. Noel 6th "	L J. Rogers 6th "
[illegible word]	Lt W. Day 1st Infy Supernumerary

Members Lt J. Pentland 6th Infy will perform the duties of Special Judge Advocate. By order of Brigr Genl Atkinson

Signed S. MacRee Lt ADCamp & A. A. A. Genl[122]

---

120. Each time the expedition stopped for several days, the site was named. Camp Teton was the first. At the Arikara village they established Camp Aricaras and at the Mandan village it was Camp Mandan. At the mouth of the Yellowstone River the expedition established Camp Barbour, a name also used for the First Infantry's 1825–26 winter camp just south of Fort Atkinson.

121. Orderly Book 25, Sheldon, "Records of Fort Atkinson," 5:124.

122. Vol. 1:68, Orders Received, Sixth Infantry, RG 391. Jason Rogers was a military academy graduate in 1821 and assigned to the Second Infantry. In 1822 he was transferred to the Sixth Infantry. He resigned in 1836, but reenlisted in the Kentucky Volunteers during the Mexican War. He died in May 1848. In 1825 he was a first lieutenant in Company E and when Larrabee retired he assumed command. Heitman, *Historical Register*, 1:843; Muster Rolls, Sixth Infantry, RG 94.

July 1st Friday [Kearny]

An Express was sent for the purpose of finding the Chayennes & inviting them to this place. A Genl. Court Martial was convened to day, by virtue of a "Right Wing order." The Court decided it was not formed consistently with the "Arts of War", & that they were incompetent to try any Prisoners and adjourned.

[Atkinson]

Saturday 2nd July. This morning the Standing Buffalo the principle chief of the Ogelallas with 5 other Indians paid us a visit at 9 o.c.[123] He came to make himself known & to ask where he should pitch the lodges of his nation. He is a dignified & well behaved man & has great influence among his people. Maj. O.Fallon three officers & myself rode out at 1/2 past 9 toward the Ogelalla Camp. The Band are covered by 110 leather lodges & are estimated at 250 warriors. Many fine cat, & other fish are taken by the men in the Teton river. Rose, Harris & three soldiers were sent this morning up the right bank of the river as high as the dirt village to assertain whether the Sioux Band under Fireheart had come in to the river & to see if any Buffalo were to be found in that quarter.[124] The party of Rose returned at 7 in the evening and reported that they had seen nothing of the Indians nor were any Buffalo to be found in that direction.

July 2d Saturday [Kearny]

A very hot day — but little wind, & that by no means refreshing.

The Ogalallas, bringing with them about 100 Lodges, arrived & pitched their Camp about a mile from us.

---

123. Except for signing the treaty, Standing Buffalo seems to have eluded historical records.

124. Later, Atkinson identifies the Fire Heart band as Saone. This band joined Leavenworth's punitive expedition against the Arikaras in 1823. Sunder, *Joshua Pilcher*, 44. They have also been identified as Yanktonai. Doane Robinson, *A History of the Dakota or Sioux Indians* (Minneapolis: Ross and Haines Co., 1956), 161. More recently it has been suggested they were Blackfeet Lakota. Anderson, "An Investigation of the Early Bands of the Saone Group," 93–94.

Brigade Head Quarters
Orders Camp Teton July 3rd 1825

While the troops lie at this place not more than three men from each Company can be absent from camp at the same time, nor for a longer time than 'till retreat on the day they go out. They are not to go more than two miles from camp and they must then take their arms with them, and are not under any pretence to go into an indian Camp or lodge. All absent Officers and men will repair to camp forthwith on hearing the discharge of a Cannon.

By Order of Brig Genl Atkinson
Signed Lt. MacRee Lt. A.D. Camp & A. A. A. Genl.[125]

[Atkinson]

Sunday 3rd. July. The Ogelalla Band came in today at 9 in the morning & pitched their lodges, in No. 110, 1/2 mile below our camp. The chiefs came into camp & invited the commissioners & officers to a feast tomorrow at 3 o.c P. M. The Tobacco, an Indian, was dispatched to day to bring in the Sione Band as early as possible.[126] They are expected to morrow evening or next day. Capt. Kennerly returned at 8 this morning from his excursion in the prairie to look for the Shians. He found the Band 60 miles up the Teton river and bro't in 5 chiefs & 11 braves of the Tribe. They sleep tonight with 7 lodges of the Ogelallas 4 miles distant. The Band is expected three days hence.

July 3d Sunday [Kearny]

The wind during the night got round to the N.W & during the day the weather was very cool — a great change since yesterday

---

Brigade Head Quarters
Orders Camp Teton 4th July 1825

A National salute will be fired at 1 Oclock pm from the 6 pr under the direction of Lt. Holmes.

---

125. Vol. 1:62, Orders Received, Sixth Infantry, RG 391.

126. George Catlin sketched Tobacco in 1832 and called him the second chief of the Oglalas. Catlin, *Letters and Notes*, 1:222.

TOBACCO, *by George Catlin, 1832. Tobacco was one of the Saones who signed the 1825 treaty. Catlin described him as "a desperate warrior, and . . . one of the most respectable and famous chiefs of the tribe."*

SMITHSONIAN INSTITUTION, WASHINGTON, D.C.

An extra gill of whisky will be issued to the troops to day, no indulgence of intemperance however will be tolerated.

By order of Brigr Genl Atkinson
Signed. S. MacRee Lt AD Camp & A. A. A. Genl[127]

[Atkinson]

Monday 4 July. At 8 this morning the chiefs & Braves of the Shyans came in and were seated at the council place & Maj. O.F. & Genl. A. explained to them the object of calling them to us. At three o.c the commissioners accompanied by most of the officers went to the Ogelalla camp by invitation of the chiefs & partook of a feast. It consisted of the <*dogs*> flesh of 13 dogs boiled in plain water in 7 kettles, much done. Our drink was water from the Missouri bro't up in the paunches of Buffalo, which gave it a disagreeable taste. Seats consisting of Buffalo robes Beaver skins & some pieces of domestic cloth were prepared in the center of the outer circle of the lodge for the commissioners immediately before which were arranged 5 entire Buffalo dungs in a row on which a pipe ready charged was laid. After being seated with the officers on the left, the chiefs of the Ogelallas, Chyenne's & Siones on the right, Standing Buffalo rose took up the pipe & presented the stem to Genl. A. & put fire to the pipe. Genl. A. took a few whiffs & passed it to Maj. O Fallon. The Chief then took the pipe emptied it of its ashes on the centre dung & presented the pipe to Genl. A. The Robes & skins on which we were seated were also presented to the Comsrs. We were occupied about an hour & a half at the feast, when ourselves & the officers returned to camp & sat down & partook of wine & fruit at a table provided by the Comssrs.

July 4th Monday [Kearny]

After breakfast went about 2 miles to see a Prairie dog village. Found it & attempted to kill some of them, tho without success. Saw two antelopes.

At noon an extra gill was issued to each man, to drink to the anniversary of the Independence of his Country. At 1 P.M. a national salute was fired from a 6 Pounder & a Howitr. About 15 of

---

127. Vol. 1:62, Orders Received, Sixth Infantry, RG 391.

the chiefs & principal men of the Chayennes arrived & a talk was held with them, preparatory to one to be had tomorrow.

At 3 P.M. the officers accompanied the commissioners to the camp of the Ogalallas, to partake of a dog feast given them by the Chiefs. After which we assembled in our Camp & drank some wine in commemoration of the day.

About 15 of the Chiefs & Warriors of the Chayennes came in to day, leaving their Nation to follow. These Indians range principally in the Black Mountains; have no intercourse & but very little knowledge with the white character. They are decidedly the finest looking Indians we have seen.

[Atkinson]

Tuesday July 5th. At 9 this morning the Brigade was reviewed in presence of all the Indians. The two field pieces mounted & served with Horses, mattrosses mounted, the pieces passed over the plain at full speed. The Indians were struck with great awe at the display. We expected to have went into council today but the Siones wished it deferred till tomorrow 'till the whole of the band should have come in.[128] In the evening the Comsrs. visited the Ogelalla Camp & invited the chiefs of the 3 tribes to our camp to witness the throwing up of some twenty rockets by Lt. Holmes, which he done with good effect.

July 5th Tuesday [Kearny]

The weather to day excessively hot — the Thermometer at 106. There was considerable air stiring during the whole day but it appeared to come from the direction that the Sun was in. In the evening a talk was held with some of the chiefs, preparatory to the Council to be held tomorrow & some Rockets were fired off. The whole command, including the artillery mounted was reviewed at 10 A.M, by the Genl.

[Atkinson]

Wednesday July 6th. At 9 this morning we counciled with the 3 tribes & concluded treaties with them. Presents were given to each of the same amount. Three Horses with Holsters, pistols & swords

128. Apparently their fieldpieces were equipped with horse drawn gun carriages. The gunner's mates or matrosses were also mounted. Although the treaty was not signed until the next day, it was dated July 5. Kappler, *Laws and Treaties*, 2:231.

were presented by Genl. A. to the three principal chiefs of these tribes. The council closed at 3. o.c. P.M. In the evening the principal chief of the Chyannes (High-backed woolf) came into camp & presented Genl. A. with a Handsome mule with rope & spanish saddle, or rather of the Indian fashion.[129] This man is one of the most dignified & elegant <*& Benigant*> looking men <*upon this earth*> I ever saw. This evening Lt. Holmes threw 6 shells from the Howitzer in presense of the Indians. They exploded handsomely & made a deep impression upon these savages.

July 6th Wednesday [Kearny]

About 7 A.M. upwards of 200 Lodges of the Saones, a band of the Sioux, arrived & encamped within a half mile of us. At 9. a council was held with the Chayennes Saones & Ogalallas, & a Treaty agreed to & signed by the Chiefs & Principal men. Presents were then made

---

Brigade Hd Quarters
Orders Camp Teton 7th July 1825.

Capt Armstrong's Command is to be dismounted, and will till further orders act as a flanking party to the Brigade.

Ten of the public horses are to be taken up the river under the care of this party. The residue of the public horses are to be sent back to the Council Bluffs under the direction of Lt Waters with a detachment of five of the mounted party, with Harris as a guide. Lt. Waters will report to Colo Woolley on his arrival at the Bluffs.[130]

---

129. High-backed Wolf, the Cheyenne chief, visited Washington in 1833 to sign a friendship treaty. He died a year later. George Bird Grinnell, *The Cheyenne Indians*, 2 vols. (New York: Cooper Square, 1962). On the 1825 treaty his name was rendered The Wolf With The High Back. Kappler, *Laws and Treaties*, 2:234.

130. Maj. Abram R. Woolley was left in command of Fort Atkinson when Leavenworth departed with the 1825 expedition. Orderly Book 25, Sheldon, "Records of Fort Atkinson," 5:91. Woolley joined the service in 1812 as an ordnance officer and was sent to the Sixth Infantry in 1823. In March 1825 he was made brevet lieutenant colonel for ten years of service and was discharged in 1829. Heitman, *Historical Register*, 1:1060.

Lieutenant Waters carried a hastily written letter by Indian Agent Peter Wilson to his sister, Mrs. Margaret Drake. Wilson apologized for having "only time to say that the expedition has advanced so far without meeting with any accident, and, I anticipate a continuation of the good luck already met with. The river is

He will draw three days provisions for his party at this place and on his arrival at Fort Kiawa, take from the depot there a quantity sufficient to subsist his command to the Bluffs.

As it may be necessary for the flankers to join the fleet when the boats are under sail, they are to be taken on board any of the boats that they may first approach.

Capt. Armstrong will call at Head Qrs daily for orders.

By order of Brigr Genl Atkinson

Signed. S. MacRee Lt AD Camp & A. A. A. Genl[131]

[Atkinson]

Thursday July 7. This morning at 1/4 before 9 the Troops embarked & moved up the river. The exhibition was beautiful. The wind being fair the boats put off in regular succession under sail & under the wheels & ran up a stretch of 1 1/2 miles in view of more than 3,000 Indians who lined the shore. Ran 12 miles & came to at 1/2 past 2 on the right bank for dinner. Proceeded at 4 o.c & ran 8 miles & came to at 7 on the left Bank for the night. Lt. Waters with 5 men & Harris as a guide were sent back with 30 of the public Horses to Council Bluffs — finding that the mounted party is rather more of trouble than profit. 13 Horses are kept for packing in meat for the comand <*of the Comses. & officers*>. Capt. Armstrongs comd. serve now as flankers.

July 7th Thursday [Kearny]

Fine morning & fair wind. Started at 9 A.M. under sail, some hundred Indians on the shore to witness our departure. On account of the extreme barrenness of the Country, & the difficulty of

---

much better above and I may conjecture (should nothing intervene to impede our progress) a possibility of reaching the Mandans by the 1st of August. Today a grand council was held — present — the Cheyennes, the Ogallallas, and a part of the Band of the Sousans, the last two being Sioux. Everything was satisfactorily accomplished and we leave here tomorrow." Katherine Gideon Colt, *The Letters of Peter Wilson* (Baltimore: Wirth Brothers, 1940), 41–43.

Atkinson must have felt supremely confident in his treaty-making to send only seven men to herd thirty horses back to Fort Atkinson. The value of these animals and the prestige acquired by their capture would have been hard to resist by the younger men of any of the tribes the soldiers might meet.

131. Vol. 1:62–63, Orders Received, Sixth Infantry, RG 391.

subsisting horses, the Horse Party has been in a great measure broken up, about 30 sent back to C.B & 10 retained to accompany us & procure fresh meat. Some given to the Indians.

Halted about 6 P. M. having made 17 miles

The weather today very hot. Some of Capt A' party fainted on the Prairies.

Brigade Hd Quarters
Flag Boat Mink (Mo River)

Orders 8th July 1825

The flotilla will come to in the evening where practicable at half past six o'clock, till further orders. The advance boat when the ground will not admit of a halt at that hour, will come to as soon after as possible.

By order of Brigr Genl Atkinson
Signed S. MacRee Lt AD Camp & A. A. A. Genl[132]

[Atkinson]

Friday 8 July. Heavy rain with much thunder at 2 o.c last night. Proceeded at 4 this morning & ran 6 miles to breakfast at 8 o.c on the right bank. Here Capt. Armstrong came to us with the Horses. Proceeded at 9 o.c and ran five miles & came to on the right bank for dinner, (wind being very strong from the north). Here the Hunters gave us two black tail deer, one very large & fat. Proceeded at 1/2 past 4 the wind having abated a little & ran 3 miles & came to on the right bank for dinner. The Hunters bro't us another large fat black tail deer. The Hunters report that they saw today a white bear [Plains grizzly].

July 8th Friday [Kearny]

During last night we had some hard wind, rain, & hail. Proceded at day break. Stopt at about 2 P.M, on the Right Bank, where we were detained for two hours in consequence of strong head winds. The hunters brought in 3 black tailed deer. Proceded about 4 & encamped at 6 P.M having come to day about 13 miles

---

132. Vol. 1:63, ibid.

[Atkinson]

Saturday 9th July. Heavy wind and rain at 3 o.c this morning. At 1/4 past 8, the weather having cleared up & the men having breakfasted, we proceeded till 1/2 past 2 o.c [and came to] on the right bank for dinner making 10 miles. Proceeded at 4 o c. & ran 5 miles & came to for the night on the right bank <*for the night*> one mile below the mouth of Cheyenne river.[133] We got 2 black tail & two common deer this evening.

July 9th Saturday [Kearny]

In consequence of strong head wind and a heavy rain, we were detained 'til 8 A.M, at which time it cleared away & the wind abated. We continued on the Right hand side of the River the whole day, & under the cord, (this being the first case of the kind, since we left Saint Louis) & halted before Sunset a mile below the mouth of the Chayenne River, having made about 17 miles

Two of the Party on Shore saw to day a White Bear which they were afraid to attack. He moved off from the men & they left him unmolested.

[Atkinson]

Sunday 10th July. Proceeded at 1/4 past 4 & ran 7 miles & came to at 8 o.c. on the right bank for breakfast. Here we found an abundance of the black currant. Proceeded at 1/2 past 9 & ran 10 miles & came to on the right bank for dinner at 1/4 past 2 o.c. Here a child of 6 months old that died last night on board the Buffalo was buried. Proceeded at 4 o.c & ran 7 miles & came to at 1/2 past 7 on the right Bank for the night. An Elk was killed today on the left shore.

July 10th Sunday [Kearny]

We proceeded at day break. Passed the mouth of the Chayenne, about 200 yards wide — near which we saw & gathered a great abundance of the black and yellow current — now ripe, & the largest about the size of a common marble — the latter kind, much

133. In 1811 the Cheyenne River was described as "one of the largest rivers that falls into it [the Missouri] being at least four hundred yards wide at its mouth, and navigable to a great distance. The banks appear to be more steep than those of the Missouri, and are clothed with trees to the water's edge." Bradbury, *Travels in the Interior of America*, 84.

sweeter than the former. Had a light wind to day for a few hours, halted at Sundown on the right bank, having made about

27 miles

[Atkinson]

Monday July 11th 1825. Proceeded at 1/4 after 4 & ran 6 miles & came to at 1/2 past 7 on the right bank for breakfast. Proceeded at 9 & ran 6 miles & came to at 2 o.c on the left Bank for dinner. Proceeded at 1/2 past 3 & ran 10 miles & came to on the left bank at 6 o.c one mile below Hidden creek where we met Fire Hearts Band of Siones consisting of 100 lodges.[134] Fire Heart & some dozen braves paid us a visit this evening. They recd. a dram each & a few plugs of Tobacco & were told that we would council with them on the morrow at 8. o.c.

July 11th Monday [Kearny]

Started at day break — fine morning. During the day a favorable wind, tho' light. About 6 P.M, halted a mile below the "Little Chayenne", on the Left side, having met here Fire Hearts Band of the Saones, with whom the Commissioners intend holding a Council.

Brigade Hd Quarters
Camp near Hiderun Creek

Orders 11 July 1825

The Brigade will appear under arms and in uniform tomorrow at 8 Oclock. By order of Brigr Genl Atkinson

Signed S. MacRee Lt AD Camp & A. A. A. Genl[135]

[Atkinson]

Tuesday 12th July. At 1/2 past 8 this morning the Brigade appeared in uniform & passed in review in the presence of the above named band of Indians. At 1/2 past 9. we went into council with the chiefs & Braves & concluded a treaty with them. Gave presents & recd. 2 pipes 2 dresses & some robes. A British medal was taken by Maj. O.Fallon from a young Indian of this band. The Troops appeared well & made a favorable impression on the Indians, as every exhibi-

---

134. Hidden Creek was also spelled Hiderun Creek. Kearny called it the Little Cheyenne.

135. Vol. 1:63–64, Orders Received, Sixth Infantry, RG 391.

tion of the sort has very manifestly done heretofore. There is not probably more than 150 warriors in Fire Hearts Band. The council was closed at 1/2 past 12. Maj. O.F. & Genl. Atkinson obtained 2 Indian horses & rode 3/4 of a mile back to the hills in rear of our position to look at the impression of foot-steps in a rock. We found the impression of three tracks of the foot of a common sized man. The first near the upper edge of the rock is made by the right foot & is about an inch deep at the heel & making a full impression of the whole track — with full impression of the five toes 3/4 of an inch deep. The next track is of the left foot & about 3 1/2 feet from the first — impression full & deep as the first. The next foot-step of the right foot is not visible but at about 6 feet from the second track an impression is again made by the left foot as deep & plain as the others. This is near the lower edge of the rock which of itself is about 11 feet by 9 lying at an angle of about 30 degrees of elevation — the length lying up & down the hill side. There are several other marks of hands &c. but these appear to have been recently made by slight scratches by the Indians, excep the impression of a hand which appears deep & full but has been newly scratched over by Indians. At 1/2 past 2 two chiefs & about 20 men of the Hukpappaws [Hunkpapa] came to us with a view of holding a council but as only a few of the Band were present & the main part of it in the country opposite the Aricaras they were told to meet us there five days hence.[136] We proceeded at 3. o.c & ran 6 miles & came to on the left Bank for the night. The Band of the Fire Heart presented us with 40 pieces of Buffalo meat.

July 12th Tuesday [Kearny]

At 8 A.M. the Brigade paraded & marched past the Genl in quick time after which the Commissioners met the chiefs, warriors & principal men of the Band & the Treaty which had been made at Camp Teton, on the 6th & signed, was explained to these men, & signed by them about 3 P. M. Some of the Onkapas [Hunkpapa], a Band of Sioux, came in & wished to have a talk delivered to them. Not willing to be detained, they were directed to meet us at the

136. The Hunkpapas numbered about 1,500. These nomads hunted an area east of the Missouri. U.S. Congress, *Expedition up the Missouri*, 10. A treaty was signed with them at the Arikara village on July 16. Kappler, *Laws and Treaties*, 2:235–36.

Ricaras, & we departed at 4 P. M, & made about 5 miles when we halted at 6.

[Atkinson]

Wednesday 13. July 1825. Proceeded at 1/4 past 4 and ran 7 miles & came to at 1/2 past 7 on the left Bank for breakfast. Proceeded at 9 & ran till 4 having had a fine wind for sailing. Made 10 miles & came to for dinner on the left bank. Proceeded at 1/2 past 4 & ran till 1/2 past 5 & came to for the night on the left bank, made 14 miles today. At 6 it rained heavily with hail & thunder. The bank was covered with black currents at this place of a size larger than we have seen before, some were of the size of a musket ball. The White Bear did not come up this evening. The Otter & Beaver were ahead of the fleet this evening.

July 13th Wednesday [Kearny]

Proceded at day break. During the morning light wind — it increased at noon, & during the afternoon, blew very fresh. About 3 P. M met a Frenchman, in a skin canoe, with dried buffaloe meat sent by the Ricaras for us. Took him & the meat aboard. Stoped at half past 5, tho' the wind was blowing fair and hard no other Boat being in sight. In the afternoon passed the Sarwarcarna, called by the French Moreau River.

Orders, Hd. Qrs. 6th Regt. Inf. Boat Elk 13th July 1825.

Order No. 4 dated 3rd June is hereby revoked. Commandants of Boats will when they deem it necessary send with their Cordell men an Officer from their respective boats. To comply with a Brigade order of today the boats belonging to the 6th Regt. of Inf. will hereafter move in the following order viz, The Elk, Buffalo, Raccoon, and White Bear. The boats will be careful not to interfere with the one preceeding them.

By Order of Col. Leavenworth

Signed J. Pentland. Adj. 6th Regt.[137]

---

137. Orderly Book 25, Sheldon, "Records of Fort Atkinson," 5:124–25. The order of June 3 called for an officer to accompany the men on the cordelle at all times.

Brigade Hd Quarters
Orders Flag boat Mink 13 July 1825

The approach of the troops to the vicinity of a tribe of Indians in hostility with the United States renders it at least prudent on the part of the General (altho' he apprehends no danger) to preserve some regularity in the movement of the Flotilla. In future the "Mink" will lead, succeeded alternately each day by the Battallions of the 1st and 6th Regts Infy. The transport boats of each to be arranged in division, by the Commandants of Corps and when thus arranged no boat will be allowed to leave its place in the line, whether running on wheels, cordelling or sailing unless an accident should occur to the preceeding boat, which would detain her more than 15 minutes, in which case the next boat would pass ahead.

By order of Brigr Genl Atkinson
Signed S. MacRee Lt AD Camp & A. A. A. Genl[138]

[Atkinson]

Thursday 14 July. Proceeded at 4 & ran till 1/2 past 7 & came to on the right bank for breakfast making 5 miles. Here we found Capt. Armstrong encamped. Proceeded at 9 o.c. & ran 6 miles 'till dinner — right bank 1/2 past 1 o.c. Proceeded at 3. o.c. & ran 5 miles & came to at 1/2 past 5. o.c. on the right bank for the night.

July 14th Thursday [Kearny]

At 8 A.M, the Boats came up & we moved on at 9. Find the Country assuming a more fertile appearance.

[Atkinson]

Friday 15th July. Proceeded at 4 o.c & ran 5 miles & came to on the left bank for breakfast at 1/2 past 7 o:c. Proceeded at 9 & ran till 2 o.c & came to on the right bank 1/2 mile below the Aricara Village. 3 chiefs of the Siones with several braves, & 2 chiefs and 4 braves & 14 men of the Hunkpappas are here to conciliate with the Aricaras, who have 'till recently been at war with them.[139] Rose

138. Vol. 1:64, Orders Received, Sixth Infantry, RG 391.

139. In 1825 the Arikaras lived in a village divided by an intermittent creek about ten miles above the Grand River. They had a population of about 2,500, raised tobacco, corn, and a few other crops, and hunted buffalo. U.S. Congress, *Expedition up the Missouri*, 10.

was sent with 2 Sioux yesterday with tobacco for the Rees. He had arrived & bro't to our camp 6 aricara chiefs who were presented to Maj. O.Fallon & myself.

July 15th Friday [Kearny]

Started at day break. Passed a River on the right bank, called by the french Grand River, near which we saw some old dirt-lodges of the Ricaras. They have been deserted for many years.[140] About noon, passed a small creek called Maripa River, & at 2 P. M. halted a mile below the Arickara village, & pitched our camp on a high Prairie considerably removed from any timber.

In the afternoon visited the Villages. There are two of them separated by a Ravine, consisting each of about 40 lodges. Each village surrounded by a slight picketing.

We are now 780 miles above Council Bluffs. From the Puncahs to this place, with but an exception here & there, the country is extremely barren & dried up. 'Tis unfit for any use, not raising even a weed.

[Atkinson]

Saturday 16. July. Held a council at 11. o.c. this morning with the Hunkpappas & concluded a Treaty with them. Made presents &c. The little white bear recognized as principal chief, to whom a medal was given by Maj. O.F. [O'Fallon][141] At 1/2 past one (after the conclusion of the Hunkpappas treaty the Commissioners & most of the officers repaird to the Aricara Village by invitation to a feast. [Joseph] Garrow, a white man living with them, had become drunk as were some of the Indians, for which cause we returned to Camp. Maj. O.Fallon & Capt. Kennerly returned to the village at 1/2 past 4 by request of the Indians (Genl. A. declining the invitation). Maj. O.F. admonished the Indians on his visit for their many offences. They offered as a present 7 Horses, a pile of Buffalo meat & some earthern

---

140. They had reached the country occupied by the Arikara for many years and archeological remains of their villages are still found. Bradbury, in 1811, noticed the remains of an old Arikara village south of the mouth of the Cheyenne River. Bradbury, *Travels in the Interior of America*, 123. In the late 1700s there may have been as many as forty Arikara villages, but smallpox decimated the tribe. Douglas R. Parks, "Bands and Villages of the Arikara and Pawnee," *Nebraska History* 60 (1979): 227.

141. Little White Bear was the first to sign the treaty. Kappler, *Laws and Treaties*, 2:236.

pots. They were told that they would be called to council at 10 the ensuing morning.

July 16th Saturday [Kearny]

Last night the weather very hot & a great numbers of mosquitoes. About noon accompanied the Genl. to the Village to partake of a feast. It soon appeared that our invitation was a mistake, it having been given by an old Frenchman (Garreau) who was drunk & forgot it, on his return to his Lodge.

Orders, Hd. Qrs. 6th Regt. Transport Elk 16th July 1825.

Commandants of Boats will drop from their Rosters all men doing the duty as Steersmen, they will not be reported on extra or daily duty except by order of Col. Leavenworth.

By Order of Col. Leavenworth.

Signed J. Pentland. Adj. 6th Regt.[142]

Brigade Hd Quarters

Orders Camp Aricara 16th July 1825

In order to facilitate the movements of the troops and to strengthen the crews of the respective boats, Capt. Armstrong's Compy of Riflemen are to be temporarily distributed among the several boats, except ten men who he will retain to carry up the public horses, at all halts of the Brigade for more than one day, the men thus distributed are to be embarked and take a position on one of the flanks of the line under Capt. Armstrong, on the Flotilla's moving the Company will be again distributed as above described. Whilst those men are serving on the boats they are to be included in the provision returns of the Compy to which they are attached. Lt Hutter will rejoin his company.[143]

The Brigade will appear under arms and in uniform tomorrow evening at 7 Oclock. The Artillery on the right under Lt Holmes and Capt. Armstrong's Rifle company on the left.

The Act. Ass. Insp. Genl will make an examination of the freight of the respective boats in order that he may equalize by distribution the same in proportion to the class of the boats.

---

142. Orderly Book 25, Sheldon, "Records of Fort Atkinson," 5:125.

143. George C. Hutter entered the service in 1820 and was a second lieutenant in the Sixth Infantry in 1825. Heitman, *Historical Register*, 1:560.

Commandants of Battallions will cause an accurate Invoice of all public stores on board of the boats to be handed in to the A. A. Insp. Genl forthwith.

By order of Brigr Genl Atkinson
Signed S. MacRee Lt AD Camp & A. A. A. Genl[144]

[Atkinson]

Sunday 17th July. The troops appeared under arms in Brigade this morning at 8 o.c. 2 pieces of artillery on the right & a compy. of Rifle men on the left (350 men under arms). The Aricaras arranged themselves on the rising ground near the parade & witnessed the review.

The artillery passed first in common time in review & in quick time, full gallop, the pieces being served with horses. After the Troops were dismissed, some 8 or 10 shot were thrown from the 6 pdr. Some racaching [ricocheting] on the river & some thrown across. The wind violent from the So. east which caused a suspension of our council with the Aricaras till the morrow.

July 17th Sunday [Kearny]

The Ricaras were much alarmed about day break by the appearance of the "Knife-chief" coming in with 200 of his Band, whom they took for the "Crows" coming to attack them.[145]

At 8 A.M. the command (with the arty on the right, the Rifle on the left) were reviewed by the Genl. & as soon as we were dismissed the wind commenced blowing so hard as to blow down the awning which had been put up on the Prairie (there being no trees) where the Council was to be held & which was therfore accordingly postponed.

[Atkinson]

Monday 18 July. This morning at 1/2 past 5 the Aricaras came into Council, 6 chiefs, 14 braves & 100 or thereabouts. A treaty of peace

---

144. Vol. 1:64–65, Orders Received, Sixth Infantry, RG 391.

145. The identity of Knife Chief cannot be confirmed, but in 1819 the principal chief of the Skidi or Loup band of the Pawnee was Knife Chief. James, *Account of an Expedition*, 243. It is possible the Skidis came from their village on the Loup River to visit the Arikaras because they are related by language and culture. On September 4 Atkinson noted some Skidi visitors.

Crow Indians hunted in the vicinity of the Bighorn River and the southern branches of the Yellowstone. U.S. Congress, *Expedition up the Missouri*, 11.

trade & friendship was concluded with them. A medal was given to the Chief (handful of Blood), arm bands to the others. 400 plugs of tobacco was all the presents given these Indians as they have so recently been committing murders of our people.[146] They appear to be impressed with deep & full contrision for their offences & it is thought they will behave well in future. Proceed on our voyage at 1/2 past 8, running on our wheels by the Villages & made 7 miles & came to at 1 o.c on the right bank for dinner. Here the Interpreters, (the Garrows) came to us accompanied by the Handful of Blood & two other chiefs to pay to us a parting respect. Proceeded at 2 o.c & ran 6 miles & came to at 1/2 past 6. on the right bank for the night. Capt. Armstrongs party, 12 in no. encamped with us. They bro't us a small deer.

July 18th Monday [Kearny]

About 6 A.M a council was held with the Ricaras & a Treaty made in which all their past offences were forgotten, & that they were henceforth, to be judged of, & acted toward, agreeably to their future conduct. A few plugs of tobacco were given to them. We started at 8 A.M. ran up about 9 miles to dinner. The River much narrower than below & the current less rapid. In the afternoon had a head wind. The Bottom Land appears more frequent & fertile & better timbered.

Garrow an old Frenchman who has been with the Ricaras for 27 years, is with us & going to the Mandans.

[Atkinson]

Tuesday 19th. Proceeded at 4 o.c & ran 7 miles & came to on the right bank at 7 1/2 o.c. for breakfast. Proceeded at 8 1/2 o.c & ran 7 miles & came to on the left bank for dinner at 1/2 past 1 o.c. Proceeded at 1/2 past 2 & ran 7 miles & came to on the right bank at 7 o.c. for the night. Capt. Armstrong encamped on the opposite shore above us. The country has materially changed since passing the aricaras, the bottoms being wider & covered with large timber,

146. On the treaty the chief's name was rendered "The Bloody Hand." Kappler, *Laws and Treaties*, 2:238. Atkinson's miserly gifts were meant to convey the army's displeasure with the Arikara attack on William H. Ashley in 1823. When Hunt and Lisa visited in 1811, the tribe was somewhat more friendly to the Americans. Bradbury, *Travels in the Interior of America*, 130.

such as cotton wood elm & ash. The land is good & the adjoining hills look fresh & green with much more grass than we found above Wooracore [Warreconne Creek] to the Rees. Many dead Buffalo have floated by us these two days & some large woolves are seen on the shore.

July 19th Tuesday [Kearny]

Started at day break and ran up about 4 miles & halted opposite to "Stone Idol creek" for breakfast. Wind ahead, tho' not very strong. Find to day but few sand bars the River generally narrow, at one place not more than 250 yards wide. The River appears entirely different from what it is below the Ricaras. It has fewer Sand bars & Islands. It is much narrower — the current less rapid, & the water not so muddy. The Bottom Lands are much more extensive. The soil more fertile — timber more abundant.

[Atkinson]

Wednesday 20 July. Proceeded at 4 o.c & ran 5 miles & came to at 1/4 past 7 on the right bank for breakfast. Here the Iroqoi [Iroquois] Hunter bro't us a fat buck. Some rain with thunder & lightning at dusk last evening & again at mid-night. Proceeded at 1/2 past 8. At one mile came to Capt. Armstrongs party *<who gave us another deer>*, ran 7 miles & came to on the right bank at 1/2 past one for dinner. Again came to Capt. Armstrongs party who gave us another deer. Proceeded at 1/2 past 2 & ran 7 miles & came to for the night on the left bank at 1/2 past 6 o.c. Here we crossed over 5 Horses from the right bank with 5 men to hunt leaving 8 Horses & men on the right bank. On this bank for some 20 miles the Indians have left marks of their recent residence in great numbers by the still existence of their bush wigwams. They are supposed to have been the Aricaras, who have hunted in this direction the past spring. Capt. Armstrong came on board & remained all night.

July 20th Wednesday [Kearny]

The musquetoes are getting so troublesome, as sometimes to deprive the men of their sleep & rest, they having no "Bars." Proceded at day break. Halted for dinner on the right hand shore where some Indians have lately been encamped, their willow shelters about 60 in number, remaining. A large trace supposed to lead to the Mandans passes here. In the afternoon Capt Gant shot at a buffaloe & wounded him. 6 others were seen by some of the party. The weather in the afternoon very hot & musquetoes troublesome.

The wolves last night came near our camp & were howling for some time.

[Atkinson]

Thursday 21 July. Proceeded at 4 o.c & ran 5 miles & came on the right bank opposite to an Island for breakfast at 1/4 before 8 o.c. Heavy rain last night at one o.c. cloudy still this morning. Proceeded at 1/2 past 9 & ran 6 miles & came to for dinner on the right bank at 1/2 past 12 o.c. Sent across the river for some deer from the hunters. Proceeded at 2 o.c. and ran till 1/2 past 5 and came to on the right bank in consequence of a thunder gust, made only 3 miles since dinner. Remained all night. Sent across the river & bro't over two deer from the hunters. Troubled today by sand bars.

July 21st Thursday [Kearny]

During last night some hard wind & rain. Started at breakfast. In the afternoon the Boats had some difficulty in getting thro' a very narrow pass, a channel being dug for the formost one. Passed by Warrenconne River, coming in on the left side. About 5 P.M a very hard blow. Slept on the Right hand shore.

Several deer & Elk have been seen in the bottoms for the last few days.

About dark some wolves assembled on the shore opposite to us & gave us a serenade. This is a good sign, indicating that we are in the neighborhood of Buffaloes, as wolves generally follow the herds in order to pick up the weak & sickly ones.

[Atkinson]

Friday 22. July. Proceeded at 4 & ran 6 miles & came to at 1/2 past 7 for breakfast. Proceeded at 9 & ran 11 miles & came to on the right bank for dinner at 2 o.c. Some 8 deer were bro't in by the hunters this afternoon. An Elk and a Buffalo were killed near us and put on board. Proceeded at 1/2 past 3 o.c. & ran three 3 miles & came to on the right bank for the night. Here seven more Buffalo were bro't in, some 2 or 3 others killed & left on the ground. Doct. Coleman, Lt. Vanswarengen & some other gentlemen who were out are of opinion they saw 10,000 Buffalo on the hills within 4 or 5 miles around.

July 22d Friday [Kearny]

Fine morning — started at day break. The men complained of having been more troubled by the musquetoes last night than ever before whilst moving up. We in the Beaver picked up a very large white wolf in the water which some of the Muskrats crew had shot! He stunk so bad (having lived of late on the carcass of a buffaloe lying near where we saw him) that we threw over. Breakfasted opposite to the Cannon Ball river. About 10 A.M. saw a herd of about 200 buffaloe, some hunters in pursuit. During the afternoon & evening the hunters brought in ten Buffalo, an Elk, several deer, & geese.

[Atkinson]

Saturday 23. July. Proceeded 4 o.c & ran 8 miles and came to at 8 o.c on the right bank for Breakfast. Here is an old village deserted some 6 years since by the Mandan Indians.[147]

Three more Buffalo were bro't in this morning & issued as were those recd. yesterday, giving 7 days rations to the whole comd. at 1 1/2 lbs. pr. rat. besides, the officers were all supplied with as much as they wanted. 3 more deer bro't in this morning. The Hunters directed not to kill any more Buffalo till further orders. Proceeded at 1/4 past 10. o.c. and ran 6 miles & came to at 2 o.c on the right bank for dinner. 4 more deer bro't to us by the Hunters on the left shore. Proceeded at 3. o.c & ran 6 miles till 1/4 past 7 making 6 miles & came to on the left bank for the night. We have been in view of large herds of Buffalo since morning.

July 23d Saturday [Kearny]

Started early & moved up about 4 miles to an old village on the Right hand side formerly inhabited by the Mandans, consisting of about [. . .] dirt lodges. 1 mile above this a war Eagle was seen in the River & it being known, that from the scarcity of feathers (at this Season) & those few he had being wet, one of the men swam ofter & caught him near the opposite shore.

[Atkinson]

Sunday 24 July. Proceeded at 4 & ran 7 miles and came to on the right bank for breakfast at 1/4 before 8 o.c. Buffalo on all the hills & plains — on the sand bars & Hundreds swiming the river. Proceeded

147. The Mandans had lived in this area of the Missouri for generations. Wood, *Papers in Northern Plains Prehistory and Ethnology*.

at 1/4 before 9 under a light breeze & ran 14 miles & came to on the left bank at 1/2 past 5 for the night. Two Buffalo were killed & bro't in. 4 calves were caught from the droves of Buffalo that were crossing the river, since breakfast. Buffalo in view all the day. Here Sergt. Moor came to us who had charge of a hunting party on the left bank & informed us that whilst the party made a halt in the morning a herd of some 2,000 Buffalo came running over the same ground he occupied & four out of the 5 Horses he had with him took fright & ran off among the herd being enclosed on all sides.[148] They carried off their packs of meat. The Herd were pursued 5 miles to recover the horses, or rather, 2 Horses & 2 mules, but they could not now be seen having not cleared themselves from the herd.

July 24th Sunday [Kearny]

Last night & this morning very cool. Started at day break. Saw many Buffaloe & several in the River. Most of the day fair wind & at no time were we more than fifteen minutes out of sight of large & innumerable herds of buffaloe. Four calves were caught, some by the men jumping upon them when in the water & putting a rope around their necks. Halted on the left bank at an old Indian encampment, surrounded by mounds in a circular form, & apparently intended for defence.[149] Opposite to this, Heart River comes in behind an Island or bar.

[Atkinson]

Monday July 25th 1825. Proceeded at 1/4 past 4 & ran under a light breeze 6 miles & came to at 7 o.c. on the left bank for breakfast. At a mile above our last nights encampment we came to a point on the left bank where an Indian village had once stood on a bluff of 40 feet which is gradually falling in. It retains a perpendicular face on the river. The upper surface for from 4 to 8 feet is filled with Bones. Appear to be mostly Buffalo. In passing we discovered a human skeleton sticking in the face of the bluff. The spine & neck

148. This is probably Corp. Thomas Moore, who had been transferred from the Sixth to the First Infantry in April. Register of Enlistments, M233, roll 19.

149. The encampment is the Double Ditch Archeological Site north of Bismarck, North Dakota. It was a large earthlodge village occupied many years before Kearny saw it. Reid and Gannon, "Journal of the Atkinson-O'Fallon Expedition," 4:34, n.51.

bones were lying nearly horizontal — the skull nearly erect with the face exposed to the river. Genl. A. directed the men to try & take up the skull when Woolly, one of the 6 Rgt., was let down by the hand over the precipice & succeeded in getting it. We have it on board. Another human skeleton was discovered in the face of the Bluff at about the same depth, 5 feet, a little above the first. The skull was not seen. 1/4 of a mile in rear of our last nights encampment stands the ruins of an old fortified Indian village. The defences seem to have consisted of a ditch with the earth thrown up on the outer part as a breastwork. Indian arrow points of flint stone, stone axes, broken earthen pots &c. were found scattered on the surface besides innumerable bones.[150] Two men were sent back this morning to try & recover our lost horses.

The Buffalo calves, which appear to be 4 months old, have become so gentle at once, as to justify a belief they may be easily reared. Proceeded at 1/2 past 8 and ran under a good breeze till 1/2 past 5. o.c. Made 30 miles today. Sergt. Harris who had been sent forward last night to kill Buffalo gave us three & a calf.[151] He had killed another but it was too far from the river to be bro't in. Buffalo in view all this day.

July 25th Monday [Kearny]

Started as usual. Soon afterwards, a fine breeze sprung up which served us most of the day. Saw many herds of buffaloe on both sides of the River & some elk. Stopt about 7 P.M. on the left bank, opposite to the remains of some old lodges.

[Atkinson]

Tuesday 26 July. Proceeded at 1/4 past 4 under a good breeze and ran 9 miles & came to on the right bank for breakfast at 1/2 past 9 o.c. Proceeded at 11. o.c & ran 5 miles & halted at 1. o.c 400 yards below the Mandan Village which is situated on the right bank of a Bluff 60 feet high with a perpendicular face. The river bearing north

150. The skeletal remains were from the Larson Mandan Archeological Site on the right bank of the Missouri, fifteen miles above Bismarck. Ibid., 34, n.50. Henry Woolly enlisted in 1812 and served until 1828. Register of Enlistments, M233, rolls 13, 18.

151. James Harris joined the military in 1815 and was in the Sixth Infantry at the founding of Fort Atkinson. Register of Enlistments, M233, roll 6.

west. This village contains 150 warriors, is formed of dirt lodges [. . .] in no. & enclosed with a slight picket work. Situated above this 4 miles is an other Mandan Village consisting of dirt lodges & has 100 warriors, not picketed in. Three Grovont dirt villages stand at intervals three miles above the latter & has 250 warriors.[152]

July 26th Tuesday [Kearny]

Started at day break — fair wind. Arrived at the Mandans about 1 P.M.

We have pitched our Camp on the Right or S. West side of the River on a handsome Plain bounded by graceful hills & protected by the River & ravines. We are two miles below the place where Lewis & Clark wintered in 1804.5.[153] & a few hundred yards from a Village which had been built within the last 8 years, & is beautifully situated on a bluff which projects for some distance over the River, & has a thorough command over it. Within 7 miles of this place are 5 Indian Villages — of which 2 are Mandans, situated on the Missouri a mile or so apart & 3 are inhabited by the Minaterees or Gros Ventres & are Knife River, which falls into the Missouri about 6 miles above here.

Brigade Hd Quarters
Orders Camp Mandan 26th July 1825

The General regrets to learn that some of the soldiers of the Brigade have been disposing of their Musket Cartridges delivered out to them for guard duties to the Indians at this place, they are also in the habit of disposing of their Clothing, both of these practices are forbid, a repetition of the offence in either case shall be met with exemplary punishment.

---

152. Atkinson estimated the population of the Mandans and "Grovont" or Hidatsas at 3,000 in five earthlodge villages near the mouth of the Knife River. They raised corn and hunted buffalo but stayed southwest of the Missouri for fear of being attacked by the Assiniboins. U.S. Congress, *Expedition up the Missouri*, 11. Archeological remains of some of the villages are now part of the Knife River Indian Villages National Historic Site. Frank H. Stewart, "Mandan and Hidatsa Villages in the Eighteenth and Nineteenth Centuries," *Plains Anthropologist* 19 (1974): 287–302.

153. Lewis and Clark built Fort Mandan in November 1804 and were there until the following April. The site has been washed away by changes in the river channel. Moulton, *Journals of the Lewis and Clark Expedition*, 3:226.

Officers commanding Corps will cause an immediate inspection to be made into the state of the ammunition delivered to their respective commands and make every man account for any present or future deficiencies of the quantity that has or may be delivered to him.

The men in future shall not be permitted to go into any Indian villages in the neighborhood only upon the business of an Officer, and then upon a pass setting forth the nature of such business and to be contersigned by the commandant of Brigade.

No Officer in future will be allowed to pass in or out of camp except at the Main guard, nor will an Indian be let in or out except at the same place.

By order of Brigr Genl Atkinson

Signed S. MacRee Lt AD Camp & A. A. A. Genl[154]

Brigade Hd Quarters

Orders Camp Mandan 27th July 1825

In consequence of the favorable report made by commandants of Corps on the state of Clothing and Ammunition for which the troops are accountable, the restriction of the order of yesterday preventing the men from visiting the neighboring villages is revoked, they will be permitted to be absent on the authority of Commandants of Corps not exceeding three hours — but not more than three men from a Company at the same time and they must be in uniform with side arms.

By order of Brigr Genl Atkinson

Signed S. MacRee Lt AD Camp & A. A. A. Genl[155]

[Atkinson]

Wednesday 27th July. Repairing Boats & repacking pork. The Mandans came in today & exhibited in a begging dance.[156] Maj. O.F gave Tobacco. 8 Crow Indians came into camp today. Some tobacco was given to each & 20 twists sent by them to the Crow Tribe who

154. Vol. 1:65–66, Orders Received, Sixth Infantry, RG 391.

155. Ibid.

156. In 1832 Catlin witnessed a beggar's dance performed to "open the hearts of the bystanders to give to the poor," but not necessarily to the dancers themselves. Catlin, *Letters and Notes*, 1:245.

are some 30 miles back in the prairie with word for the tribe to come in as soon as possible.

July 27th Wednesday [Kearny]

The Mandans & Gros Ventres are clearly allied in friendship & confirmed by intermarrages. Their 5 villages may average about 40 Dirt lodges each & each of these containing about 3 Warriors & [. . .] souls. From here to the British factories or Trading House on the Assiniboin is but 150 miles & over a good country & a large trace leading to it. An American Trading House is located here, of which Mr McKenzie has the charge — who gets his goods from Saint Louis, via Saint Peters & Lake Traverse.[157]

From the Rickarees here, the Country appears much better than we saw it below the former place — the soil more productive & better timbered.

We are now 1600 miles above the mouth of the Missouri.

Around the Village is an extensive Prairie, level & bounded by a range of hills, 2 miles in the rear. On this Prairie their horses feed in the day time.

Hd. Qrs. Camp Mandan 27th July 1825.

The Transport White Bear will be left at this Place until the return of the troops, her crew and cargo will be distributed amongst the boats of the Regt. including the Mink, according to the tonnage. Sergt. Fleming, Dennis of Comp D. will be left here to take care of the Transport, The White Bear and for other purposes as may be hereafter directed. Lt. Crossman is assigned to the Raccoon. Capt. Gray and Pentland will remain at this place until the Flotella returns. The individuals left here will be subsisted to include the 30th

157. The British trading post was possibly Brandon House, built in 1794 by the Hudson's Bay Company on the Assiniboine River, nearly opposite the mouth of the Souris. It was almost 200 miles from the Mandan villages. Wood and Thiessen, *Early Fur Trade on the Northern Plains*, 11.

The American trading house belonged to the Columbia Fur Company. Their first post, built in 1823, had been abandoned and a new one was erected early in 1825. Thomas D. Thiessen, "Historic Trading Posts Near the Mouth of the Knife River," *The Phase I Archeological Research Program for the Knife River Indian Villages National Historic Site, Part II* (Lincoln, Nebr.: National Park Service Midwest Archeological Center, 1993), 59–60

Sept. By Order of Col. Leavenworth. Signed Thos. Noel. Adj. 6th Regt.[158]

[Atkinson]

Thursday 28 July. This morning the Mandans went out to kill Buffalo, by making whats called a surround, at 8 miles distant from hence. Maj. Kearny, Capt. Mason & Doct. Gale went out to witness the affair. This party & the Indians returned at 3 o.c having killed some 50 Buffalo. Chabanno came in from the Crows today & informs us that the tribe will be in within two or three days. An Indian was dispatched to hurry them in. Violent storm of wind & rain at 4 o.c this afternoon. Blew down most of the tents & drenched everything with wet.

July 28th Thursday [Kearny]

At Sunrise went with a party of the Mandans about 100 to hunt buffaloe. We rode down the River 8 miles where we found them in great numbers. Several were killed. The Indians show some skill & dexterity in pursuit & shooting their arrows into the mortal parts of the animal.

In the afternoon a very severe storm of wind & rain — which upset our Tents & for a time delayed our camp.

[Atkinson]

Friday 29th July. Morning fine & cool. Sergt. Harris was dispatched this morning at Reveille with 6 men (mounted for the purpose of going to the ground occupied by the Buffalo, with instructions to kill and bring in as many as 7 horses would pack.

The hunting party did not return today. Campbell who went out with them came in after night having been taken sick.[159] Noth-

---

158. Orderly Book 25, Sheldon, "Records of Fort Atkinson," 5:125. Pvt. James Dennis enlisted in 1822 and was assigned to Company D of the Sixth. Muster Rolls, Sixth Infantry, RG 94. George Hampton Crossman or Crosman was a second lieutenant in Company F of the Sixth Infantry. Orderly Book 25, Sheldon, "Records of Fort Atkinson," 5:125. He would go on to serve in the war against Mexico and in the Civil War, where he was promoted to the rank of major general. Heitman, *Historical Register*, 1:340. A year before going to the upper Missouri with Kearny, Crossman was searching for some deserters from Fort Atkinson when he was captured and briefly imprisoned by the Grand Pawnees at their village on the Platte River. Morgan, *The West of William H. Ashley*, 258 n.26.

159. Oran Campbell of Company K, Sixth Infantry, enlisted in 1824 and served his enlistment. Register of Enlistments, M233, roll 18.

ing occurred today worthy [of] notice. The Indians bring in squashes, corn, robes &c. expose them for barter before the main guard — our market place at all camps we make before Indians.

July 29th Friday [Kearny]

Mr. Gordon, a citizen whom we left at Fort Kiawa, came in to day bringing our letters which had been sent there from "C. B." [Council Bluffs][160] He traveled alone & in [. . .] days.

Several rumors of Sioux & Assinoboins being in the neighborhood are afloat. No doubt they are false & are spread by the Mandans, (who are at War with both Nations) to make us believe they are bold & fearless.

The River rose this afternoon a foot, in consequence of the rain of yesterday.

[Atkinson]

Saturday 30th July. Today at one o.c. P.M. the Mandans & Grovonters came into council & treaties of peace & Trade & friendship we concluded with them.[161] They disavow the act of killing some of Genl. Ashleys party and explain the offence away by attributing it to the imprudence of their young men who were on war excursions and further state that these parties fired in the night upon the camps of the whites under the impression that they were Indians.

Large presents were given to the Tribes. Two of the hunters came in this evening with one deer & some Buffalo meat. Sergt. Harris & the rest of the party went further on in pursuit of Buffalo.

---

160. William Gordon, a civilian traveling with the expedition, witnessed the treaty with the Ponca and the Sioux, and stayed with the troops until they reached the Mandan villages. He remained there until the soldiers returned and then went with them to Fort Kiowa. Gordon had been in Indian country since 1822 and had just returned from the Rocky Mountains after the collapse of the Missouri Fur Company. Morgan and Harris, *The Rocky Mountain Journals of William Marshall Anderson*, 320–22.

Colonel Leavenworth believed Gordon was one of the two men Joshua Pilcher ordered to set fire to the Arikara village at the end of Leavenworth's campaign against the tribe in 1823. Vol. 5, Dec. 28–Feb. 24, 1836, Thomas Sidney Jesup Papers, Library of Congress, Washington, D.C.

161. Kappler, *Laws and Treaties*, 2:239–44, gives the date of the treaty as July 13, which is clearly in error.

July 30th Saturday [Kearny]

About 1 P.M a council was held & a Treaty concluded with the Mandans & Gros Ventres. About 200 were assembled.

[Atkinson]

Sunday 31 July. Sergt. Harris came in this morning with some Buffalo meat. The Crows still unheard from. We are awaiting their coming in. Some Rockets and shells were thrown across the river at 9 o.c. this evening.

July 31st Sunday [Kearny]

A very cool day resembling autumn. In the evening about 9 some rockets were fired off & a few shells. The latter frightened the Indians considerably, they not being able to imagine how it could go off twice.

[Atkinson]

Monday Aug. 1, 1825. Capt. Riley was dispatched this morning into the plains to bring in the Crows. He is accompanied by a Crow Indian, one of the two who arrived this morning from the Crow Band who are some 15 miles from this. Also he is accompanied by Mr. Gordon & four soldiers.

August 1st Monday [Kearny]

A flag was sent this morning by Capt Riley of the 6th Infy in order to meet the Crows & hurry them in. They are supposed to be about 10 miles off & as Buffaloe are known to be in that direction & quarter, 'tis feared they may make a delay there.

[Atkinson]

Tuesday 2 Augt. We are yet waiting for the Crows to come in. Capt. Riley has not returned. Nothing has occurred today worthy of notice.

Augt 2d Tuesday [Kearny]

Went to day for the first time into the adjoining Village. Visited 20 lodges. Found them so dirty, was not tempted to remain long. Every evening their horses are brought in from the Prairie & for the sake of safety & security are suffered at nights, to partake of part of their lodges.

A report was made to day to the Genl. that the Assiniboins had scalped, in the morning, two squaws of the Gros Ventres, as they were attending the corn adjoining the Village.

[Atkinson]

Wednesday 3rd Augt. Capt. Riley returned with the Crow Tribe today at 1/2 past 2 o.c. All the lodges are here except six which [are] with Rotten Belly and 40 warriors near the mountains.[162]

Augt 3d Wednesday [Kearny]

The report of yesterday, of the Assiniboins proves unfounded. Almost every day furnishes similar false rumors.

The Crows arrived about 10 A.M, bringing 300 Lodges, 600 Warriors & about 3000 souls.[163] They are fine looking Indians & well mounted.

[Atkinson]

Thursday 4th Augt. The Brigade appeared under arms at 1/2 past 7. o.c. The artillery on the right served with Horses. At 11 went into Council with the Crows & concluded a Treaty with them.

Two Iriquois prisoners were demanded of the Crows; from this or some other cause unknown to me the Crows became very hostile in their conduct, and from their attempting to take the presents before they were told to do so Maj. O.Fallon struck three or four of the chiefs over the head with his pistol. About this time Genl. A. who had been a few minutes absent from the council, to get his dinner, in returning to the council saw the commotion & ordered the troops under Arms. This probably saved blood-shed.[164]

---

162. Rotten Belly was a highly successful warrior who became chief of the River Crows by age thirty. Denig, *Five Indian Tribes*, 162. He was not present when the 1825 treaty was signed.

163. In 1833 Denig estimated there were 800 lodges and 6,400 Crows. Ibid., 169.

164. James P. Beckwourth, one of William H. Ashley's trappers, heard about the incident a few days later. Recalling it thirty years later, Beckwourth blamed O'Fallon for issuing an ultimatum calling for the Crows to prepare for a fight or surrender the prisoners who Beckwourth said were a mixed blood woman and child taken from the Blackfeet. The Crow chief maintained the soldiers were no match for his warriors, who could whip the whole army. At this affront O'Fallon lost his temper, aimed his pistol at the chief, and pulled the trigger, but the weapon failed to fire. O'Fallon then used the gun as a club to pummel the chief on the head. When Atkinson discovered what had happened he was able to placate the Crows. Beckwourth believed the Crows anticipated trouble, recalling they stuffed grass and wooden pegs in the cannons so they could not be used. T. D. Bonner, *The Life and Adventures of James P. Beckwourth*, ed. Bernard DeVoto (New York: Alfred A. Knopf, 1931), 53.

Reuben Holmes wrote about the event some years later, but claimed Edwin

Augt 4th Thursday [Kearny]

The Command was reviewed this morning at 7 by the Genl. after which a Council was held & a Treaty made & signed by the Commissioners & the Chiefs & Principal men of the Crow Nation. Afterwards a very serious difficulty ensued, by Mr. O. F striking 3 or 4 of the Chiefs on the head, & one so severely that the blood ran down his face very free. The long Role was beat — the Battalions paraded. Three or four officers of us alone remained with the Indians, who were prepared & ready for fight — their guns cocked, their arrows ready for use. By some trouble & exertion, a partial reconciliation was effected which was afterwards matured by Genl. Atkinson, meeting & talking to some of the Principal men outside of camp. At one time, it was considered that the result, Peace or War was as uncertain, as in throwing up a copper, wheither it comes head or tail. The Nation moved about a mile further from our camp. A Capts guard was mounted & our chain of sentinals increased.

Rose wielded the gun and it was O'Fallon who prevented him from striking the Crow chief, Long Hair. This was in keeping with Holmes's portrayal of Rose as a "savage" and O'Fallon as "civilized." Reuben Holmes, "The Five Scalps," *Glimpses of the Past* 5 (1938): 3–54.

O'Fallon was not one to restrain himself when dealing with Indians. In 1819 he visited the Pawnees on the Loup River and a journalist described his actions when "A half Breed . . . boasted of having Killed a prisoner at the Massacre at Chicago in 1812, and of other heroic feats of a like nature, used every exertion to instigate the Indians there assembled to rise against the Agent. This being communicated by a chief, Mr. O Fallon promptly cut off the fellows ears, gave him one hundred lashes, threw his arms [weapons] in the river, and set him loose." Nichols, *The Missouri Expedition*, 35.

The August 4 incident was not the only outburst of O'Fallon's temper. A few days earlier at Camp Mandan, sutler George H. Kennerly described another incident: "What I have long expected has at last taken place, on the evening before last [July 30, 1825] while at the supper table the Genl. and Majr. O'F. came to an open rupture after the most harsh, and angry conversation had taken place, they mutually siezed, one a knife, the other a fork, and made the attempt to stab — fortunately I was siting near, and threw myself between them runing myself the risk of receiving the blows of one, or both, I stoped them at the time, they have not since spoke to each other, and how it will end God only knows. . . . it is evident that he had provoked the Genl. to this line of conduct, by his continual bad humor, and unnecessary interferance with his duties as a military officer." G. Kennerly to J. Kennerly, Aug. 1, 1825, James Kennerly Papers, Missouri Historical Society, St. Louis.

[Atkinson]

Friday 5th Augt. All the chiefs & braves came in this morning & recd. additional presents, said their wounds were covered & they would throw all that had passed behind them. Genl. A. went out at 11 & visited the Crow camp & called on the long hair.[165] He recd him friendly. Genl. A. does doubt somewhat whether the Crows are yet reconciled & that it is necessary to be on the alert. Many of the Crows came in this afternoon & appear to be quite friendly. I think they are.

Augt 5th Friday [Kearny]

A warm day. The difficulty of yesterday was adjusted & considered finally settled. Presents were made to the Chiefs & Principal men of the Crows who appeared satisfied. Genl A rode to their Village & was politely treated in the Chief's Lodge. In the evening some Rockets & shells were fired off.

A capts guard being mounted, I went upon duty as officer of the Day.

[Atkinson]

Saturday 6th Augt. At 1/2 past 7 this morning embarked & proceed up the river for the Yellow Stone. Passed the encampment of Lewis & Clark of 1804 at 9 o.c situate 4 miles above the present lower Mandan Village & 4 miles below the 2 Mandan Villages. We see nothing of the remains of the old Fort & picket work erected by them. Passed the upper Mandan Fort at 11 o.c & the 1 Grovont at 12 o.c. Halted on the left shore at 1/2 past 12 for dinner. Proceeded at 1/2 past one. Passed the mouth of Knife river on which the two Villages are & came to 6 miles above them, making 18 miles today. The Crow Tribe of Indians encamped today, this evening 3 miles from us & one above the Grovont Village. Several of their braves came into camp this evening & left us at dusk. Hairlip a Crow brave accompanied us on board the Mink from Camp Mandan to our camp this evening. He is a dignified & well behaved man of a begging disposition as most Indians are. A young Mandan accompanied us also from the 2nd Mandan Village — a modest well behaved man. Shabano [Chaboneau]

165. Long Hair was chief of the Mountain Crows and the first signer of the 1825 treaty. Denig, *Five Indian Tribes*, 194.

& his wife & her brother came to us here & staid all night. <*The weather very hot.*>

Augt 6th Saturday [Kearny]

Our business here being terminated we started at 7 A.M. The White Bear, one of the Boats belonging to the 6th Infy being considered unable to keep up with the others, was left behind. Passed the Mandan & Gros Ventres Villages, the latter being on Knife River which empties in to the Missouri 9 miles above our late encampment. Overtook & passed the Crow Nation, who were moving up on the bank of the River, being about to return to the Mountains. Had some wind & sailed a part of the day. Halted at 6 about 3 miles distant from the Crow Camp, having made 20 miles

[Atkinson]

Sunday 7th Augt. Proceeded at 4 o.c. all persons having left who does not belong to the expedition. Halted at 3/4 past 8 on the right bank for breakfast having ran 10 miles. Passed this morning coal Banks on the right bank in strata of 6 in. to 6 feel at different elevations. Proceeded at 1/4 past 10 & ran 7 miles & came to on the <*right*> left bank for dinner 1/4 mile below Miry River at 1/2 past one o.c. Proceeded at 3 o.c & ran 8 miles & came to at 1/4 past 7 on the right bank for the night. Here the hunters bro't us the hind quarters of a Buffalo, the other part being left as the animal was poor. Passed below this & Miry river banks of coal.

Augt 7th Sunday [Kearny]

Proceded at day break; a little lightning & some rain after which the Sun came out very hot. Made ten miles for breakfast. Had some sailing. In the afternoon passed Miry River & encamped on the Right bank a mile or two above it. About Sun down the mosquitoes in the evening very numerous & troublesome.

The Camp Guard was this evening reduced from a Capts to a Subalterns, as usual.

[Atkinson]

Monday 8th Augt. Proceeded at 4 & ran 5 miles & came to on the left bank for breakfast at 8 o.c. The navigation is bad hereabouts. Proceeded at 1/2 past 9 & ran 8 miles & came to on the left bank for dinner at 2 o.c. Proceeded at 1/4 past 3. & ran 7 miles & came to for the night on the left Bank at 1/2 past 6. Our hunters bro't in three deer and one Elk. The Bluffs thro' this days run have coal.

Augt 8th Monday [Kearny]

Morning clear & cool. As we were about starting, some one killed a Porcupine. Proceded a little after day break. Strong water during the day. Passed on the Left bank some considerable quantity of coal. Halted in there about Sun down. Two Deer were killed to day — very fat & large. Tracks of the grizly Bear were seen on the sand bars. Stopt at the lower end of the "Island, in the Little Basin."[166]

[Atkinson]

Tuesday 9th Augt. Proceeded at 4 under a pretty Breese & passed little basin Island at 1/2 mile from our camp. The breese increased at 8 o.c & the men breakfasted on board & we continued to sail till <*1/2 past*> 2 which bro't us to the mouth of the little Missouri River. Here the Missouri turns to the north & a little above the bend we encountered the most difficult snaggy bend & rapid water we have met with. Most of the boats however pass thro under their wheels. The Buffalo & Otter by the cordel. Crossed to the right bank & came to for dinner at 1/2 past 3. Proceeded at 1/4 past 4 & ran 7 miles & came to on the right bank at 7 o.c. for the night. The hunters brot us a very fine Elk.

Augt 9th Tuesday [Kearny]

About day break some lightning. Started as usual. Fair & stiff breeze. Breakfasted on board while sailing. At 3 P.M passed the mouth of the "Little Missouri," near which we saw on one side of the River, several rafts, & on the opposite, painted sticks put there about 6 weeks since, no doubt, by a war party of the Assiniboins. Above the mouth of the "Little Missouri" we found many snags & a very narrow gorge thro' them. Dined a mile above this & then proceded 'til Sundown, having made a better run than on any day previous viz 35 miles

---

166. In 1805 Lewis and Clark camped in this vicinity and mentioned "a remarkable bend in the river to the S. W. which we called the little bason." Moulton, *Journals of the Lewis and Clark Expedition*, 4:20.

[Atkinson]

Wednesday 10th Augt. Proceeded at 1/4 past 4 — the morning foggy. Ran 6 miles & came to on the left bank for breakfast at 8 o.c. Proceeded at 9 & ran under a pretty light wind 15 miles & came to on the left bank for dinner at 1/2 past one. The river turning here to the south the wind became adverse. Proceeded at 1/4 before three & ran 7 miles & came to on the right bank at 6 o.c for the night, an half hour earlier than usual to wait for the transport Buffalo to come up who had injured her machinery. Our hunters brot us one buffalo and three deer today. Buffalo scarce. Elk & deer, particularly the latter abound here as they do for an hundred miles back. It is however very difficult to kill them as the hunters are too much anoyed by the Musquitoes to remain in the bottoms any length of time. These insects are more numerous in this river from the Puncars up indeed on the plains and on the highest hills than I have witnessed any where in my travels. They make no singing noise, but strike you as soon as they come up & penetrate the skin at once. The navigation today has been very good. At the entrance of the mouth of Goose Egg lake we saw several swan.

Augt 10th Wednesday. [Kearny]

A heavy fog at day break. Started about an hour after it. Had some difficulty in getting over sand bars. Passed "Wild Onion creek", coming in on the Left Bank & stopt for breakfast, a short distance above it. Afterwards had some sailing. In the afternoon passed near "Goose Egg Lake" & halted at 6 P.M on the Right Bank — a few miles below "Chaboneaus creek", having made about 30 miles

Our hunters to day killed a Buffaloe & some deer & antelopes.

[Atkinson]

Thursday 11th Aug. Proceeded at 4 and ran 7 miles and came to on the left bank at 8 o.c. for breakfast. Light wind & the appearance of rain. One of the hunters bro't us a fine black tail deer this morning. Two white bear were seen on an Island opposite the mouth of Shabanos creek two miles below this point. Proceeded at 9 & ran under a fine wind till 6 o.c & came to on the right bank for the night having made 40 miles today. Our hunters gave us three Buffalo & an Elk today.

Augt 11th Thursday [Kearny]

Started as usual. Passed Chaboneaus creek, so called from a frenchman who accompanied Lewis & Clark across the mountains and whom we saw at the Mandans residing as a Trader amongst them. Saw two White Bear — they appeared to be yearlings, & at 200 yards distance on account of sand bars, we could not, without going back, approach nearer to them so we continued on. The hunters killed several Buffaloe & deer & at night upwards of 3 pounds of fresh meat was furnished to each man of the command. Had a fair wind & good sailing most of the day & stopt at Sundown, having made about 30 miles.

[Atkinson]

Friday 12 Augt. Proceeded at 1/4 past 4 and ran 8 miles and came to at 8 o.c on the right bank for breakfast. Here two Elk & one deer were bro't in. Great sign of Buffalo and other game in this part of the country. Buffalo are seen on the bottoms & on the hills in small herds. We have so much fresh meat that we discourage hunting. Proceeded at 9 o.c and ran three miles and came to at 1/2 past 10 on the right bank in consequence of strong head winds. Here an Elk & a Buffalo was killed & brot to us. Proceeded at 4 o.c & ran 5 miles and came to at 7 o.c on the right bank for the night. Two Elk & a deer were bro't in this evening.

Augt 12th Friday [Kearny]

Last night very warm. Proceded at day break head wind. Had good banks for cordeling & easy water. About 11 A.M, in consequence of the strong head wind, were obliged to lay to until 4 during which time a large Buffaloe bull ran down very near to our Boats. He was afterwards killed. Stopt at Sun down. Our run to day has been but short.

[Atkinson]

Saturday 13th Augt. Proceeded at 1/4 past 4 under a good Breeze. The Muskrat halted at 2 miles distance from our last nights encampment & twelve below Pumice Stone Creek and took in two Elk three white Bear & one deer that our hunters had killed yesterday. The Bear was an old female & two young ones or Cubs. These are the first of that animal killed by any of the expedition altho several have before been wounded. The Elk (transport) halted a mile above our last nights camp to take in game. Ran twenty-four miles — fresh Breeze — and came to on the right bank at 2 o.c for dinner — the wind having become adverse by the turns of the river to the south. The Elk came up at 1/4 before 4. She brot 5 Elk & one buck killed by Sergt. Harris & Rash and one Elk & 4 deer killed by other hunters.[167] We passed Hall's strand lake & creek at 1/2 past 10 this morning. The river appears to have washed the bank on the left shore opposite Halls strand lake, perhaps swallowed the whole of it up as we could not discover any standing water thereabouts. Proceeded at 1/2 past 4 and ran under cordelle and wheels 6 miles and came to at 7 on the left bank for the night.

Augt 13th Saturday [Kearny]

Started as usual. Fair wind hoisted sail. About 7 the hunters brought in 3 White Bear, which they had killed yesterday. Breakfasted on board. Passed the Burnt Hills, & Halls strand creek.[168] Sailed til 1 P. M, when we stopped for dinner. Proceeded at 3 & halted at Sun down on the left bank, having made 30 miles
Had some white Bear cooked for supper — found it tough & not as good as the common Black Bear. Passed to day the most Northern point in the Missouri, being upwards of 48 & less than one degree from the line that separates the U.S. from Canada.

[Atkinson]

Sunday 14th Augt. Proceeded at 20 minutes past 4 and ran 8 miles and came to at 1/4 before 10 on the right bank for breakfast. Here Maj. O.Fallon, Maj. Ketchum, Capt. Gantt, Doct. Gale & Lts. Crossman & Pentland left the Boats and proceeded with the mounted party at 1/4 past 11 for the mouth of the Yellow Stone taking the road by the river route. Proceeded with the flotilla at the same hour and ran 9 miles and came to at 1/4 before 7 on the left bank for the night. Here we found a pen made of drift wood which appears to have been occupied by white men as some letters were visible on the logs & the name of Thompson written with a fire coal. Crossley of the crew of the Rackoon killed a white bear two miles above this encampment this evening.

---

167. Wilborn Rash began his second enlistment in the Sixth Infantry eight days later and would continue serve as a private until his discharge in 1840. Register of Enlistments, M233, rolls 18, 19.

168. Lewis and Clark mentioned the Burnt Hills and the large quantities of pumice floating in the river. Moulton, *Journals of the Lewis and Clark Expedition*, 4:48.

Augt 14th Sunday [Kearny]

During last night some rain & at day break, a shower. Proceeded as usual. Had a little wind & continued 'til 10 A.M, when we halted for breakfast on the Right bank. Several of our party here left the Boats in order to walk & hunt to the Yellow Stone. A Beaver trap was found this morning with the foot of the animal in it. A White Bear was seen on the bar; stop't at 6 P.M, on the Left bank, where we found a small pen made of logs about 8 foot diameter, evidently intended to protect some Trappers from surprise from the Indians. One of the logs had a name written on it with a coal, but so badly we could not make it out. A. R. in capital letters were easily distinguished. A White Bear was killed two miles above here.

[Atkinson]

Monday 15. Augt. Proceeded at 20 minutes past 4 & ran 5 miles and came to on the right bank at 1/2 past 8 for breakfast. Light rains this morning. The navigation difficult on account of sand bars. Sergt. Harris bro't in a deer this morning. The white bear killed by Crossby last evening was put on board of the Rackoon this morning.[169] This animal's flesh is tolerable food. We had at our table yesterday for dinner part of one killed two days since. The men prefer the flesh to that of Elk or Buffalo. The rearety however is the cause, as the flesh is certainly not as well flavored as either Buffalo or Elk. Proceeded at 1/2 past 9 and ran under a light breese & occasionally on the wheels & cord 18 miles and came to on the right bank at 1/2 past 3 for dinner. Sergt. Harris bro't us another deer since breakfast. Proceeded at 1/2 past 4 and ran after the first mile under a good wind 7 miles and came to at 1/2 past 7 on the left bank for the night. The young Oto Indian and Corpl. Wear, who were of the party that went across by land for the Yellow Stone, came to us this evening & state that they were sent into the bottom to hunt & from the mist and rain were unable afterwards to rejoin the party.[170] Rain this day from 8 till 12 o.c.

---

169. John Crosby enlisted in 1817, wintered with the Rifle Regiment in 1818 at Cantonment Martin, and was present when Fort Atkinson was built. He served two five-year enlistments. Register of Enlistments, M233, rolls 14, 18.

170. William Weir enlisted in 1817 and spent ten years in the Sixth Infantry. Descriptive Books no. 5, no. 62, Sixth Infantry, RG 391.

Augt 15th [Kearny]

Started at day break. The white Bear killed last eve was brought aboard — very large, weighing about 400 cwt. The River full of turns & some very short. About Noon passed the mouth of White Earth River coming in on the left. Sailing for most part of the day. Stopt after Sun down on the N.E. shore.

[Atkinson]

Tuesday 16 Augt. Rain & wind last night. In consequence of the wind continuing & the men & baggage being wet the troops breakfasted at their encampment. The wind abating we proceeded at 1/2 past 6 under the wheels, hoisted sail at a miles distance & ran around the sand bar. Put out the cordel & ran 12 miles & came to on the right bank at 1/2 past 3 for dinner. Ran under sail part of the time. Proceeded at 1/2 past 4 & ran 6 miles & came to on the left bank at 7 o.c. for the night. 4 deer were brot in by the hunters today.

Augt 16th Tuesday [Kearny]

Rain last night & strong wind at day break. Breakfasted early and proceded at half past 6 A.M. Passed a Slough on the Left bank (which several of the Party suppose to be White Earth River) saw a large White Bear on the Right shore. The River has many & short turns. Dined at 2 P. M, about which time it cleared up & the Sun shone warm & bright. Halted at Sun down on the Left Shore.

[Atkinson]

Wednesday 17 Augt. Proceeded at 1/2 past 4 and ran 6 miles and came to on the right bank at 1/2 past 8 for breakfast. Proceeded at 1/2 past 9 and ran under the cordelle & wheels 2 miles, thence 5 miles under sail, fresh wind & passed the mouth of the Yellow Stone at 2 o.c. & came to at Ashley's old fort 1/4 mile above the mouth of that river on the right bank of the Missouri.[171] Sergt. Harris bro't in four deer. This position is the most beautiful spot we have seen on the river being a tongue of land between the two rivers — a perfect level plain elevated above high water & extending bank [back] two miles to a gentile ascent that rises at the distance of three miles 100 feet. This gorge of bottom is a quarter of a mile across where we are encamped & gradually opens out to a mile & 1/4

171. Ashley's old fort was Fort Henry, built in 1822 a short distance above the Yellowstone on the right bank of the Missouri. Morgan, *Jedediah Smith*, 40.

where it joins the rising ground to the rear. A heavy timbered bottom flanks the Yellow stone in the forks & on the opposite side — a heavy timbered bottom on the left bank of the Missouri & prairie in the forks on its right bank. This river at the points trends north west & the Yellow stone <*so. so*> west so. west. The bottom on the Yellow stone extends 60 miles on its left bank before the hills intersects the river & is 1/2 mile to a mile wide. 3 sides of the fort or picket work remain entire. The west side has been burnt down. One house is standing. Three appears to have been burnt, as also the gate of the work. A large herd of Buffalo is seen in the bottoms between the rivers. Four hunters are sent out to kill as many of them as possible. Maj. O Fallon and party arrived on the opposite side of the Yellow stone yesterday evening & are encamped 1/2 [mile] above its mouth. Our skiffs are sent up to cross the party with three horses to us.

Maj. O.F. & party arrived at sun set. The Horses were left at the crossing place on this side the Y. stone 1 1/2 miles above us. Sergt. Davis killed 2 Buffalo this evening.[172] Capt. Gantt & Maj. Gordon & Capt. Armstrong, 4 others.

Augt 17th Wednesday [Kearny]

Started at day break. The wind blowing moderately & fair, tho' as the River makes such short turns, what is fair one mile is often ahead the next. Arrived at 2 P. M, at the mouth of the Yellow Stone River & encamped a short distance above it, on the Right bank of the Missouri, near an old Picket enclosure made by Henrys party in 1822, & which they abandoned the following year in consequence of the defeat of Ashley by the Ricaras & the "Black Feet" stealing their horses &c.

Hd. Qrs. Camp Barbour Mouth of the Yellowstone, 17th Aug. 1825.

Commanders of boats will cause their cargoes to be landed early tomorrow morning and their boats well cleaned. They will also deliver to the A. A. C. before 7 O'clock tomorrow morning an accurate statement of all subsistence stores on board of their respective boats. . . . Lt. Holmes will cause a Blacksmith's forge to be

172. William Davis served in Company I of the First Infantry from 1823 until 1828. Register of Enlistments, M233, roll 18.

erected and have such articles made and repaired to put the transports Elk and Raccoon in the best possible order. . . . The Elk and Raccoon will be repaired to ascend the Missouri from this place on the morning of the 19th Inst. By Order of Col. Leavenworth. Signed Thos. Noel. Adj. 6th Regt.[173]

Brigade Hd Quarters, Camp Barbour
Mouth of the Yellow Stone River
Orders 18th August 1825

The transport Beaver, Muskrat, Elk, Raccoon and Mink will be held in readiness to proceed up the Missouri at an early hour on the morning of the 20th Inst.

The crews of the two former will be strengthened from that of the Otter at the discretion of Major Kearny. The transport Buffaloe and Otter with the officers and men attached to them (except the men to be drawn from the latter by Major Kearny together with the mounted men, will remain at this place untill further orders under the command of Captn Riley who will call on the Commanding General for special instructions. Asst Surgeon Coleman is temporarily assigned to this command under whose care the sick will be left [illegible words] not allowed to perform actual duty.

By order of Brigr Genl Atkinson
Signed. S. MacRee Lt ADCamp & A. A. A. Genl[174]

[Atkinson]

Thursday 18 Augt. The Buffalo killed yesterday were brot in this morning, also 2 large fine Elk killed by Burns, Capt. Riley's Hunter.[175] Issues made of the flesh of both to the troops. Troops reposing & cleaning their cloths & persons.

Aug 18th Thursday [Kearny]

Our Camp lies near the River on a most beautiful & level Prairie bounded in the rear by the Missouri, on the Left by the Yellow Stone, in front by a handsome wood three fourth of a mile distant,

---

173. Orderly Book 25, Sheldon, "Records of Fort Atkinson," 5:126–27.

174. Vol. 1:66–67, Orders Received, Sixth Infantry, RG 391.

175. Samuel Burns entered the army in 1818. He reenlisted at Fort Atkinson and was assigned to Riley's Company B. Register of Enlistments, M233, roll 18.

& on our right, the Prairie extends for several miles, & passes over a gentle & smooth Ridge. We have plenty of game near us, viz, Buffaloe, Elk, Deer, Big Horns, Ducks, Pigeons &c as well as fish, of which we get abundance from the two Rivers.

We were engaged to day taking the freight out of our Boats & cleaning them.

[Atkinson]

Friday 19 Augt. Three men from Genl. Ashleys party arrived at 9 this morning. At 11 Genl. Ashley with a party of 24 men arrived with 100 pack of Beaver.[176] Genl. A. offered him transportation for his fur & for his party if he would await the return of the troops to C. Bluffs, which proposition the Genl. acceeds to. 2 Elk & one deer were brot in today. Genl. Ashleys Beaver was put on board of the Buffalo this evening. No occurrance of moment.

Augt 19th Friday [Kearny]

Genl. Ashley & his party arrived to day about noon with 100 pack of Beaver skins from the Mountains. He left Council Bluffs last Novemb. & wintered near the head waters of the Platte. He has met with several Nations of Indians & had his horses stolen & his party fired upon by the Black feet. One of his men is seriously injured from an attack by a White Bear.

[Atkinson]

Saturday 20 Augt. Proceeded at 1/4 before five this morning on an excursion up the Missouri with the Mink, Beaver, Muskrat, Elk & Rackoon manned with 330 men & one piece of ordnance. The Buffalo & Otter with 125 men, with Genl. Ashleys men, were left

---

176. Ashley had eighty to one hundred packs of beaver worth $40,000 to $50,000. *St. Louis Beacon*, Oct. 3, 1825. His arrival at the mouth of the Yellowstone at about the same time as Atkinson may not have been a coincidence. Ashley was on his way to trap west of South Pass when he stopped at Fort Atkinson in the fall of 1824. Atkinson was there and they had ample opportunity to discuss the upper Missouri expedition. Harrison Clifford Dale, *The Ashley-Smith Explorations and the Discovery of a Central Route to the Pacific, 1822–1829* (Cleveland: Arthur H. Clark Co., 1918), 117.

James P. Beckwourth was with Ashley. Many years later Beckwourth recalled it was the noise they made in an attempt to save the furs from one of their sinking boats that alerted Atkinson's men to their presence. When they began their descent of the river the trappers rode as passengers. Bonner, *The Life and Adventures of James P. Beckwourth*, 52.

at Camp Barbour under Capt. Riley for the purpose of procuring meat for the troops.[177] Genl. Ashley accompanies us. Halted after having run 6 miles at 1/4 before 8 on the left bank for Breakfast. Proceeded at 9 o.c. & ran 8 miles & came to on the right bank for dinner at 1/2 past 1 o.c. Proceeded at 1/2 past 2 and ran 11 miles and came to at 3/4 past 7 on the right bank for the night. Our hunters bro't in today 2 fine Elk, one deer & one antelope. Hot sultry day.

Augt 20th Saturday [Kearny]

We started shortly after day break. The Otter, one of the boats of the 1st Infy, & Buffaloe of the 6th being left behind our object from this, to ascend the Missouri for a few days. Genl. Ashley (who has determined to detain his party & furs til we go below, in order to be sure of a safe passage) is with us. Ran up 6 miles to breakfast. Found the River narrow & shallow & but little current. Continued during the day under the wheels & cordell. The weather very warm & no wind. Handsome Prairies on either side of the River. Halted at dark on the Right bank having made 25 miles

[Atkinson]

Sunday 21. Augt. Proceeded at 1/4 before 5 and ran 8 miles & came to on the left bank for breakfast. Here our hunters killed & brot in 11 Elk. Capt. Armstrong also killed 2 very fine deer. Proceeded at 11, having been detained to take our meat, and ran 8 miles and came to on the right bank at 1/4 past 3 for dinner. Proceeded at 1/4 past 4 and ran 8 miles and came to at 7 o.c. for the night on the right bank.

Augt 21st Sunday [Kearny]

Started at day break. 6 miles above stopt for breakfast, at which time 10 large Elk were killed near our Landing & brought in. Saw two White Bear who came within about 150 yards of us & then ran off before we could load our guns. The Banks generally bounded by high, rough & precipitous barren hills. Current is gentle & the River narrow. In these respects, the character of the Missouri is totally changed above the Yellow Stone from which it is below. Passed on the Left bank a long range of hills 150 feet high, containing coal &

---

177. Atkinson said 300 men went an estimated 120 miles farther on this last portion of the trip. He hoped to find the Blackfeet and sign a treaty, but Ashley told him the tribe was too far away. U.S. Congress, *Expedition up the Missouri*, 6.

Saltpeter, & which appears to have been much burnt. At Sundown, encamped on the left bank. Day very warm & no wind.

[Atkinson]

Monday 22nd Augt. Proceeded at 1/4 past 4 & ran 8 miles & came to at 1/4 past 8 for breakfast on the left bank. Proceeded at 1/2 past 9 & ran 10 miles & came to at 2 o.c for dinner on the right bank. Proceeded at 3 o.c & ran till 7 making 9 miles & came to on the left bank for the night. Two Elk were killed today.

Augt 22d [Kearny]

During last night we had much wind. Started at day break. Passed Marthas River on the N.E. Wind light, tho fair. The River Bottoms begin to widen; in the afternoon passed thru a part of the River cut up with Sandbars, & at one point, the Missourri could not have been more than 100 yards wide. Sun very warm. In the evening the Beaver, Muskrat & Racoon had a race, of about a mile — little or no difference in their running. Halted at dark on the Left bank.

[Atkinson]

Tuesday 23rd Augt. Proceeded at 1/2 past 4 under light breeze. Breakfasted on board at 8 continuing to run till <*1/2 past*> 3 o.c & came to on the right bank for dinner. Proceeded at 4 & ran till 8 o.c & came to on the right bank for the night making 30 miles today. Porcupine River is a mile above us & we are at the mouth of a creek which we take to be 2000 mile creek supposing this creek to have changed its entrance into the Missouri a mile below its old mouth.

At 12 o.c tonight a heavy thunder gust came up from the N. West & drove the Mink from her moorings. She had only 12 men on board but she was laid across the river by their exertions on the slides with safety on the opposite shore.

Augt 23d Tuesday [Kearny]

Supposing that we are not more than 25 or 30 miles from Porcupine River we started at day break, with the intention of pushing hard & endeavoring to reach there, which is to be the extent of our journey. Had a good wind & breakfasted whilst under way. Made good progress under sail 'til about noon when the wind died away. The River full of turns, which led us towards every point in the compass. At Sundown reached a creek which we suppose to be the "2000 Mile creek," but as we have not seen the Porcupine River tis determined that we continue on.

We are now 2000 miles from the mouth of the River.

[Atkinson]

Wednesday 24 Augt. The Mink was bro't over to the right shore at dawn this morning and at 1/4 past 4 the flotilla moved up the river to assertain whether we have yet arrived at 2000 mile creek. Ran 7 miles & came to on the right bank where we dismantled our boats, as we intended not to ascend higher than 2000 mile creek and now finding we were 7 miles above it.[178] Genl. A. & Lt. Rogers each killed a Buffalo cow this morning.

Turned about and commenced our descent of the river precisely at midday & ran down till 6 o.c when we came to on the left bank in consequence of a thunder gust from the west. Remained here all night. Made 35 miles. Our boats were aground several times this afternoon but detained us only a little.

Brigade Head Quarters Mo River
4 miles above 2000 Mile Creek

Orders 24 Aug 1825

The Commissioners having ascended the river as high as the advanced state of the season & the reduction of the subsistence will justify, as well as the improbability of meeting with either of the Blackfeet or Assinniboins Indians; the flotilla will commence the descent of the river today at an hour that will be communicated in subsequent orders.

The Boats will descend in the same order of movement as when ascending observing to preserve at least 200 yards between each boat: and any boat running against another which may be obstructed by sand bars or otherwise detained will be held in error and her commandant held accountable for the act.

By order of Brigr Genl Atkinson

Signed S. MacRee Lt AD Camp & A. A. A. Genl[179]

---

178. Two Thousand Mile Creek, present Red Water Creek, is opposite Poplar, Montana, about 1,600 miles up the Missouri. Reid and Gannon, "Journal of the Atkinson-O'Fallon Expedition," 4:43, n.68. Atkinson's remark that "we dismantled our boats" refers only to the sailing and cordelling gear. Kearny mentions that masts were taken down because they would not be needed on the trip down the river.

179. Vol. 1:67–68, Orders Received, Sixth Infantry, RG 391.

Augt 24th Wednesday [Kearny]

During the night a hard rain & a very severe blow, which caused the Mink to drag her cable & the wind drove her over to the opposite shore. It was so dark that she could only be seen during the flashes of the lightning. A few men had slept on board of her, & who were in her when she drifted off. These brought her back by day break when we all proceeded a mile or so. Brought us to Porcupine River which we passed without knowing it. It comes in behind a bar. Continued 'til 8. when we halted for breakfast. It was now ascertained we had passed the Point we had been aiming, & a return decided on. Our Masts were taken down, & our Boats dismantled, & at 12. we turned round, each Boats crew giving 3 hearty cheers, when we commenced descending. A hard blow storm at 5 P. M which detained us an hour. Slept on the Left bank.

[Atkinson]

Thursday 25th Augt. It rained all night, held up at 4 o.c. At 1/2 past 4 we set out & ran 20 miles & came to at 8 on the right bank for breakfast. At this point two large Buffalo Bulls swam across the river & landed fifty yards below the Mink. Genl. A. shot one of them from the Boat & Sergt. Harris the other. The first Genl. A's. fell from the single shot after going 100 yards. The other was 3 times shot by Genl. A. & twice by Capt. Armstrong & Sergt. Harris before it fell. It would have died from the first shot. These animals were butchered & distributed to the Boats. The one Gen. A. killed weighed more than 1000 lbs. The other 750 lbs. 4 hunters that were sent down the river yesterday morning to kill game (in a skiff) succeeded in killing only a grizzly Bear, having seen nothing else but one deer. A soldier of the 6th Rgt. by the name of Piper killed the Bear.[180] Proceeded after breakfast at 10. o.c. & passed Marthas river at 11. Very strong wind from the west. Saw Buffalo on Marthas river. Ran on till 7 o.c & came to on the left Bank 12 miles above the mouth of the Yellow Stone with the Mink, Rackoon & Muskrat. The Beaver & Elk were detained by the winds.

180. John Piper had just begun his second enlistment in the Sixth. Private Piper died in 1827. Register of Enlistments, M233, roll 18.

WOLF CHIEF, *by George Catlin, 1832. Called by Catlin "the first chief of the Mandan," Wolf Chief was the second signatory on the 1825 treaty.*

SMITHSONIAN INSTITUTION, WASHINGTON, D.C.

Augt 25th Thursday [Kearny]

Rain & Lightning during the night. Wind in the morning from N.E. Proceded at 4 A.M, at 7 it cleared away. Cool & feels like Autumn. Stopt at 9. for breakfast. Two Buffaloe bulls were killed where the current is strong & snags thick, Find much difficulty in preventing the Boat from running on them. At 12 the wind blew so hard as to compel the Elk & Beaver to lie to 'til 3 P. M (the other

Boats being ahead continued). We stopt at 7 P.M, on the Left bank. Passed to day Marthas River which is not more than a yard broad at its mouth.

[Atkinson]

Friday 26. Augt. Proceeded at 1/2 past 4 and ran down to the mouth of the Yellow Stone at 1/4 before 6. o.c. The Beaver came in at 10 o.c. & the Elk at 1/2 past 10. They encamped 30 miles distant last night.

Capt. Riley who was left at this point with the Buffalo & Otter to kill & salt down game has succeed in curing but 4 barrels of Buffalo Beef. The Game in this neighborhood having disappeared since the arrival of the troops 8 days ago. Sent off one of the skiffs this morning to descend the river some 20 miles for the purpose of killing game by the time the flotilla [comes] down tomorrow. Gen. Ashley shipped his furs this afternoon on board the Mink, Muskrat & Rackoon.

Augt 26th Friday [Kearny]

Started this morning earlier than usual in order to reach the Yellow Stone for breakfast. The Beaver & Elk arrived at 10 A.M, the other three Boats had reached there at 7. Found the Otter & Buffaloe which had been left behind when we went up. Arrangements were made for starting off tomorrow.

Brigade Hd. Qrs. Mouth of Yellow Stone
Orders. River, Camp Barbour 26 Aug. 1825

The Flotella will commence descending the river for Fort Atkinson (Council Bluffs) at an early hour tomorrow morning.

The public horses will be transported on board the Elk, Buffaloe, Beaver and Otter; five to the boats of the 6th and four to those of the 1st Infy. General Ashley's furs will be taken on board of the Mink, Muskrat & Raccoon.

The A. A. Insp. Genl will in distributing the subsistence & other stores make allowance for the weight of the horses and furs in favor of the boats in which they are transported.

By order of Brig. Genl Atkinson
Signed S. MacRee Lt. ADCamp & A. A. A. Genl[181]

---

181. Vol. 1:67, Orders Received, Sixth Infantry, RG 391.

[Atkinson]

Saturday 27. Augt. Embarked the horses on board of the Buffalo, Otter, Elk & Beaver & commenced our descent of the river at 40 minutes past 5 o.c. A.M. and ran till 9 o.c & came to on the left bank for breakfast. Sergt. Harris who had been sent forwarded yesterday bro't in part of an Elk at this point. Proceeded at 10. At 1/2 past ten took a small deer & at 11 a deer & one of Gen. Ashleys hunters who had killed them. Came to on the left bank at 1/2 past 3 in consequence of a heavy squall & with rain & hail. Proceeded at 4 & ran till 3/4 past 6 & came to on the left bank for the night having we supposed made 65 or 70 miles today. Sent a skiff & three hunters forward this evening to hunt in the morning before the boats should get up.

Augt 27th Saturday [Kearny]

At day break, embarked 10 horses aboard our Boats & then proceded down the River, taking with us Genl Ashleys party of 22 men, & the furs, which they had brought from across the mountains.

In the morning had some rain, when it cleared away & remained so 'til about 4 P.M when the clouds thickened, & we experienced for half an hour a very severe wind, which compelled us to lay bye. About this time a large water spout was seen in the [illegible word]

We had passed White Earth River about 3 P.M & encamped 15 miles below it, on the Left bank.

[Atkinson]

<*Monday*> Sunday 28 Augt. Proceeded at 1/4 past 4 & ran till 1/4 before 7 & came to with the Mink on the right bank to take in the hunters who had killed but one deer. Burns one of the hunters has not come in. The other transports ran till 8 & came to on the right bank for breakfast. Came up to them & all proceeded at 1/2 past 8. & ran till 10 minutes past 2 & came to on the right bank for dinner. Proceeded at 3 o.c & ran till 1/2 past 6 & came to on the right bank for the night. We have made (we suppose) 65 miles today. Our hunters bro't us this morning 4 deer & one Elk (they were sent forward last night in the skiffs.)

Augt 28th Sunday [Kearny]

The weather last night very cool. Proceded as usual. Breakfast at 8 AM & at 9 took in our hunters who had left us last night in a skiff, bringing with them two large deer & an elk.

[Atkinson]

<*Tuesday*> Monday 29th Augt. Proceeded at 4 o.c. passed Charbano's creek at <*1/2 past 7*> 8 o.c. Halted for breakfast a short distance above on the right bank. An Elk was killed here by Corpl. King. Proceeded at 9 & ran 4 miles and came to with the Mink, Beaver & Muskrat on the left bank for the purpose of obtaining some fresh meat seeing a large herd of Elk on the sand bar. Hunters sent in to the bottom who with the aid of Capt. Armstrong, Lt. Harris & Vanswarengen & Genl. A. killed 12 fine Elk. Capt. Armstrong killed 3. The Lieuts. & Genl. A. one. The flesh was bro't on board of the 3 boats & we followed the other transports (who had proceeded on) at 3 o.c. Came to at dusk 3 miles above the mouth of the little Missouri on the left bank. The fires of the other boats in view to whom we sent the skiff ladened with Elk meat.

Augt 29th Monday [Kearny]

Started as usual. About noon met with a herd of Elk, & our Boats, (excepting those, of the 6th Infy, & the Otter) stopt; we killed about a dozen & took them on board, which detained us two hours. We then proceded 'til dark, which brought us within 3 miles of the Little Missouri, & where we encamped on the Left bank, on a Sand bar, & separated from the remainder of the Boats.

The afternoon warm & found in the evening, some mosquitoes.

[Atkinson]

<*Wednesday*> Tuesday 30th Augt. 1825. Proceeded at 4 & ran three miles & came up with the rear boats (that left us yesterday) just as they were passing the snaggy obstruction at the mouth of Little Missouri. All the boats passed in safety. The Otter losing two buckets the whole injury. Passed the mouth of Little Missouri at 10 minutes before 5. Weather very fine for the last 48 hours. Halted at 8 for breakfast on the right bank. Fresh tracks of a small party of Indians were seen at this place. Proceeded at 9 & ran till 2 & came to on the left bank for dinner. The hunters killed a Buck at this

place. Proceeded at 3 & ran till 1/2 past 6 & came to on the right bank for the night 30 miles above the lower Mandan Village.

Augt 30th Tuesday [Kearny]

The morning cool & some wind. Started at daybreak & passed a snaggy place at the Little Missouri where we found the Boats of the 6th Infy & the Otter. Continued on; wind ahead which drove the Beaver against the shore & broke the yoke of her rudder. Stopt at dark, on the Right bank.

[Atkinson]

<*Thursday*> Wednesday 31st 1825. Proceeded at 1/2 past 4 passing the Grovonts & upper Mandans from 7 till 9 & arrived at the lower village at 10 o.c. Fired a gun (swivle) on passing each village & on our arrival at this point. The Boats were ordered to be put in order & held in readiness to proceed at 4 tomorrow morning. We find here some 40 Sioux Indians of the Sione & Hunkpapas bands who are on a friendly visit. We understand that the Chayanne Tribe is at a short distance (30 or 40 miles) hence. Some of the tribe were here a few days since to make a peace with the Mandans & Grovonts. They have succeeded & Yellow Belly (the young Grovont Chief) with a party of warriors have now gone to visit the Chayennes. The Asyniboines are said to be 7 days journey from this across towards Red River. The Sub. agent Mr. Wilson sent two white men three days ago to invite them to pay a visit to this place & for the purpose of effecting a peace between the Indians here & them.[182] 300 lodges of the Assinibonis are said to be at the point mentioned.

Augt 31st Wednesday [Kearny]

Proceeded at day break. At 7 A.M, passed the Gros Ventres Villages on Knife River, & at 9 stopt at our old encampment below the lower Mandan Village. The remainder of the day was occupied in repairing the White Bear.

'Tis understood that the Chayennes are within 15 miles of here, in order to make Peace with the Mandan & Gros Ventres, & that

182. The commissioners had returned to Fort Atkinson when Peter Wilson concluded a treaty with the Assiniboin on September 29, 1825. Although the treaty was similar to the others signed in 1825, the one with the Assiniboin was not recognized because Wilson did not have the authority to conclude a treaty. Lowrie, *American State Papers: Indian Affairs*, 2:671–73.

300 Lodges of the Assiniboins are on the opposite side of the River, & within ten days travel. Tho' we are anxious to see these Indians, yet the delay is more than we can afford.

Lt. R. Holmes a. a. Qr Mr. In consequence of a deficiency of shoes among the troops will issue to the Brigade Commanded by Brigdr Genl H. Atkinson Three Hundred & Ninety three pairs of Buffaloe Mockasins as an extra issue.

Mandan Village H. Atkinson
Aug. 31, 1825 Br Gen U.S. Army[183]

[Atkinson]

<*Friday*> Thursday 1 Sept., 1825. Proceeded at 10 minutes past 5 A.M, taking on board of our transports some 20 of the Sioux who are returning to join their friends below. Halted on the right bank at 8 for breakfast. The hunters bro't us 4 deer & one Elk this morning. Proceeded at 9 & ran till 2 & came to on the <*right*> left bank for dinner. Several of the Sioux left the boats & went down by land on the right bank. Proceeded at 3 & at 5 miles passed a party of Sioux on the left bank. Halted on the <*left*> right bank at 1/2 past 4 for the night in order to repair the machinery of the Mink. Sent forward the skiffs to procure game. This evening a Buffalo Bull ran from the plains thro' our Camp knocking nearly down the marque of Maj. Kearny & leaped into the river. He was shot & taken. Some Sioux came to our camp & traded a little Buffalo meat.

Septr 1st Thursday [Kearny]

Started about an hour after day break, the number of our Boats being increased to 8. Stopt at 8 A.M for breakfast where we found our hunters, who we sent out yesterday, bringing an Elk & a deer. We took with us about a dozen of the Sioux who are going from the Mandan to join their Nation. At half past 4 P.M, the Pitman of the Mink broke, & we halted on the right bank on a high Prairie. Saw during the day several scattering buffaloe, & sent out hunters

---

183. Atkinson to Holmes, an enclosure from Holmes to "Sir," Oct. 5, 1827, Commission Accounts, a/c 12969/1829, RG 217. This was not the first time Atkinson found it necessary to purchase moccasins for the troops. At Fort Kiowa he bought 108 pairs for $27 from Joseph Sire. Voucher 2, abstract A, account 5020/1825, ibid.

in the skiff to descend the River this evening & hunt to morrow morning. At Sundown, a Buffaloe Bull that had been chased from the hills entered our Camp & was killed directly alongside one of our Boats.

[Atkinson]

<*Saturday*> Friday 2 Sept. Proceeded at 1/2 past 4 & ran till 8 & came to on the left bank for Breakfast.

The hunters brot us three Elk this morning whilst the men were breakfasting. Genl. Atkinson went out & killed a very large Buck Elk — Capt. Armstrong a deer. Several other deer were killed by others.

Proceeded at 10. & ran till 2 & came to on the right bank for dinner at 3 o.c. Proceeded at 4 & ran till 1/2 past 6 & came to on the right bank for the night.

Sept. 2d Friday [Kearny]

The Mink being repaired we started as usual. Our hunters brought us two Elk about 6 A.M. At 12 we passed an "old Mandan Village" on the right bank, & at 5 P.M, the mouth of Cannon Ball River, & slept ten miles below it on the left bank.

[Atkinson]

<*Sunday*> Saturday 3 Sept. Proceeded at 1/2 past 4 and ran till 9 & came to on the right bank for breakfast. The wind which was blowing hard from the So. increased & we lay to till 1/2 past 2 when we proceeded against a strong wind and rain till 6 & came to 25 miles above the Aricara Village on the right bank for the night. We saw Elk & many deer at this point but succeeded in killing one deer. We found here a frenchman trapping beaver. He had taken 4 last night. Genl. A. procured from him 3 Beaver tails & some of the flesh.

Sept 3d Saturday [Kearny]

Started at day break & at the distance of two miles passed the "Warreconne creek." Head wind. Our hunters report that there is no game to be seen. Halted at 8. for breakfast & were detained 'til 11 A.M waiting for the Boat Elk; when she came up, the Mink got under way but immediately came to in consequence of strong head wind which detained us 'til 2 P.M. We passed at 4, a <*Ricara*> Chayenne encampment of about 200 souls on the right bank, & halted at 6 on a Prairie on the left, near a large herd of "Elk." Several of the party went in pursuit but were unsuccessful.

[Atkinson]

<*Monday*> Sunday 4 Sept. Proceeded at 1/2 past 4 & arrived at the Aricara Village at 1/2 past 9. The 6 chiefs of this tribe visited us on board of the Mink & recd. presents — 5 guns & 2 pistols — Blankets — scarlet Chiefs Coats — powder — Ball & other small articles. They appear decidedly friendly & are greatly pleased with the presents. 6 lodges of Cheyennes are here & the principle man & 8 others visited us & recd. small presents. 3 Sioux are here. We recd. from the Aricaras a pouch of plain & a pouch of sweet corn. Having finished all our business here we proceeded on our desent of the river at 3 o.c & ran till 7 & came to on the right bank for the night. We have on board of the fleet 4 Pawnee Loups who had been on a visit with some 20 other to the Aricaras.

Sept 4th Sunday [Kearny]

Arrived at the Ricaras about 8 A.M & remained 'til 3 P.M. Saw many of the Nation & some of the Chayennes, the latter having 6 lodges here. The Commissioners held a talk with them & made them presents, as well as to the Ricaras, who obtained none on our former visit. Descended about 20 miles. In the afternoon the wind occasinally strong & ahead. A few Pawnee Indians, who have been on a visit to the Ricaras, & anxious to return home, have taken passage on board one of the Boats.

[Atkinson]

<*Tuesday*> Monday 5. Sept. Proceeded at 1/4 past 4 & passed the Moro [Moreau] at 1/2 past 7. Came to at 8 on the right bank for Breakfast, proceeded at 9 & ran till 2 & came to on the right bank for dinner. Proceeded at 3 & ran till 7 o.c for the night on the right bank. Squally & rain in the evening & night.

Sept 5th Monday [Kearny]

Proceded as usual; breakfasted below Moreau River. Dined opposite the Little Chayenne, & encamped on the right bank (opposite to an Island) 20 miles below it. The water has fallen several feet since our passing up. The River is now filled with Sand bars which renders it very difficult, at some places, to find the channel.

[Atkinson]

<*Wednesday*> Tuesday 6 Sept. Proceeded at 1/2 past 4 and ran till 1/2 past 7 & came to on the right bank where were 20 lodges of

<*Yantona*> Sione Sioux who had been up to the Aricara village to trade for corn & were on their return to their own district of country. Six Braves — there being no chief, came on board & expressed both by words and actions great friendship. We gave them a present of tobacco some balls & a case bottle of whiskey. They gave us some fresh Elk meat & offered us a dog feast which last we declined as we are in a hurry to get on. Proceeded at 1/2 past 8 and ran till 1/2 past 10 & came to on acct. of very strong head wind. 3 boats on the left & 5 on the right shore. Proceeded at 1/2 past 5 & ran till 7 & came to on the left shore for the night.

Sept 6th Tuesday [Kearny]

During last night, high wind & rain. Morning cool. Ran about 15 miles & halted for breakfast on the right shore, where we found 15 lodges of the Saones, a band of the Sioux. At this place the Elk joined us, having been absent (in the rear) since yesterday morning. Put off at 9 & at 11 A.M, were stoped by the wind which detained us til 5 P.M, after which we ran down to the upper end of the Chayene Bend, & halted after dark on the left bank.

Flag Boat Mink
Sir Sept. 7th 1825

The Officer of the Day, on duty last night reports that Lt. Nute, 6th Infy., who was detailed & mounted Guard, absented himself from his post for some two or three hours & that during the same time most of the Guard were also absent. You will cause Lt. Nute to be put in arrest & charges will be preferred against him for neglect of duty.[184]

Very respy. your Obed. Servt.
Signed H. Atkinson Brig. Genl. U.S. Army[185]

---

184. Lieutenant Nute was released from arrest by an order issued on September 23.

185. Atkinson to "Sir," Sept. 7, 1825, entry 5587, Letters Received by Henry Atkinson, 1825–31, Records of Named Departments, Records of U.S. Army Continental Commands, Record Group 393, NARA (hereafter cited as Letters Received by Atkinson).

[Atkinson]

<*Thursday*> Wednesday 7th Sept. A little rain & some wind at 4 this morning. Proceeded at 1/2 past 4. Passed the mouth of Shyenne river at 7 & came to a 1/2 mile below on the right bank to speake with some Sione Indians. Here we breakfasted & 5 Sioux came on board & recd. a present of Tobacco & some whiskey to drink. Sent by them 60 Twists & a bottle of whiskey for the chief of the party who with 40 lodges is 20 miles up the Shyenne river where there are plenty of Buffalo. Proceeded at 8 ran till one o.c and halted on the left bank for dinner. Here we had to wait till the ensuing morning for the Muskrat to repair her rudder — having by running on a sand bar & swinging against the bank broke the tower iron attached to the rudder.

Sept 7th Wednesday [Kearny]

Started at day break. Passed the Chayenne River at 7. & breakfasted a mile or two below it where we found a few Sioux, & who were very desirous of hearing an account of the difficulty we had with the Crows at the Mandan Village. This story we find has already been circulated amongst all the Indians, thus far. After breakfast experienced much difficulty with Sand bars. Halted at 2 P.M, about 10 miles above Teton River for dinner where we found the Iron hoop of the rudder of the Muskrat was broken. The forge was put up & it was night before she was repaired.

[Atkinson]

<*Friday*> Thursday 8 Sept. Proceeded at 1/2 past 4 & ran till 8 and came to below the mouth of Teton river on the right bank for Breakfast. The rackoon did not come up till 1/4 before 9 o.c having been detained on a sand bar. Proceeded at 1/2 past 9 & ran till 1/2 past one o.c & came to on the right bank for dinner. Proceeded at 1/4 past 2 & ran till 7 & came to on the left bank for the night and about 10 miles from the commencement of the great Bend. The Hunters brot in a large Elk today.

Sept 8th Thursday [Kearny]

Last night very cool & the first frost that we have experienced. Started at daybreak, passed Teton River at 7 A.M. The navigation of the river getting much better. Sun during the day, warm & pleasant

— no wind. Reached Medicine or Tyler River at dark, & stopt on the opposite shore — having made to day 66 miles

[Atkinson]

<*Saturday*> Friday 9th Sept. Proceeded at 3/4 past 4 & ran till 8 & came to on the left bank for breakfast. Proceeded at 1/4 before 9 & ran till 2 & came to on the right bank for dinner. Proceeded at 3 & ran till 5 & came to at Fort Kiawa. Here we took in 8 days provisions that we had deposited in our ascent. Repaired the crank of the Racoon which had partly given way. Discharged Mr. Gordons horse from the Otter, he intending to stay here. 7 lodges of Sioux are here. No news.[186]

Sept 9th Friday [Kearny]

Proceded at day break. 6 miles below entered upon the "Great Bend." Dined at the foot of it & arrived at Fort Kiawa at 5 P.M.

The gorge of the Big bend is laid down on all maps from N. to S which is incorrect. It should be from E. to W.

[Atkinson]

<*Sunday*> Saturday 10th Sept. Proceeded at 9 o.c and ran till 1/2 past one o.c & came to on the left bank for breakfast 3 miles above the mouth of White river. Proceeded at 1/4 past 2 & ran till 7 & came to on the right bank for the night. We suppose we are 20 miles below White river. Saw three Indians on the hills to our right a little below White river. Impeded & perplexed this evening with sand bars. The Elk, Buffalo & Otter in consequence thereof halted on the left bank 2 miles in our rear, it becoming too dark to run later.

Sept 10th Saturday [Kearny]

During last night the wind blew very hard & we had some rain. The crank of the Racoon being broken, we were detained 'til half past 8 A.M when we proceded, & ran down to White River for dinner after which we had much difficulty, wind sand bars. Stopt after dark on the right bank under a high bluff; we had no place for a camp, but were necessarily compelled to halt here, in consequence of the darkness & a fresh breeze, just springing up.

---

186. James Beckwourth recalled spending the night at the fort. He said Joshua Pilcher was there and presented William Ashley with a large grizzly bear "for a plaything." The bear was chained to the deck of one of the boats and was taken to Fort Atkinson, where it was turned over to Major Biddle. Bonner, *The Life and Adventures of James P. Beckwourth*, 54–57.

[Atkinson]

<*Monday*> Sunday 11. Sept. Proceeded at 1/4 past 4 and ran till 3/4 after 8 & came to on the right bank for breakfast. The Otter, Elk & Buffalo came up here. Made 20 this morning. Proceeded at 9 o.c. Strong wind down the river. Ran till 1/2 past one & came to on the right bank for Dinner. Proceeded at 1/2 past 2 & ran till 1/2 past 6 & came to on the right bank for the night. Made 65 miles today.

Sept 11th Saturday [Kearny]

The Elk & Buffaloe, boats of the 6th Infy & the Otter of the 1st remained in the rear last night. They came up about day break, when we proceded. Passed Cedar Island at 10 A.M. Saw a flock of Turkies near it. Some wind during the day but fair, River getting better — less obstructed with bars & current stronger. Stopt after dark on the right hand shore under high Bluffs.

[Atkinson]

<*Sunday*> Monday 12th Sept. Proceeded at 1/2 past 4 & ran 2 miles & were bro't up by sand bars, which all the boats did not get over till 1/2 past 8. The Mink came to at 7 on the left bank 6 miles from our last nights encampment to await the coming up of the Beaver, Otter & Buffalo. The came up at 1/2 past 9 & after breakfasting proceeded at 10. The Elk, White Bear, Rackoon, & Muskrat are 3 hours before us. The Beaver also passed us without stopping. She is 3/4 hour ahead. Very strong blustering wind from the West. Came up with the head boats at 20 minutes past 3. Halted & dined on the right bank & proceeded at 1/4 before 4 and arrived at the Poncar Village at 6 o.c. where we encamped for the night. Gave the chiefs this evening a present of Tobacco, 5 blankets, 4 Chiefs Coats & various small articles.

Sept 12th Monday [Kearny]

Proceded at day break & were detained 3 hours in getting a mile & a half out of a slough, into which we had entered last night. Wind fresh & fair. Dined near Puncah creek. Passed the Leau qui coure & arrived at the Puncah Village on White Paint creek at 5 P.M.

[Atkinson]

<*Wednesday*> Tuesday 13th Sept. Our horses were disembarked here & Maj. Ketchum, Lts. Kingsbury & Wragg & two soldiers sent across to the bluffs with them, by the way of the Maha Village

with instructions to turn Harris, our express, who we expect on his way to the Great Bend with the mail. 5 lodges of Yankton Sioux are here. 3 of them go with Maj. Ketchum to make peace with the Mahas. After having given a present of two kegs of mixed liquor to the Poncars & a bottle to the Sioux & recd. presents from them of Buffalo meat, melons & pumpkins, we proceeded at 1/4 before 7 and ran till 1 o.c. & came to on the <*left*> right bank for dinner. Proceeded at 2 & ran 'till 3 o.c & came to on the right bank two miles above the river a Jacque in consequence of the Muskrat having run upon, what is called a hidden snag. She was perferated in three places in her bottom forward of her machinery & filled with water & sunk, her bows in 2 feet water & her stern in 4 feet. The Beaver & Otter who were near ran to her relief, recd. her cargo & by 7 o.c succeeded in stopping the leaks temperarily, raised & free'd her from water, when she was ran to a sand bar on the left shore & the damages repaired during the night. About 25 packs of 45 of Beaver, belong to Genl. Ashley, became wet by the accident, some fixed ammunition damaged & the officer's baggage. Nothing was lost.[187]

Sept 13th Tuesday [Kearny]

The horses which we brought in our Boats from the Yellow Stone, having been disembarked, & a party started by land for Council [Bluffs]. We proceeded after breakfast. Passed Bon Homme Island & dined near the Calumet Bluffs — after which, about 3 P.M & 5 miles above the River Jacque, the Muskrat struck a snag which made 6 holes in her. She was imediately run on a Sand bar, in about 3 foot water, when she filled & settled on the Bar. Being unloaded, she was hauled up, & blankets &c being stuffed in, she was bailed out, & by dark, we succeded in getting her ashore. The above happened in the middle of the River, & the Beaver & Otter being near, immediately halted along side, & by the assistance of the three boats crews she was saved, tho with difficulty. She must certainly have been lost, had she been alone. She had the greater part of Genl Ashleys Beaver on board of her, which was not injured.

---

187. James Beckwourth remembered, "Again all our packs were afloat, and General Atkinson, witnessing the accident, ordered every man overboard to save the peltry, himself setting the example. In an instant, mountaineers, United States officers and soldiers plunged in to the rescue. Fortunately it was shoal water, not more than waist high, and all was speedily saved." Ibid., 53.

Snags on the Missouri, *by Karl Bodmer. Watercolor and pencil, 1833.*
Joslyn Art Museum, Gift of the Enron Art Foundation

[Atkinson]

<*Thursday*> Wednesday 14th Sept. The Mink, Elk, Buffalo, White Bear & Buffalo proceeded at 1/2 past 5 this morning. The Beaver, Otter & Muskrat that are on the opposite shore not yet being quite ready did not proceed till 7. Ran till 1/2 past 12 & came to on the right Bank with the first 5 boats. The other three came up at one o.c. Remained till 4 for Genl. Ashleys furs to be dried that got wet yesterday when we proceeded. Met 4 Keel Boats one mile below our halting ground belonging to Pratte & Co. & Mr. Tilton, two each. Maj. O.Fallon & Capt. Kennerly went in a Skiff on board of these boats. The flotilla went on & halted at 1/2 past 6 on the right bank opposite the burning bluffs for the night.[188] The Elk came to a mile above to take in 7 Elk killed this evening by her hunters.

188. The Burning Bluffs was the result of oxidation of certain shales exposed to the air by erosion. Moulton, *Journals of the Lewis and Clark Expedition*, 2:506.

Sept 14th Wednesday [Kearny]

The Muskrat having been last night hauled out of the water, a new plank put into her & being caulked, she was again launched, & being reloaded, we having breakfasted, proceded. At half past Six passed the Jacque, near which we found a snaggy place & stopt at noon, on a Sand bar, for dinner, & for the purpose of drying Genl. Ashleys furs, which were wet yesterday in the Muskrat. This detained us til 4 P.M when we put off & shortly passed 4 Boats on their way to the Mandans, Rickaras, & Sioux belonging to the Trader a few miles below. Passed Vermillion or White Stone River, & reached the Burning Bluffs at Sun down & halted on the opposite shore.

An hour after dark we experienced a very heavy blow accompanied by rain, thunder & lightning which lasted for an hour.

Seven black bears were seen to day and five of them shot.

[Atkinson]

<*Friday*> Thursday 15th Sept. Proceeded at 1/4 before 5. & ran till half past 8 & came to on the left bank for breakfast. The Elk came up at 1/4 after 9. At 1/2 past 9 the flotilla proceeded & ran till 1/2 past 1 o.c & came to on the <*right*> left bank for dinner. Proceeded at 1/2 past 2 & ran till 1/2 past 6 & came to on the left bank for the night.

Sept 15th Thursday [Kearny]

Received this morning at day break several news Papers, brought up by the Boats which we passed yesterday, & obtained from them, by one of our party, who visited them in a skiff, & overtook us this morning. Proceded as usual & ran down about 15 miles to breakfast when the Elk rejoined us, which had been absent from yesterday & bringing 7 elk which some of her Crew had shot. Passed the Iowa about 2 P.M. Reached the Big Sioux at dark & halted on the left bank a mile below it. Made to day about 60 miles. The current is strong & we find many snags and sawyers.

[Atkinson]

Friday 16 Sept. I have committed an error back in this journal having run a day a head, which I will correct at leisure. Proceeded at 1/4 before 5 & ran till 1/2 past 9 & came to on the right bank for breakfast. Proceeded at 1/4 before 11. Here Fitzgerald & Williams were sent across on the Maha trace to meet Harris, the express, should he come that route.[189] Halted at 2 o.c on the left bank for dinner. Proceeded at 3 & ran till 1/2 past 6 & came to on the left bank for the night.

Sept 16th Friday [Kearny]

Proceded at day break morning foggy. Ran down about 20 miles when we passed the old Maha Village & breakfasted a mile below it. From this place, two men were started by land, for Council Bluffs in order to meet the Express, should he come up by this route, & turn him back. Passed Black birds Hills in the afternoon, & stopt at Sun down on a high Sand bar on the left hand shore. Geese, ducks & Turkeys seen in great abundance to day.

[Atkinson]

Saturday 17th Sept. [Proceeded] at 1/4 before 5 & ran till 7 & came to on the right bank 3 miles below Woods hills to await the coming up of the White Bear which had been detained by breaking the arms of one of her wheels in passing a snaggy bend this morning. The wind rising high by 8 she came to at Woods Hills & lay to till 1/2 past 4 which detained the fleet till 5 except the Beaver which went on to the lower end of pratts bend. The fleet proceed at 5 & ran till 1/4 after 6 & came to on the right bank in pratts bend for the night.

Sept 17th Saturday [Kearny]

The Boats proceded this morning at day break. The Beaver being the rear one, as she was about to start, a large part of the Sand bar fell in & broke some buckets. Soon after starting entered into a very snaggy bend & ran on a sawyer which knocked out an arm & broke some more buckets. Whilst these were repairing we breakfasted. Afterwards, & about 8 miles below, passed the fleet which had stopt for breakfast. We continued & halted at half past 12 at the lower end of Pratts bend (which is 20 miles round, & the gorge 360 yards) & which we found full of snags, & in some places dangerous.

[Atkinson]

Sunday 18. Sept. Proceeded at 1/4 before 5. Came up to the Beaver at 7. Here the Otter halted to repair her paddles which she broke in passing a snaggy bend. The fleet went on and halted at 8 on the right

---

189. William Williams enlisted in 1819 and served at least until 1835. Register of Enlistments, M233, roll 17. At this time there was a John S. Fitzgerald and a Thomas Fitzgerald in the Sixth Infantry. The former enlisted in 1824 at Fort Atkinson, while the latter enlisted in the same year in Ohio. Ibid, roll 18.

bank for breakfast. The Otter came up at 9 & the fleet proceeded and ran till 1/4 before 2 & came to on the right bank for dinner. At a snaggy bend a 1/2 mile in the rear of this position the Rackoon sprung her main shaft, being cracked & partly broken near the centre. The cogs of both wheels were much broken & injured by the accident. The Boat was bro't down to our position & mechanics put to work repairing the machinery. At 1/4 before 4 o.c the other 7 boats proceeded & ran till 1/2 past 6 & came to on the left bank for the night. Orders were left with Capt. Gantt to bring the Rackoon on as soon as she should be repaired.

Sept 18th Sunday [Kearny]

About 7 A.M, the Boats made their appearance, when we proceded passed the Little Sioux River. The Racoon struck a log which broke her main water shaft & knocked out about 30 of her cogs. Being so near C.B we proceded, leaving her behind, & to man oars & follow us. Halted at Sun down on the right bank.

[Atkinson]

Monday 19th Sept. Proceeded at 1/4 before 5 and ran till 1/4 after 8 & came to on the left bank for breakfast. Proceeded at 1/2 past 9 & ran till 3 o.c and arrived at Council Bluffs. The troops were disembarked & the 6th went into quarters. The first under tents.

Sept 19th Monday [Kearny]

Proceded at day break. About 12 passed the "devils race ground" & reached Council Bluffs at 2 P.M. a month earlier than we expected when we left there, in May.

The Racoon arrived the following day. Thus a little upwards of 4 months, we have traveled above 2,700 miles — made several stops. Treated with all the Indians on that part of the River. Met with no serious accident, excepting that of the Muskrat, which was shortly repaired & all returned in good health — no lives having been lost.

[Atkinson]

Sunday 20th Sept. Heavy rains last night.

Head Quarters Right Wing, Western Dept
Orders No 9 Fort Atkinson 19th Sept 1825

The Detachment of the 1st Infy, under the Command of Majr Kearney, will remain at this Post til further Orders.

The commanding officer of the Post will furnish Quarters for this detachment, as soon as possible.

By order of Brig Genl Atkinson
S Macree A d Camp[190]

Head Qrs Right Wing West. Dept
Orders Fort Atkinson 20 Sept. 1825

The Brigade composing the Missouri expedition is hereby dissolved and the Corps composing it will report separately 'till further orders to the Commandant of this post. The public stores are to be landed from the transports by the Corps who occupied them and each description Ordnance, Quarter Master's and Commissary stores turned in to the proper Officers of this post.

The General takes this occasion to express his thanks to the Commandants of Corps (of the Brigade) and to the Officers & men under their respective commands for their indefatigable zeal and perseverance in discharging the fatiguing duties connected with the expedition and for the soldierly appearance of the men on the frequent occasions that they were required to appear in uniform.

By order of Brigr Genl Atkinson
Signed S. MacRee Lt & ADCamp[191]

Sir, Fort Atkinson Septr 21st 1825

By order of the Commissioners, General Atkinson, and Major O Fallon I have the honor of reporting that they arrived at this post on the 19th instant having very fully achieved the object of their mission.

They have treated with the Poncars — with the Teton, Yancton, Yanctonies, Augallallas [Oglalas], Saones and Hunkpapas tribes of the Sioux — with the Chayennes — the Ricaras — the Mandans — Minetarees, and Crow nation of Indians.

The Commissioners ascended to the two thousand mile creek.

At this place they will treat with the Mahas, Ottoes, Missouris, and Panis tribes; within twelve days, after which they will descent to St Louis, from which place they will report to you in detail.

---

190. Vol. 1:308, Orders by Atkinson, RG 393.
191. Vol. 1:70, Orders Received, Sixth Infantry, RG 391.

I have the honor to be
Sir, yr obt Servt
A. L. Langham Secy

The Hon.
James Barbour &c &c[192]

Head Quarters Right Wing W. Dept
Orders No 12 Fort Atkinson 23 Sept 1825.

Major Kearney will proceed with the detachment of the 1st Regt. Infy to the Lime Kilns and put his command under cover, for which purpose he will erect temporary huts. Six months provisions will be drawn for his command.

The Asst Quarter Master of the 6th Infy will furnish, on Maj Kearny's requisition, such transportation and tools as he may deem necessary.

Lieut. Levi Nute of the 6th Regt Inft is relieved from arrest and will report for duty.

By order of Brigr Genl Atkinson
S. MacRee AdCamp[193]

Sept 23d Friday [Kearny]

The Detachment of the 1st Infy being ordered to remain, to await the directions of the Gov't, & the Cantonm't at C.B. not being large enough to contain all the Troops, it was determined that the 1st should build huts for wintering Quarters near the Lime Kiln, & we accordingly started at half past 3 P.M, & reached the Kiln at 5. We encamped on a handsome table Land on the right bank about 8 miles (by water) below Fort Atkinson. At this Place we built Cantt Barbour, in less than 4 weeks, spacious & comfortable Quarters, Store Houses &c for the 4 companies, rafting all our Logs across the Missouri, & sawing the Plank by hand.

Head Quarters Right Wing, West Dept.
Orders No 13 Fort Atkinson 7 Oct 1825

The post established by Major Kearney, near Fort Lisa, is a seperate Command and will report thro' the Head Quarters of the Right Wing at St. Louis accordingly; the detachment composing its

---

192. Letters Received, M234, roll 429, 401–2.
193. Vol. 1:311, Orders by Atkinson, RG 393.

Garrison, however will be subject to the orders of Lt Col Woolley, who is charged with the general duties of this Station, whenever he may think it necessary in the discharge of those duties to call them into active service.

The troops under Major Kearney, beside the six months supply of subsistence already ordered to be taken below from the depot here, are to be furnished by the A. Comy at this post, weekly, with fresh beef, delivered in quarters at this Post; they are to be supplied also, with two pair of Shoes each man, on the requisition of Major Kearney, by the Act Asst Quarter Master, who will also furnish, Carts, and work oxen, for the use of that Command, not to exceed four carts and six yoke of oxen, with the proper allowance of forage.

The public Boats are to be moored for the winter, in a safe harbor near the lower Post under charge of the 1st Infy.

By order of Brigr Genl Atkinson
S. MacRee AdCamp[194]

With the conclusion of the expedition, Kearny discontinued his journal but would resume it in the spring. Atkinson made one brief entry concerning the Oto and the Pawnee treaty before beginning a record of the return trip to St. Louis.

[Atkinson]

Counciled, on the 26th Sept. with the Otos, on the 30th with the Pawnas & on the 6th October with the Mahas.

Friday Oct. 7th 1825. Set out this day at 8 minutes before 4 o.c P.M. in the Antelope for St. Louis. Genl. Atkinson, Maj. O.Fallon, Capt. Riley, Lt. McRee & Rogers, with 10 invalids and 8 effectives composing her crew, on board. Arrived at the Cant. First Infy at 1/2 past 5 & came to for the night. Maj. Kearny has erected huts for his command & a s[t]orehouse & Sutlers shop. The officers quarters are yet to be put up. It is supposed these & the other buildings will be completed in three weeks.

Saturday 8th Oct. 1825. Proceeded at 1/2 past 5 & ran till 7 o.c & came to at Mr. Cabana's establishment for breakfast. Proceeded at

---

194. Vol. 1:312, ibid.

1/2 past 8 & ran till 1 o.c & came to at Mr. Pilchers & handsome trading House & out buildings. Proceeded at 2 o.c & ran till 5 o.c & came to 8 miles below the Platte on the right bank of the river. Heavy rains during the whole day.

Sunday 9th Oct. 1825. The rain continued to fall heavily all night. Proceeded at 1/4 past 5 & ran till 8. o.c & came to on the right bank for breakfast. Proceeded at 9. Met Mr. Curtis' boat at 10. o.c. Halted 15 minutes to see him on business with Maj. O.Fallon. Ran till 1/2 past 12 & came to on the right bank for dinner. Wind very strong from the So. Proceeded at 1/2 past one & ran till 1/4 before three when we were compelled to come to on acco. of the wind blowing a gale. Proceeded at 1/2 past 4, the wind having abated a little, & ran till 6. o.c & came to on the left bank for the night.

Monday 10th Oct. The weather cleared up last night & we proceeded this morning at 1/2 past 5 & ran till 1/2 past 6 & came to on the right bank, there being two large flocks of Turkeys at this point that had come in for water & we were desirous to kill some of them for our Table. The men ordered to get their breakfast & Lt. Rogers went in pursuit of the Turkeys, but succeeded in getting but one, shooting it thro' the head that its body should not be injured by the ball. Proceeded at 1/2 past 7 o.c & ran till 12 & came to at the mouth of the Nishanabotana for dinner. Proceeded at 1 o.c & ran till 1/4 past 5 & came to on the right bank a mile below the big Nemanha for the night. This day has been very fine. It is worthy of remark that in passing from the Bluffs to this point we have seen no game but Turkeys. These however have shown themselves frequently in flocks on the banks of the river.

Tuesday 11th Oct. Proceeded at 1/2 past 5 & ran till 1/4 past 6 & came to on the lower point of an Island in consequence of the fogg becoming too dense to proceed. Here Genl. A. killed a fine goose. Proceeded at 1/2 past 7 and ran till 1/2 past 12 & came to on the left bank for dinner. Genl. A. & Maj. O.F. hunted in the bottom for an hour but saw no game. In returning the former killed a duck & the latter a prairie Hen. Proceeded at 1/2 past 1 & ran till 1/2 past 5 & came to at the foot of a bluff, right bank for the night. Met a large canoe belonging to Welch at 11. o.c this morning, on her way to the C. Bluffs, ladened with apples & comd. by one Irving, Welches Jack one of the hands which leads us to think that Welch has some illicit views in his intercourse with the Bluffs.[195] Passed the Nadowa at 3 o.c this afternoon.

Wednesday 12th Oct. Proceeded at 1/2 past 5. Ran till 8 & came to on the left bank at 8 for breakfast. Proceeded at 9 o.c. At 11 saw a deer come into the water from the right bank, pursued it with the Antelope[,] came up with & succeeding in taking it after it was twice shot by Maj. O.Fallon. The deer had been driven into the water by a panther as appeared on examination the deer being wounded by the claw of the animal on the thighs & around the tail. Passed Cow Island at 5 & halted 2 miles below on the right bank for the night. Saw several Indians on the lower point of the Island & some 20 Horses.

Thursday 13th. Proceeded at 1/2 past 5 & ran till 8 & came to on the right bank for breakfast. Proceeded at 1/2 past 8. Saw a party of Kansas on the right bank. Arrived at Curtis & Elys establishment at 12. o.c. Here we saw the White plume & several other Kansas Indians.[196] Proceeded at 1/2 past 12, passed the Kansas river & arrived at Choteau's place at one o.c & halted for dinner. F. Choteau had gone with his Father across to the Osage river.[197] Proceeded at 1/2 past one & arrived at Galatin opposite to Liberty at 1/2 past 4. Here Genl. A. procured a horse & rode up to Liberty to get letters & papers from the post office. Capt. Riley & Lts. McRee

---

195. John Welch had a farm about three miles south of Fort Atkinson. *Missouri Republican*, Jan. 10, 1825. He sold corn and beef to the army. Leavenworth to Atkinson, Feb. 1, 1825, Letters Received by Atkinson, RG 393. There was also a suggestion that he was a bootlegger. Orderly Book 20, Sheldon, "Records of Fort Atkinson," 4:15. Jack was probably Welch's slave. Order No. 101, Apr. 12, 1822, 25, Orders Issued, Sixth Infantry, RG 391.

196. White Plume was an influential Kansa leader during the 1820s and 1830s. Unrau, *The Kansa Indians*, 118–19.

197. Francis Gesseau Chouteau was the son of Pierre Chouteau. The family had a post near the Kansas River and another on the Osage River for the Osage trade. Lecompte, "Auguste Pierre Chouteau," *Mountain Men and the Fur Trade*, 9:64.

& Rodgers walked up as did Thomas and Parsons two of the men, the whole of [whom] remained all night.[198] Capt. Armstrong arrived from across the country at dusk from the Bluffs. He left Maj. Langham & Lt. Pentland at crossing of the Tarico. The former had lost his Horse in the mud in crossing a branch beyond 42 mile creek. He was remounted on the pack Horse.

Friday 14th Oct. Wrote to Col. Wooly & Maj. Kearny, left written orders for the express to wait at Liberty till Sunday week for Maj. Ketchum, & then get the mail & return to the Bluffs with the Major. Proceed to the boat at Galitin at 1/2 past 6 & reached the landing at 8. Proceeded with the Boat on our voyage at 9 & ran till 1/2 past <one o.c> 12 & came to at the Ferry below Fort Osage for dinner. Proceed at one o.c & ran till 5 & came to on the point of an Island for the night 2 miles above Jacks ferry.[199]

Saturday 15th Oct. Rain last night with thunder & lightning. Sergt. Ceders, sick, Lt. Rogers indisposed, William sick.[200] Several of the men have also been sick since our departure from the Bluffs. Proceed at 1/2 past 5 & ran till & 8 & came to on the right bank for breakfast having passed Jacks ferry at 6 where we saw two moving waggons. Proceeded at 1/2 past 8 & ran till 1/2 past 12 & came to opposite Davises, Tilson, & came to on the right bank for dinner. Proceeded at 1 o.c & ran till dark & came to at Patricks old place on the right bank for the night 3 miles below the mouth of the Grand river.[201] Just before coming to we ran upon a sawyer & unshipped our rudder & lost our skiff. No other damage, put to shore where we encamped for the night, reshipped the rudder.

---

198. William Thomas enlisted in the Sixth Infantry in July 1824 and was discharged at the expiration of his term in July 1829 while on the Santa Fe Trail. Register of Enlistments, M233, roll 18.

At this time there was a Robert Parsons and a Richard Parsons in the Sixth Infantry. Descriptive Books no. 6, no. 40, Sixth Infantry, RG 391.

199. A ferry between Bluff Town and Lexington was operated by a Mr. Jack. *Missouri Intelligencer*, Dec. 10, 1822.

200. Solomon Cedars was a career soldier, who enlisted in 1814 and remained in the army until at least 1839. Register of Enlistments, M233, roll 3. Sergeant Cedars accompanied the expedition in 1825. Muster Rolls, Sixth Infantry, RG 94.

201. Davises and Tilson are not clearly written and the transcription is uncertain. These sites, like Patrick's old place, do not seem to have been mentioned elsewhere.

Sunday 16th Oct. Proceeded at 1/4 past 5 and after running some 5 miles the paddles of our left wheel struck a snag, split one paddle & broke one of the arm-braces. Halted at 8 o.c on the right bank at Jefferson for breakfast. Put on a new paddle & put in a new brace. This is the first breakage we have experienced since we set out on the 7th & this of very immaterial consequence. Proceeded at 9 & ran till 1/2 past 12 & halted at the arrow rock left bank for dinner. Proceeded at 1/4 past one o.c & arrived at Franklin at 20 minutes past 3 to remain for the night. Visited Genl. Smith, Capt. Wetmore, Maj. Ketchum &c.[202]

Monday 17th Oct. Set out this morning at 1/2 past 8. much troubled to collect the crew, the whole being drunk from indulging last night. Purchased 115 [pounds] beef & Whiskey for the remainder of the voyage. 4 of the discharged men left us here, rather an unprincipled piece of conduct on their part having been bro't down in the boat with an understanding that they would work their passage to St. Louis. Halted at 1/2 past 10 on the right bank for the men to eat their breakfasts. Proceeded at 11 o.c. & ran till 2 o.c. & came to on the left bank for the men to get their dinners. Proceeded at 1/2 past 2 & ran till 1/2 past 5 & came to on the left bank for the night, 5 miles above the city of Jefferson.

Tuesday 18th Oct. Proceeded at 6 o.c. dense fog, ran 2 miles & came to on the right bank in consequence of the fog becoming too thick to run. Proceeded at 1/2 past 7 passed Jefferson at 8. The Governor's House appears to be completed, it is a Handsome brick building 60 by 40 feet, two stories. A stone building is in progress standing a 100 yards above. We have met Mr. Ranney in a Keel Boat on his way to Council Bluffs ladened with goods for the sutler — Mr. Culbertson. In company with it was a Mackanaw boat engaged in the Indian trade & destined for the Iowas on the river. Passed the mouth of Osage River at 10 minutes past 10 o.c. Ran till

202. This is certainly the Gen. T. A. Smith mentioned by Titian Peale in 1819. A. O. Weese, ed., "The Journal of Titian Ramsay Peale, Pioneer Naturalist," *Missouri Historical Review* 42 (1947): 227. Heitman, *Historical Register*, 1:903, lists Thomas A. Smith, but gives a death date of 1818.

Alphonso Wetmore enlisted in the army in 1812 and was now the Sixth Infantry's regimental paymaster. Heitman, *Historical Register*, 1:1021.

one o.c. & came to on the right bank for dinner. Proceeded at 1/2 past one & ran till 1/4 past 5 & came to on the right bank for the night 5 miles below the mouth of Gasconade.

Wednesday 19th Oct. Proceeded 1/2 past 5 and ran till 8 & came to on the right bank for breakfast & here Gen. A. killed two wild turkeys. Proceeded at 9 & ran till 1 o.c. & came to on the right bank for dinner. Proceeded at 1/2 past one & ran till 1/2 past 5 & came to on the right bank for the night 12 miles above St. Charles.

Thursday 20th Oct. Proceeded at 1/4 past 5 & ran till 1/4 past 7 & came to on the left bank for breakfast. Proceeded at 10 minutes before 8 & ran till 1/4 past one & came to on the left bank of the Mississippi 1 1/2 miles below the mouth of Missouri for dinner. Proceeded at 2 o.c. and arrived at St. Louis at 5 o.c.

This ends General Atkinson's journal.

In the spring of 1825 Kearny's detachment of the First Infantry abandoned their winter quarters. They boarded wheel boats for the trip back to Bellefontaine and Kearny resumed his diary.

May 2d 1826 — Cantonment Barbour

Having received an order yesterday from Genl Head Qrs to repair with my Command to Belle Fontaine, we started at 8 A.M in the Elk, White Bear & Muskrat Transport Boats: when within 2 or 3 miles of Mr Cabannes, the wind blowing strong from the South, & the waves running tolorably high, we were very near being lost in the Elk, she springing a leak in several places, & for a few moments leaning her starboard side, so much over, as to have the running board considerably under water, & shipping some of it. From Mr. Cs sent back for the Beaver, & taking the Elks load into her proceded at 3 P.M. A slight rain & wind strong from the North. Were obliged to put to a few miles below Harts Hills, which was effected with considerable difficulty.

The River, which has been higher this Spring than ever before known, appears to be falling fast.[203]

---

203. The Franklin *Missouri Intelligencer*, May 12, 1826, reported the river was the highest it had been in thirty years and all the bottomland was flooded be-

May 3d Wednesday

Proceded at 4 A.M. Breakfasted near Mr Robideaux.[204] At 8. passed the Platte; & about 5 P.M, the <neck> narrows of the Nishnebotona. In the afternoon rain & hard wind. In consequence of the storm we were desirous of stopping but had run about 15 miles before we could find dry Land & this is only to be seen when the Hills came in to the River.

May 4th Thursday

Started at 5. A.M. Passed the mouth of the Nishnabotona & at 7 halted for breakfast on the Right bank, & were detained here the remainder of day in consequence of hard wind.

May 5th Friday

Started at 4 A.M. About 7 when turning a point to the right, the White Bear fell into an eddy which turned her around like a top, her larboard side bent over. She shipped considerable water & was in much danger of being lost. Stopped at 8. below Wolf River for breakfast. Killed a Deer swiming in the River. At 2 P.M, when halted for dinner one of the men was bitten by a Pilot Snake & several of them, & the Rattlesnakes, were discovered & killed. In the afternoon passed Independence creek & halted at Sun down on the Right bank, a few miles above Cow Island. Clear sunshining day — little wind. 106 miles

May 6th Saturday

Proceded at day break. Passed Cow Island & breakfasted a short distance below it. Afterwards passed the Little Platte & halted for dinner at Mr Ely's establishment, the wind strong ahead. At 1 P.M moved on, passed the Kansas; stopt at the landing near Liberty for 2 hours, during which rode to the Town (4 miles) to the Post office. There has been no communication between this & Franklin for a

---

tween Franklin and Fort Atkinson. The source for the news item was identified only as "a gentleman from Council Bluffs." Considering the date of the report it could have been Kearny or one of his men.

204. There is no evidence for a Robidoux trading post in this vicinity, so Kearny must be referring to a campsite. It is more likely to have been Francois or Antoine, rather than their brother, Joseph, who spent most of his time in St. Louis. Mattes, "Joseph Robidoux," *Mountain Men and the Fur Trade* 8:196–98.

fortnight & 2 mails are due. The high water has overflowed the Country. Reached Fort Osage at Sundown & visited my old friend Mr. S[ibley]. 100 miles

May 7th Sunday

Took in Mr. Ss brother & his horse, & proceded at day break.[205] At 7, in passing down a slough, the Beaver ran on a snag which broke out two of the Arms of the wheel — repaired it and continued on at 8. At 11 the Pitman of the Muskrat broke in two and her forward slide went to pieces! Detained 'til 1/2 past 2 P.M. in mending it & then proceded. Passed Grand River in the afternoon & slept 10 miles below it.

In the morning passed two Keel Boats on their way to Council Bluffs. The water is so high that they are compelled to warp their Boats the whole distance.

May 8th Monday

Started at day break, passed the Chariton at 7 A.M, & breakfasted a mile below it. Reached Franklin at 1/2 past 11 dined & left there at 1/2 past 1 P.M. The skirts of the Town are over flowd — not much damage done. Passed Jefferson in the afternoon & halted at 7 on the right bank 5 miles below it.

During the evening much lightening & in the night a very heavy rain.

We have overtaken the rise of the River. The water appears now to be at its height.

Tuesday May 9th

Proceded at day break — clear morning. Passed the Osage at 6 A.M. Breakfasted near the Gasconade & halted at 7 P.M. about 5 miles above Saint Charles. Day clear & but little wind.

Wednesday May 10th 1826

Started at day break. Passed Saint Charles & arrived at Belle Fontaine at 7 A.M. & breakfast. Found the Cantonm't in a very

205. His brother was probably Samuel Hopkins Sibley. Gregg, "The War of 1812 on the Missouri Frontier," 191.

decayed state but being more comfortable than Tents, moved into it.[206]

Remained here 'til July 10th when we moved down the Mississippi & encamped about 4 miles below Carondelet. Commenced the erection of Jefferson Barracks.[207] The 3d Infy arrived here from Green Bay, in Septr.

This concludes the Atkinson and Kearny journals.

206. Two years earlier Atkinson assured his superior that the barracks at Belle Fontaine were repaired and would be serviceable for ten years. Atkinson to Brown, Jan. 5, 1824, Letters Received, M567, roll 9.

207. Jefferson Barracks was a new infantry school. Atkinson supervised the construction. Nichols, *General Henry Atkinson*, 11.

APPENDIX A
THE LANGHAM JOURNAL

Angus Lewis Langham was appointed by General Atkinson to be the expedition's secretary. Langham had served three enlistments in the army beginning in 1808 and ending in 1816, when he resigned as a brevet major of infantry.[1] Upon his return to civilian life, he worked as a real estate agent and surveyor in Missouri.[2] After the completion of the trip up the Missouri River, he returned to surveying, including a survey for a part of the Kansa Indian reserve.[3]

Langham's journal covers the passage of the wheel boat *Antelope* from St. Louis to Fort Atkinson in the early spring of 1825. Because Langham recorded little more than each day's camping place, it did not seem necessary to transcribe the entire diary. His first entry begins, "Thursday March 17th The 'Antelope' a boat intended for the accommodation of the Commissioners left St. Louis. Lt. Bloodgood comd."[4] The list of campsites follows until they reached Fort Atkinson on Friday, May 13, 1825. Langham then writes, "Sat & Sun. 14 & 15th Rain & head winds prevailing, prevented the departure of the Military Escort. The boat Antelope was deemed unfit for the expedition." The next day he mentioned the departure of the boats for the upper Missouri and continued with the list of campsites until the expedition was near the Ponca village on June 1, at which point the travelogue ends abruptly.

1. Heitman, *Historical Register*, 1:615.

2. *St. Louis Enquirer*, Oct. 25, 1823.

3. Barry, *The Beginning of the West*, 134.

4. Lt. William Bloodgood graduated from the military academy in 1819 and served in the First Infantry until his resignation in 1836. Heitman, *Historical Register*, 1:226.

At the request of Atkinson and O'Fallon, Langham made a copy of the legislative act authorizing the expedition.[5] This was followed by copies of four letters, reproduced below, containing Atkinson's and O'Fallon's appointment as commissioners, their general instructions, and an explanation of the funding for the expedition.

James Monroe, president of the united States of America.

To all to whom these presents shall come Greeting Know Ye that reposing special Trust and confidence in the Prudences, Abilities and Fidelity of Henry Atkinson and Benjamin O'Fallon, and according to the provision of the Act of Congress of the 25th May last entitled "An Act to enable the president to hold treaties with certain Indian Tribes, and for other purposes," I do appoint them jointly and severally Commissioners for the purposes designated in the said Act, requiring them to transmit any Treaty or Treaties which they may conclude and sign agreeably thereto, to the President of the United States for his final ratification by and with the advice and consent of the Senate of the United States: this commission to continue in force during the pleasure of the President of the United States for the time being In Testimony whereof I have caused these Letters to be made patent and the Seal of the United States to be hereunto affixed. Given under my hand at the City of Washington the fifth day of June A. D. 1824: and of the Independence of the United States, the forty Eighth

By the President (Signed) James Monroe
(Signed) John Quincy Adams Secretary of State[6]

To Brigt. Genl. H Atkinson War Department
& June 1 1824
Majr. Benjamin O'Fallon

Gentlemen, The President by virtue of the Act of Congress of the 26th Ultimo authorizing him to appoint suitable persons for Commissioners to negotiate Treaties of Trade and friendship with the Indian Tribes beyond the Mississippi and to fix their compensation &c, has appointed you to the execution of this trust.

5. Peters, *Public Statutes at Large*, 4:35–36.

6. Another letter copied by Langham, not reproduced here, contained the same information in similar wording. It was dated Jan. 26, 1825.

Your Commission is herewith endorsed. By the same act the sum of ten thousand dollars is appropriated to carry this object into effect. The designs of Congress being expressed in the act (a copy of which I herewith transmit to you) it is not deemed to be necessary to dwell in detail upon the objects to be effected.

You will exercise a sound discretion in the prosecution of this undertaking, and accomplish whatever may be deemed by you to be necessary in carrying the views of the government, as those are conveyed to you by the act of Congress, into effect.

The sum appropriated, viz: ten thousand dollars is intended to cover all expenses (excepting those connected with the military escort for which provision is made) as well those embraced by your compensation as commissioners which will be to Genl Atkinson for the time actually employed, a sum equal to the difference between his present pay and the pay and emoluments of his Brevet rank; to Major O'Fallon a sum which added to his present pay as Agent will make it equal to Genl Atkinsons, and to the Secretary five dollars a day, on accounts made out in the usual form accompanied by your Certificate of honor that the Sums to each, respectively are for services rendered under the commission.

The time of entering upon this Commission is left to your discretion; but the sooner the duties assigned to you can be accomplished, the better. If it be practicable, this Summer or Autumn — but if not at the earliest period thereafter which it may be within your power to command.

Your bills on this Department as you may find it necessary to make them from time to time to carry into effect this commission will be duly paid. You will preserve in distinct forms the various kinds of expenditure under the appropriate heads of presents, military escort, pay of commissioners, Secretary &c &c which you may make, and so express it in your letters of Advice, also, making them to correspond with the payments in the several branches of the expenditure.

The bills will be sold at the market value and if there should be a premium it will be accounted for to the Government

I have the honor to be
Very Respectfully
Yr. Obt. Servt.
(signed) J. C. Calhoun

P.S. Your Commissions not having been received from the State Dept will follow next mail.

To Brigt War Department June 2 1824

Genl. H Atkinson

Sir Yesterday I addressed a joint letter to yourself and Major Benjamin O'Fallon informing you that the President had appointed you joint Commissioners under the act of Congress of the 26th Ultimo, to negotiate Treaties of Trade and Friendship with the Indian Tribes beyond the Mississippi, and that ten thousand dollars the amount appropriated by that act, was to embrace all the expenses arising out of your own pay as Commissioners, the pay of your Secretary, and such contingent expenses as may arise out of the prosecution of the trust

The 6th Section of the act, appropriates ten thousand dollars to enable the President to furnish a competent military escort to the commissioners authorized to be appointed by the same act if in his opinion the same shall be necessary

The numbers and description of the escort are left to your discretion, and selection the expenses of which you will take care shall not exceed the appropriation.

The charges upon the $10,000 are intended to embrace the extra costs arising out of the movement, such as transportation, contingent expense &c, and not such as would be incurred if the troops had remained stationary. The accounts will be kept separately, and accounted for distinct from the ordinary items of appropriation and the sum amy be drawn in like manner as you are authorized in relation to the $10000 for the expense of holding the Treaties.

I have the honor to be
Sir very respectfully
Yr. obt Sert
J. C. Calhoun

Department of War, Off. Indian Affairs

Gentlemen 9th March 1825

Your appointment as Commissioners to hold treaties of trade and friendship with Indian tribes beyond the Mississippi, made during the last recess of Congress, was submitted by the President as required by the Constitution, to the Senate at the late session and received the advice and consent of that body. I am therefore directed by the Secretary of War to transmit to you the enclosed Commission and to instruct you to proceed in the execution of the duties assigned you under the instructions which you received with your former commission from the Department of War

I have the honor to be
Your Mo. Obt Servt
Tho L. McKenney

Genl H. Atkinson &
Major B. O'Fallon } Comms &C

This ends Langham's journal.

APPENDIX B
THE WHEEL BOATS

After Congress authorized the expedition to the upper Missouri, carrying out the mission became the responsibility of Gen. Henry Atkinson. While the general would face many challenges, his first and possibly greatest concern was providing transportation for approximately 475 troops on a trip of more than 3,000 miles. It seems no consideration was ever given to any means of transport other than boats, but ascending the Missouri River would provide a test of strength and will. Experienced river pilots admitted the Missouri was an exceptional stream. In 1820 riverman John D. Cummins had "no hesitation in saying that the Missouri River is four times as bad to navigate as the Mississippi, owing to the strength of the water, the many sand bars, changing of the channel, falling in of the banks; the many logs, snags, and roots, and many of them concealed under water, and the water being so muddy that they cannot be seen, which subjects boats very often to run on them, and be greatly delayed, and sometimes destroyed."[1]

Artist George Catlin went up the Missouri in 1832 and formed a similar opinion. He described the river as "perhaps different in appearance and character from all other rivers in the world; there is a terror in its manner which is sensibly felt, the moment we enter its muddy waters from the Mississippi." Suggestions for improving navigation on the treacherous Missouri had been offered from time to time. The *St. Louis Enquirer* urged Congress to appropriate thirty thousand dollars to pay for the removal of dead trees

1. *Annals of the Congress, 16th Cong., 2nd Sess.*, H. Doc. 110, 92.

embedded in the river bottom that posed a serious danger to boats. The *Enquirer* suggested work crews be sent out in the dead of winter, when the river was at its lowest and frozen. The men could then cut off "all the planters and sawyers" level with the ice. It was assumed the spring rise would cover the stumps deeply enough to make navigation safe. The scheme did not receive congressional support.[2]

In addition to the threats posed by the river itself, there were limitations in the craft used to navigate the stream. Keelboats had been primary cargo vessels on the Missouri River for a century, used first by French, then Spanish, and finally American explorers and merchants. The boats were sturdy craft made of planks pegged to a wooden rib frame. The bows and sterns were generally pointed and the bottom slightly rounded. A four-inch-square wooden beam extending from bow to stern projected from the bottom and tended to hold the craft on a straight course. Most keelboats had a cabin high enough for a man to stand upright comfortably. The boats' size and capacity varied greatly, some being one hundred feet long and able to carry forty tons.

The most frequently used method of propulsion against the current was the cordelle. The crew walked along the bank pulling a mile-long length of rope, which was tied to the mast and passed through a ring in the bow. When extra men were available they went ahead and cleared a path for the men on the cordelle.[3] Under the best of circumstances cordelling was exhausting work, with an added risk of injury and disease. In a discussion of the problems faced by river travelers, Senator Thomas H. Benton noted that men on the cordelle "are exposed to sun and water all day, lay down wet at night, and at the end of the voyage, or sooner, they gather the fruit of these exposures in a bountiful crop of agues and bilious fevers."[4]

Although there were other means of propelling a keelboat upstream, they could be used only under certain conditions. A large,

2. Catlin, *Letters and Notes*, 1:17; *St. Louis Enquirer*, Jan. 13, 1824.

3. Leland D. Baldwin, *The Keelboat Age on Western Waters* (Pittsburgh: University of Pittsburgh Press, 1941); Seymour Dunbar, *A History of Travel in North America* (Indianapolis: Bobbs-Merrill Co., 1915); Hiram M. Chittenden, *History of Early Steamboat Navigation on the Missouri River* (reprint, Minneapolis: Ross and Haines, 1962); James A. Hanson, "The Keelboat," *Museum of the Fur Trade Quarterly* 30 (1994): 9–25.

4. Benton to Calhoun, Sept. 22, 1824, box 64, Consolidated Correspondence File, RG 92.

square sail was unfurled whenever the wind was blowing from the boat's stern, but its usefulness was limited. Paul Wilhelm traveled the Missouri in 1823 and noted, "The sails used on the boats . . . are much too simple and awkward to permit a rapid journey, for they can be used only when the wind blows directly from the back of the vessel. The boats themselves, very clumsily built, are calculated only for safety to meet the extreme dangers of navigation on hazardous rivers."[5] In addition to a sail, most boats carried oars as well as poles. Rowing against the Missouri River current was generally futile, but when descending the river the oars were effective. Poles could be used only in the late summer and fall when the river was shallow. The warp was used when all else failed. A warp or rope would be run out and tied to a stout tree, while the other end was wound on the boat's capstan to winch the craft slowly up the river.[6]

Atkinson felt conventional, medium-sized keelboats should be able to ascend the river from St. Charles to the Council Bluffs in forty-two days, an average of fifteen miles per day.[7] The general expected more than most crews could produce. The 1818 advance party of the army's Yellowstone Expedition crept along at a snail's pace, requiring sixty-seven days to make the journey. Civilian boats generally made better time. In 1812 John Luttig made the same trip in fifty days, which may have been about average.[8] It took Wilson Price Hunt and his fur traders forty-nine days to cover the same distance. Manuel Lisa left St. Charles a few days after Hunt and was determined to overtake his competitor. By offering his crew every inducement and threat, Lisa reached the Bluffs in forty-one days, which may be a record still unbroken. It was possible to travel four times as fast on a downstream trip. Boats drifted with the swift current and the crews manned oars to provide some added

---

5. Wilhelm, *Travels in North America*, 211–12.

6. Donald Jackson, ed., *Letters of the Lewis and Clark Expedition* (Urbana: University of Illinois Press, 1962), 317; Wilhelm, *Travels in North America*, 292.

7. Nichols, *The Missouri Expedition*, 107. In 1820 the distance from St. Charles to Council Bluffs was estimated at 630 river miles. *Annals of the Congress, 16th Cong., 2nd Sess.*, 223–24. A survey published in 1896 tallied the distance at 662 miles. J. V. Brower, *The Missouri River and Its Utmost Sources* (St. Paul, Minn.: Pioneer Press, 1896), 119. Kearny reckoned it to be about 670 miles.

8. Nichols, *The Missouri Expedition*, 5–6; John C. Luttig, *Journal of a Fur-Trading Expedition on the Upper Missouri, 1812–1813*, ed. Stella M. Drum (St. Louis: Missouri Historical Society, 1920).

speed. Under the most favorable conditions a downstream boat could travel one hundred miles or more in a day.[9]

Atkinson was determined to provide his troops with transportation that was faster, less hazardous, and less taxing than pulling a thirty-five ton boat up the Missouri. He was wary of steamboats after the disastrous gamble with steam power during the 1819 Yellowstone Expedition. By 1825 several steamboats had reached Fort Atkinson, but they were not dependable and delays were frequent. The *General Neville* set out for the fort in the spring of 1824, but was grounded on a sandbar for several weeks before it was finally freed and completed the trip.[10] No steamboats had yet been tested on the upper river.

Atkinson turned his attention to a recent innovation called a wheel boat, occasionally referred to as a team boat or horse boat. These were keelboats with paddle wheels fitted to each side. A variety of mechanisms had been devised by which animal power, or occasionally human power, was transferred to the wheels through a system of gears and driveshafts. The most common power trains were treadmills for horses, although a capstan was sometimes used. Patents for wheel boats had been filed in the United States before the end of the eighteenth century, and the boats were soon common on the rivers, lakes, and canals of eastern states. Under certain conditions, wheel boats proved so successful that they continued to be used well into the twentieth century.[11]

Using horses on treadmills was considered by many as a marvelous advancement. In 1814 a New York reporter described the maiden voyage of an eight horsepower craft that went up the East River "against a very rapid flood tide to the admiration of a numerous assemblage of spectators on the wharves. Thus in a few years we have witnessed the wonderful improvement from sails to

---

9. Bradbury, *Travels in the Interior of America*, 185. Brackenridge, *Journal of a Voyage up the Missouri*, 147, estimated they went approximately twelve miles an hour.

10. Wesley, "Diary of James Kennerly," 69, 73, n.86.

11. Donald G. Shomette, "Heyday of the Horse Ferry," *National Geographic* 176 (1989): 548–556. Shomette has found patents in the U.S. Patent Office dating from 1791 for animal-powered wheel boats. An advertisement in the *Edwardsville Spectator*, Mar. 19, 1822, promised "Cash for Horses. Wanted at the St. Louis and Illinois Team Boat Ferry, twenty large, sound, blind horses, in good condition, for present use."

Detail of the Wheel Boat Mechanism, *by Curtis Peacock. Pen and ink, 1992. Based on the Atkinson and Kearny journals and other archival sources, this sketch is a reconstruction of the wheel boat mechanism. Built by a millwright, the metal parts were limited to nails, bolts, the wrists at the ends of the pitman or connecting rod, and the iron and brass "boxes" or bearings on the ends of wooden axles. The paddle wheels attached to the largest cog wheel by a wooden axle, while the large flywheel was securely attached to the boat's keel. An axle extended through the flywheel to the side of the boat to provide additional strength. The rectangular piece on the side of the flywheel was a metal plate that balanced the mechanism. A pitman connected the flywheel to the center slide. Additional slides on either side of the boat prevented the dowel crossbars from twisting. Soldiers sat under canvas awnings at the crossbars and pulled them forward and back to propel the boats.*

Nebraska State Historical Society, Lincoln

steam, and from steam to animal power, which is calculated to supersede the necessity and expense of steam, particularly for these short ferries." The concept was not limited to boats. As early as 1817 the *Missouri Gazette* carried advertisements for a horse-powered treadmill to drive a flour mill or sawmill. The advertiser hinted that the system was superior to steam power.[12]

12. *Long-Island Star*, Aug. 10, 1814, typed copy provided by Donald G. Shomette; *Missouri Gazette*, May 24, 1817.

Atkinson certainly had ample opportunity to examine these boats at Louisville, Kentucky, the headquarters of his command. A horse-powered wheel boat ferry had been in operation at Louisville since 1807. Wheel boats were also used as ferries at St. Louis, probably for two years before Atkinson arrived there in 1819.[13]

During that summer the general built his first wheel boat, powered by men walking on a treadmill. After a test on the Missouri River the *Edwardsville Spectator* carried a laudatory report:

> St Louis, June 28, 1819. Last week Col. Henry Atkinson, on seeing the ferry-boat at this place worked by wheels, immediately conceived the idea of applying that improvement to his barges bound up the Missouri with United States' troops and public stores. In about three days he had one of them rigged with wheels, and a trial made, which was successful beyond expectation. The barge was run up the Missouri about two miles against as rapid water as there is at any other point on that river, and returned to the place from whence it started in the space of thirty minutes. This improvement, simple in itself, promises fair to be an incalculable advantage to the government in the conveyance of troops and stores up those vast waters, the Missouri and Mississippi, where such advanced positions are about to be made. Two other barges, engaged in the same expedition, are nearly completed in the same manner. Three pair of wheels are fixed to each barge, and five men tread at a time at each pair of wheels.[14]

---

13. *Mississippi Free Trader*, Jan. 30, 1845. The paper copied a historical note about the Louisville ferry from an unnamed New Orleans newspaper dated 1807. John Perry, *American Ferryboats* (New York: Wilfred Funk, Inc., 1957), 55–71, has cautiously concluded that wheel boats were first used in the United States in 1814, although he acknowledges that the principle, if not the actual use, dates to the mid-sixteenth century in Europe.

Missouri Gazette, June 2, 30, 1819; Robert A. Tyson, *History of East St. Louis* (n.p., 1874), 21. The *St. Louis Enquirer*, Apr. 19, 1820, carried an item about the "new" eight-horse ferry boats operated by a Samuel Wiggins. He was operating a horse-powered ferry at least until March 1825. Agnes Wallace, "The Wiggins Ferry Monopoly," *Missouri Historical Review*," 41 (1947–48): 5.

14. *Edwardsville Spectator*, July 3, 1819. The *Missouri Gazette*, June 30, 1819, filed a similar report:

"Last week Col. Henry Atkinson, on seeing the ferry boats worked by wheels, immediately conceived the idea of applying them to the barges bound up the Missouri with U. States troops, stores &c. In about three days he had one of the barges rigged with wheels and a trial made in which she was run up the Missouri about two miles and back in 30 minutes. . . . This improvement which he has put

Apparently the *Spectator* exaggerated the success of the boats because they were not used on the expedition, though Atkinson was not ready to give up.[15] He built another treadmill prototype in 1823 and in a letter to the Secretary of War John C. Calhoun, described the boat and its many advantages:

> Dear Sir: My attention has been engaged since I arrived on the Missouri, in 1819, to ascertain some mode of overcoming the difficulties of navigating the western rivers with Troops. Upon reflection I concluded that the power derived from a wheel on the incline plane might be applied to propelling Keel Boats. I accordingly engaged a Mechanick and have had the experiment tried, and the result fully answers my expectations.
>
> The Machinery for a twenty five Ton Boat (the size on which I made the experiment) consists of an inclined wheel twenty feet in diameter, attached to a vertical shaft, to which is also attached, below, a cog wheel, eight feet in diameter; these wheels have an inclination of twelve degrees, and a motion of three and a half revolutions in a minute, and revolves a horizontal shaft, that is cogged and to which the water wheels is attached, twenty times a minute, giving a velocity to the Boat sufficient to advance her ascent of the Missouri at the rate of 2 1/2 to 3 miles an hour.
>
> My first experiment was made in company with the detachment of the first Regt. in its ascent for the Bluffs. The company that embarked in this boat was able to make Belle Fontaine in much less time than the other Boats. The detachment being halted at Belle Fontaine this Boat was used two trips to St. Louis and back to transport materials for repairing the Barracks; both trips were made in good time, but believing that the Boat would run

---

on these barges will prove of vast importance to the government, both in expedition and saving expense."

15. There were other mentions of the wheel boats. Titian Peale passed Atkinson's camp on June 22, 1819, before the expedition set out, and noted, "Col. Atkinson is contriving his boats to go by wheels turned by soldiers. Each boat is to have two pairs of wheels and 8 men at each pair." Weese, "The Journal of Titian Ramsay Peale," 162. Another newspaper reported that the expedition left "in three steamboats and four keelboats, propelled by wheels and sails." *Missouri Gazette*, July 14, 1819.

A secondary source, perhaps based on the *Missouri Gazette* article, mentioned "four barges propelled by wheels and sails." Frederick L. Billon, *Annals of St. Louis in Its Territorial Days*, 2 vols. (St. Louis, 1888) 2:96. While Atkinson was experimenting with wheel boats at this time, the military records of the Yellowstone Expedition clearly show they were not used.

much better by adding to her power, I had the inclined wheel increased from 18 to 20 feet in diameter. After the alteration I had her loaded and ascended in her on the 4th inst. from St. Louis to Belle Fontaine the same day, a distance of twenty four miles with only twenty four indifferent men, they being men of the Band of the Regt., running the whole distance with her wheels alone and encountering as rapid and difficult water as any in the Missouri. If I had have had a crew of forty effective men, which would have formed two relieves for the wheel, I would have proceeded thirty miles with ease. I have not the smallest doubt but a Regiment with a boat of 25 to 30 tons to each company would make an average, in all weather, twenty five miles per day, a distance more than twice as great as Keel Boats ordinarily make. Besides the facility gained by Boats on this plan, the fatigue to the men is in a great measure done away, and some five to six thousand dollars worth of clothing saved to a Regiment in ascending from St. Louis to Council Bluffs. The risk of losing Boats is also greatly lessened.

I have observed above that the wheel has an inclination of only twelve degrees. A man can walk upon it with his hands resting upon a cross bar a whole day, therefore if relieved every hour the exercise would not be more than would be necessary for the health of the crew.

Having made the above statement upon actual experiment and being willing to vouch for the success and practicability of the plan, I have to request (in case troops ascend the Missouri next season) authority to prepare all our transport Boats in the same way. Expense will amount to $150 to $200 per Boat, a sum about equal to the expense of rigging a Boat with mast and sails. With a flotilla of this description I will venture to affirm, and I am sustained by the opinion of the officers of the detachment of the first Regt., that I could arrive at Council Bluffs in thirty days from St. Louis with a Regiment, transporting eight months provisions. This facility would carry us to any point on the Missouri early in the season and enable us to effect any object that might be pointed out. Indeed I consider the great difficulty of navigating the Missouri with Troops as overcome and a new era in that respecting presented to us. . . .

I am now on my journey to Council Bluffs, where I shall obtain the best information relative to Indian affairs there and above, which shall be communicated on my return to St. Louis, about the first of December, by which time I request you will let me know your determination on the subject of this letter, that in case you approve of my proposition I may lose no time in having the necessary machinery prepared for the Boats.[16]

On the same day, Atkinson sent a letter to Quartermaster General Brig. Gen. Thomas S. Jesup, in which he copied the first five paragraphs of the above letter, and then added a further endorsement of the boats:

> Dear General. . . . The above is an extract of a letter to Mr. Calhoun respecting a proposed improvement on our transport boats for the Missouri. I have tried the experiment fully and am satisfied with its great utility. Will you favor me with your approbation to carry this object into effect. It will more than double our progress, save our clothing & lessen our fatigue. Besides making ultimately a great saving in your Dept.
>
> The experiment has been tried upon a public boat that had neither mast or rigging, the expense of completing it has been rather more than rigging a boat in the ordinary way but I must request that you will have the amt. allowed which you will find in bills accompanying Capt. Brants returns.[17]

Atkinson's proposal to modify boats was approved by the quartermaster general, but Secretary of War Calhoun misunderstood the scope of the plan.[18] An expedition to the upper Missouri had only been considered by the army, and the secretary thought Atkinson was about to undertake the trip. In early February 1824 Calhoun called a halt to the entire project, but the interruption was only temporary and may have been for the best.[19]

---

16. Atkinson to Calhoun, Oct. 11, 1823, Hemphill, *The Papers of John C. Calhoun*, 8:304–6.

17. Atkinson to Jesup, Oct. 11, 1823, book 4, no. 43-a, Letters Received by the Office of the Quartermaster General, Records of the Office of Quartermaster General, Record Group 92, NARA. Joshua B. Brant joined the army in 1813 and worked his way through the ranks. In 1824 he was assistant deputy quartermaster general. Heitman, *Historical Register*, 1:241.

18. Jesup to Atkinson, Nov. 26, 1823, vol. 3:432, Letters Sent by the Office of the Quartermaster General (Main Series), 1818–83, Records of the Office of Quartermaster General, Record Group 92, NARA (hereafter cited as Letters Sent, RG 92). Q. M. Gen. Jesup questioned the price of the machinery, but an aide stationed in St. Louis defended the cost-effectiveness of the boats. Brant to Jesup, Oct. 13, 1823, Commission Accounts, 2565/1823, RG 217.

19. Calhoun to Atkinson, Feb. 6, 1824, vol. 12:24, Letters Sent by the Secretary of War Relating to Military Affairs (National Archives Microfilm Publication M6, roll 12), Records of the Office of the Secretary of War, Record Group 107, NARA.

Despite Atkinson's laudatory remarks about his treadmill boat, he must have recognized some problems because it was never used again. Perhaps the boat was unstable because the treadmill exceeded the maximum beam of the boat by several feet. In Atkinson's last adaptation, the possible problem of instability was solved by putting the crew on benches. They pushed and pulled on crossbars connected by a pitman to gears driving the side-mounted paddle wheels. The new design was described in some detail by the *National Daily Intelligencer*:

> St. Louis, Sept. 27 — A detachment of the 1st Regt. Infantry, consisting of four companies, and 60 recruits of the 6th Regiment, embarked at this place, under the immediate order of Maj. Kearny, for Council bluffs, on the 17th inst. in four keel boats of the first and second class. This detachment, we understand, is to form part of the military escort that is to ascend the Missouri early next spring from Council Bluffs, with Gen. Atkinson and Maj. O'Fallon, Commissioners appointed under the act of Congress of the 26th of May last, to hold treaties of trade and friendship with the Western tribes of Indians.
>
> The keel boats which compose the transportation of the troops, are provided with machinery on a new and improved plan, invented by Gen. Atkinson, and executed by Gregg M'Daniel, a skilful mechanic. The machinery consists of a shaft, thrown across the centre of the boat, with a water wheel at each end; a five feet cog-wheel in the centre of the shaft, and put in motion by another cog-wheel three feet four inches, resting on an iron shaft, which supports a fly wheel at one end, of eight feet in diameter. The fly and small cog-wheel are moved by a crank projecting from an arm of the fly-wheel, with two pitmans, which are impelled by soldiers seated on from eight to ten benches, four abreast, with a succession of cross bars before each bench, contained in a frame that moves on the slides, with a three feet stroke of the crank. The men are comfortably seated under an awning, sheltered from the sun and rain; the labor much lighter than rowing with a common oar, and the boats are propelled with a velocity sufficient to stem the most rapid currents in the Missouri. The flotilla made St. Charles from this place in about two days, a distance that requires at least four days by boats propelled in the ordinary mode. It is ascertained these transports will make twenty miles a day, and thirty in cases of emergency.[20]

---

20. *Daily National Intelligencer*, Oct. 22, 1824. The *Niles Weekly Register*, Nov. 6, 1824, published a slightly shortened version of the article. Part of the *Intelligencer* article was copied from a letter by Atkinson to Norse, Oct. 13, 1824,

Thomas Hart Benton, the influential senator from Missouri, lent his support to the novel craft in a letter to the secretary of war. Benton claimed the boats were twice as fast as ordinary keelboats and since the crew did not have to walk on the bank pulling the cordelle, they were protected from the "bountiful crop of agues and bilious fevers."[21]

Not everyone was convinced the boats were a great improvement. An anonymous bit of doggerel, found in the collections of the Missouri Historical Society, St. Louis, expresses one derisive opinion of the wheel boats:

And now, enough! of Wiggins' ferry
And John Day's treadmill too,
And Atkinson, who retrogressed
A century or two;
By putting men on horses' work
(No labor saver *he*),
He sent his boats a-wheelin' up
The dark, wide Missouree.[22]

Letters Received, M567, roll 9, 162–69. A similar letter was quoted in Grant Foreman, "River Navigation in the Early Southwest," *Mississippi Valley Historical Review* 15 (1928–29): 37–38.

In the 1880s James Haley White recalled that in 1822 William Henry Ashley's fur trappers went up the Missouri River in keel boats "fitted out with side wheels, like our present Steamers, with shaft, crank, and fly wheels and sliding frames erected upon the top deck of the boats attached to the cranks and to move back and forward. They had seats made across the boats under the frames fore and aft of the shafts, to accommodate forty men sitting; with round cross pieces as handles for the men to move the frames and propel the boats." Although White's recollection of a wheel boat is accurate, there is no evidence that Ashley ever used the craft, and White must have been thinking of Atkinson's boats. James Haley White, "Reminiscences, 1822–1823," St. Louis Reminiscences Envelope, Missouri Historical Society, St. Louis.

Two letters confirm the receipt of a written description and drawings of the machinery in the office of the quartermaster general. Jesup to Brant, Dec. 13, 1824, and Feb. 5, 1825, vol. 7:204–5, 301, Letters Sent, RG 92. One of the more frustrating aspects of the research on this book was the inability to locate these descriptions and drawings despite an exhaustive search of the National Archives.

21. Benton to Calhoun, Sept. 22, 1824, box 64, Consolidated Correspondence File, RG 92.

22. The limerick was found by Mrs. Ernst A. Stadler, former archivist, Missouri Historical Society, St. Louis. Although undated, the mention of Wiggins's ferry suggests it could have been authored by a contemporary of Atkinson.

Atkinson wasted no time in preparing for the trip after President Monroe signed the bill authorizing the upper Missouri expedition on May 25, 1824. In St. Louis the keelboats *Otter*, *Beaver*, *Mink*, *Muskrat*, and *Raccoon* were put in dry dock where repairs were made and the wheels added. The boats were caulked, planks were replaced, and decks were repaired. Windows were installed in the cabins of some boats. The company of Laveille and Morton, which provided much of the lumber, also made five steering wheels that Atkinson incorporated into his design.[23] A "deadwood" had to be installed on the *Otter* and the *Raccoon*, and awnings were attached on all the boats to protect the soldiers from the sun and rain.[24]

Installing the paddle wheel machinery required a small army of carpenters, painters, and mechanics. A construction crew of up to twenty civilians, plus fifteen army privates and a sergeant, were under the supervision of Gregg McDanel. They spent just over 700 man-days on the work and McDanel's bill for labor was approximately $1,125, which included his own princely salary of $3.50 a day for seventy-four days. The wheel boat work was not McDanel's first contract with the military. He was also a master millwright, and had spent nine months supervising the construction of a grist and sawmill at Fort Atkinson, which was completed in December 1821. He had also worked on the prototype treadmill boats in 1823, and Atkinson considered him to be "absolutely necessary to the completion" of the retrofitted boats in 1824.[25]

---

23. Voucher 12, Commission Accounts, 10987/1824–25, RG 217. Steering oars costing about $8 were also listed on some of the vouchers covering the expenses of the expedition. Voucher 7, Commission Accounts, 488/1825, abstract A, RG 217.

Five skiffs were also built. Their use was limited to traveling between the wheel boats or other short trips. Most of the time they were towed. Voucher 15, Commission Accounts, 10987/1824–25, RG 217.

Three more boats, the *White Bear*, *Elk*, and *Buffalo*, were fitted with wheels at the fort. Orderly Book 25, Sheldon, "Records of Fort Atkinson," 5:64.

24. Voucher 15, Commission Accounts, 10987/1824–25, RG 217. The deadwood was a fin attached to the keel in front of the rudder to give the boats additional stability. Voucher 14, ibid. The awnings were waterproofed with a sizing of flour paste and then painted. Ibid.

25. Voucher 20, ibid; Voucher 1, 42, 59, Commission Accounts, 11483/1822, abstract B, RG 217; Atkinson to McDanel, Aug. 12, 1823, Commission Accounts 3020/1824, RG 217; Brant to Jesup, July 17, 1824, Commission Accounts, 3389/1824, RG 217.

Another important craftsman was Joseph Bates, who had worked on McDanel's crew. Bates left St. Louis for Fort Atkinson in December 1824 and spent nearly four months in the employ of the army constructing the machinery for the boats already at the fort. There was a rush to complete the task, and Colonel Leavenworth ordered as many men as could be spared from other duties be assigned to the construction crew. Bates completed his contract on time, and his workmanship was approved.[26]

All of these craft were older boats, to which the paddle wheels were added. In the closing months of 1824 in St. Louis, construction began on a completely new boat. Christened the *Antelope*, it was to be the flagship of the fleet taking Atkinson and O'Fallon to the upper Missouri. According to the Missouri *Advocate*, it "was built with much mechanical skill, and fancifully finished for the accommodation of the Commissioners, a beautiful Barge, the *Antelope*, 46 feet keel, and 9 feet beam; propelled after the manner of those boats which have gone before." The boat had a crew of twenty-three.[27]

By mid-March 1825 the *Antelope* was on its way to Fort Atkinson with the commissioners. The boat did not live up to expectations, and the crew spent much of their time on the cordelle. After reaching Fort Atkinson Angus Langham, the commission secretary, tersely noted, "The boat Antelope was deemed unfit for the expedition" to the upper Missouri.[28] Apparently the only other time it was used was to take Atkinson and some soldiers back to St. Louis at the conclusion of the expedition.

Although the *Antelope's* dimensions were published, there are only scattered clues concerning the size of the other wheel boats modified by Atkinson. There are references to the cargo capacity and occasionally to the dimensions, but both numbers are rarely provided for a given craft. In 1820 Dr. John Gale considered evacuating Fort Atkinson soldiers stricken with scurvy. He estimated fifty soldiers could be sent down the river in a keelboat.[29] These

26. Voucher 46, Commission Accounts, 10987/1824–25, RG 217; Leavenworth to Atkinson, Feb. 1, 1825, Letters Received by Atkinson, RG 393.

27. *Missouri Advocate*, Mar. 19, 1825. A note on the back of a bill of lading gives the length of the *Antelope* as twenty-seven and one-half feet, but this is unusually small and must have been an error. Bill of lading by W. Bloodgood, Mar. 7, 1825, Consolidated Correspondence File, RG 92.

28. Langham, "Journal of the Commissioners," 3.

were the thirty-five ton boats used to bring the troops to the Council Bluffs the previous year. Apparently the army preferred this tonnage because there are references in army records to a number of boats of about this size.[30] One report described a thirty ton boat as being one hundred feet long and fourteen feet wide with a seventeen inch draft. The report noted that it was the usual length for a thirty ton boat, but added that it had an unusually shallow draft and was therefore wider.[31]

The boats used on the expedition were of two slightly different sizes. One of Atkinson's orders specified that fifty-eight men were to be assigned to the larger boats, while the smaller boats were to have forty-eight, not including officers. These numbers would account for the detachment going to the upper Missouri, excepting Company A of the Sixth, which followed along on horseback. When most of the horses were left at a trading post in central South Dakota, the company was distributed among the boats, bringing an average crew to about fifty-nine.[32]

Although the evidence is rather limited, it is possible to estimate some dimensions for Atkinson's wheel boats. The four men abreast on the crossbars, as mentioned in the *National Daily Intelligencer* quoted above, would require at least eight feet. An additional four feet would have been required for the slides, as well as for catwalks along the sides of the boat for those rare times when the boats were poled. It seems unlikely that the beam could have been less than twelve feet. Space for men on ten benches and the three foot stroke of the crossbars would require perhaps sixty feet. The boats carried an enormous amount of cargo, so it is reasonable to assume that the cabins were large, as well as the storage

---

29. Nichols, *The Missouri Expedition*, 5, 119, 124. When the troops were preparing to go up the Missouri in 1819, Atkinson reported that one keelboat could carry 200 barrels of clothing and provisions. Ibid., 105.

30. Lt. Nicholas J. Cruger, Sixth Infantry, Fort Atkinson, vol. 2, abstract A, Commission Accounts, 3053/1824, RG 217.

31. Berry to Jesup, June 10, 1821, entry 225, Consolidated Correspondence File, RG 92. The dimensions of the boat are more suggestive of a mackinaw, but being a boat-builder Berry could hardly be expected to be in error.

32. Orderly Book 28, Sheldon, "Records of Fort Atkinson," 5:4. *Niles Weekly Register*, Nov. 6, 1824, reported thirty-two to forty men were required to "row" the boats Kearny used in 1824. When the Rifle Regiment went upriver in 1818, a crew of twenty was assigned to cordelle the conventional thirty-five-ton boats.

lockers, which were common features of keelboats. There would also have had to be room for the flywheel, connecting rods, and gears. The cabins and machinery could easily add another thirty or perhaps forty feet, bringing the length of the boat to nearly one hundred feet. The boats had a shallow draft, as was shown when one of them sank in three feet of water. It would seem then that, excepting the *Antelope*, Atkinson's wheel boats were nearly one hundred feet long, at least twelve feet wide, and had a draft of perhaps two feet.

The machinery installed in the boats functioned admirably except for a few minor problems. An initial weak point was the "slides," that part of the mechanism carrying the crossbars the soldiers grasped and moved back and forth in a rowing motion. Occasionally these cross-pieces broke, but more frequently they would bind or pull loose from the slides, the channels in which they were supposed to travel. The slides must have been improved, because they performed flawlessly during the 1825 trip. On this second leg of the expedition the flywheels caused most of the problems. Breakage occurred on the flywheel shaft, the bearing boxes, and the pitmans attached to the wheel. The Atkinson and Kearny journals mention approximately twenty malfunctions of the machinery during the entire voyage. Considering the thousands of miles the eight boats traveled, the reliability of the machinery was extremely good.

One problem was probably the fault of the crews. In 1824 the *Mink* could not keep up with the rest of the flotilla. At first Kearny suspected the problem was with the boat, but then he began to think the problem might be a lazy crew. Kearny exchanged twenty-four men from the *Mink* with soldiers from other boats, but by this time they were so near Fort Atkinson that a fair test could not be made before the trip ended. It is likely the crew was at fault. In 1825 the *Mink* served as the command boat carrying the treaty commissioners, and there was no further mention of its lagging behind.

Other problems were of a kind that could have occurred on a standard keelboat. Masts, rudders, and cordelles broke a total of twelve times. On one occasion, when a cordelle broke, the current was so strong the boat floated downstream for one-quarter of a mile before it could be brought under control, even though an anchor had been dropped. The most nagging problem was running aground on sandbars. Once the *Beaver* was so firmly grounded that three hundred men were unable to pull it off until the boat was unloaded. A more serious danger was from logs, either floating or anchored in the river bottom. Only good fortune saved the *Muskrat* when it hit such a snag that opened six holes in the hull below the water line. Fortunately the boat sank in only about three feet of water, which saved the craft, its cargo, and possibly some lives.

Atkinson never lost confidence in the superiority of his boats. When the first flotilla of wheel boats reached Fort Atkinson in the fall of 1824, Atkinson wrote to the adjutant general, describing the success of the trip. He claimed his boats made the trip in three weeks less time than boats then on the river manned by "select French crews," which were accepted as the elite boatmen of the day. Atkinson went on to say, "Besides the facility of movement gained by the new mode of propelling the Boats, the health of the troops is preserved, and their clothing from the wear and tear incident to Boat hands who navigate the river in the ordinary way. The men were in order for review of inspection the day after their arrival."[33] Another letter by the general, at the conclusion of the trip to the upper Missouri, carried the same tone: "We performed our trip with great facility and ease, owing partly to the manner our transports were propelled, that is by wheels, and it is remarkable that a body of more than 550 [*sic*] men should have encountered the dangerous navigation of the Missouri, ordinary casualties, etc., with out losing on the whole voyage a single soul, or meeting with any accident to our transports."[34]

Atkinson's assurances of the boats' seaworthiness won him accolades in Washington. In January 1825 he received a letter from the adjutant general stating, "I am further directed by the Commanding General to express to you the great satisfaction which both himself & the Government feel in the complete success of your improvement in propelling boats, as exhibited in the late ascent of the Missouri, an improvement which must produce almost incalculable advantages not only to the Army in its movements upon the western waters, but to the whole of that section of the country."[35]

---

33. Atkinson to Norse, Dec. 16, 1824, Letters Received, M567, roll 9, 228–31.
34. Henry Atkinson, "Letter from General Atkinson to Colonel Hamilton," *Nebraska History* 5 (1922): 9–11.
35. Nourse to Atkinson, Jan. 6, 1825, vol. 7:45–47, Letters Sent, M565, roll 7.

At times Atkinson made exaggerated claims concerning his boats' advantages. He had alleged the wheel boats would save $6,000 worth of clothing because the men would not be using the cordelle, which quickly wore out uniforms as they struggled through brush and brambles.[36] Apparently the savings were negligible because at the end of the expedition Colonel Leavenworth asked that new uniforms be issued due to the "extraordinary destruction of their clothing incident to preforming the duty" on the expedition. The crew of the *Antelope* fared no better. Not long after leaving St. Louis the crew was "destitute of Shoes and Overalls," and new clothing had to be purchased at Liberty, Missouri.[37]

Atkinson also claimed the paddle mechanism would replace the standard rigging necessary for cordelling and sailing. The money saved on rigging could be used to pay for the machinery, and therefore the boats would be no more expensive than the standard models. Nonetheless, the paddle wheel fleet was rigged in the conventional manner, so no savings were realized.[38]

The wheel boats were faster than conventional keelboats, but they did not live up to Atkinson's prediction that they could make the trip from St. Charles to Fort Atkinson in thirty days.[39] Kearny was able to make the ascent in forty-three days, nearly matching the fifteen-year-old record set by Manuel Lisa. The mechanically-plagued *Antelope* made the ascent in fifty-one days, about average for an unmodified keelboat.

The journals kept by Atkinson and Kearny are frustratingly silent concerning the wheel boats' capabilities. Atkinson would not have been likely to reveal shortcomings of his own design, and Kearny mentioned complaints by his officers on only one occasion. Adjustments were made to the machinery, after which the complaints stopped, or Kearny chose not to record them.

---

36. Atkinson to Calhoun, Oct. 11, 1823, entry 225, Consolidated Correspondence File, RG 92.

37. Leavenworth to Scott, Nov. 6, 1825, Orders Issued, 314–17, Orders by Atkinson, RG 393; Brant to Jesup, Sept. 5, 1825, Consolidated Correspondence File, RG 92.

38. See Appendix C. For example Peter Burtlow of St. Louis was paid $10 for making a sail and $5.25 for rigging a boat. Vouchers 24, 29, Commission Accounts, 10987/1824–25, RG 217.

39. Atkinson to Calhoun, Oct. 11, 1823; Hemphill, *The Papers of John C. Calhoun*, 8:306.

The army ceased using wheel boats at the conclusion of the Atkinson-O'Fallon expedition, which does not necessarily imply the boats were grossly inferior. By 1825 improved technology had enabled steamboats to provide for most of the needs of Fort Atkinson. When the fort was abandoned in 1827 and Fort Leavenworth was established at its present-day site, the new post was within easy range of the rapidly improving steamers. If Atkinson had been ready with his improved wheel boats in time for the 1819 Yellowstone expedition, they might have served the army regularly until steamboats made them obsolete. As it was, Atkinson's innovation was a modest success, but one that came too late.

APPENDIX C
FINANCIAL RECORDS

The financial records of the Atkinson-O'Fallon expedition provide a nearly complete statement of prices and expenditures, as well as a bonus of other useful data. Among the unexpected information were several clues concerning construction details of the wheel boats, which could not be found elsewhere. For example, rudders and steering wheels were added, showing that the boats were guided much like steamboats, rather than with the sweeps common to conventional keelboats. Glass windows were installed in the cabins of at least some of the craft, and the boats were painted, but unfortunately the color was not mentioned. There was also information on such diverse topics as the presents given to the Indians, the equipment the army took on the expedition, the civilian contractors who provided the equipment, and insights into some of the problems encountered during the voyage.

The act that authorized the Atkinson-O'Fallon expedition allocated $20,000 to cover the cost, an amount Atkinson considered to be "quite ample."[1] Secretary of War John C. Calhoun explained that one-half of the fund was "intended to embrace the *extra* costs arising out of the movement, such as transportation, contingent expense &c, and not such as would be incurred if the troops had remained stationary."[2] Much of this portion of the fund was spent in retrofitting the boats. The remaining $10,000 was to be used to

1. Peters, *Public Statutes at Large*, 4:35. Section six of the act deals with funding. Atkinson to Calhoun, July 14, 1824, Letters Received, M221, roll 99.
2. Journal of the Commissioners, 9.

defray expenses incurred in making the treaties. Most of this money was spent for presents given to the Indians.[3]

Atkinson spent approximately $14,500 from the funds allocated for the expedition. Over one third of the expenditures ($5,810) were for the boats. This amount included $843.62 to build the *Antelope*, which proved unsuitable, and $1,500 to buy three keelboats. The remainder went for equipment and labor to convert the keelboats to wheel boats. The second largest expense was $3,635.59 for gifts to the Indians. Of this, $764 was spent for fifty-five Northwest guns and forty other assorted guns. Nearly a ton of tobacco was charged to the account for Indian presents. There were also gifts of cloth, blankets, and shirts plus some unexpected items, such as eight dozen black silk handkerchiefs. The commissioners also paid for more than sixty gallons of wine and forty gallons of whiskey from the Indian account. Another major expense was the purchase of forty-four horses and equipment totalling $2,507. The animals were for Capt. William Armstrong's mounted infantry, but halfway through the expedition Atkinson admitted that the horse company was more trouble than it was worth and the horses were sent back to Fort Atkinson. As with any expedition of this size there were many incidental expenses, for example, $53.75 for paper, pencils, pens, and ink.

In the following section the expedition's financial records are given, along with a few additional documents that provide supplemental data. The first document is an estimate of the cost of sending a keelboat to the Yellowstone River. It was provided by the assistant quartermaster in St. Louis a year before the Atkinson-O'Fallon expedition was authorized. The documents that follow it relate more directly to the expedition. The original spelling and the format of the documents has been retained as closely as practical.

Estimate of expenses in fitting out and navigating a Keel Boat of 35 Tons carrying 28 Tons inclusive of Subsistence Stores for crew, from Saint Louis Mo. to the mouth of the Yellow Stone river or intermediate points viz.

3. Secretary of War Calhoun ordered the drafts on the fund to be kept separately. Ibid. The two accounts are now numbered by the National Archives, as 9534/1824–25 and 10987/1824–25 in Record Group 217, Records of the Accounting Officers of the Department of the Treasury.

1 35 Ton Keel boat with new rigging, Sales, Poles, Oars, 2 Anchors and Skiff	$ 800		
4 Twine Warps of the best quality	80		
4 do Cordelles do	80	160	$ 960 -
Crew			
1 Patroon capable of taking charge of the Boat		$ 240	
15 Hands of the cordell or Warp, 1 Bowsman and 1 Cook in all 17 at 80$ each		1360	1600
Subsistence			
Boat			281.50
Probable expenses to Great Bend of Missouri			$2841.50

From Big Bend of The Mandan Villages

The estimate to Big Bend being $2041 50/100 exclusive of the cost of Boat, add to that sum 33/3 % the [illegible words]	680.50
Cost to the Mandan Villages	$ 3522.00
From the Mandan Villages to Mouth of Yellow Stone Add to $ 2722 the cost of transportation to the Mandan Villages 16 2/3%	453.67
	$3975.67
Add for risk and profit 13%	516.75
Charge to freight 28 Tons pr St. Louis to Yellow Stone Dolls	4492.42

From the above the average amount [illegible word] would be nearly as follows, viz.

From St. Louis to upper part of Great Bend Mo	5 cents per pound
From Great Bend to Mandan Villages	1 3/4 cents per pound
From Mandan Villages to mouth of Yellow Stone	1 1/4 cents per pound
Total amount for St. Louis to Yellow Stone	8 cents per pound

Duplicates Asst. Qr. Mas Office

St. Louis 17 June 1823[4]

The United States, pr Genl Atkinson

In Acct with Scotts & Rule Dr

1824				
July 27th	6 lb Bolts & Nuts	@ 25		1.50
	9 3/4 do do			4.93 3/4
	6 small do do			1.50
	6 small do do			1.50
	2 Bands for Brass Gudgeon		10 lbs	2.

4. Brant to Jesup, June 17, 1823, Consolidated Correspondence File, RG 92. On November 5, 1823, Col. Henry Leavenworth approved the $700 purchase of a keelboat complete with sails, rigging, warp, anchor, poles, and oars from James Kennerly, sutler at Fort Atkinson. Voucher 2, abstract A, Commission Accounts, 3053/1824, RG 217.

	16 lb Bolts & Nuts			[illegible]
	5 1/2 do do			1.37
	16 do do			4.50
	3 do do			.75
	4 Slides 35 lbs			8.75
	4 do & 8 small Bolts	39 lbs		9.75
	2 plates for Balance Wheel	9 1/2		2.37
	12 Bolts for plates to Balance wheel & turned head	7 3/4 lbs		1.93
	2 plates	7 1/4 lbs		1.81
	29 1/2 lb Bolts & slide plates			7.37
	32 wedges 5 1/4 lbs			1.38
	8 slide Bolts 5 1/4 lbs			1.06
Aug 13	4 Boxes		13 lbs	
	4 ditto		15	
	Double crank		50	
	Wrist & Key for ditto		10	
	8 Bolts for [illegible word] Block		11	
	Wedges for Crank		4	
	3 washers		2	
	2 Pitman Irons		36	
			141 lbs @ 25	35.25
	2 Cast Iron pillow Blocks			
	Turnings Shafts & wrist		5	

St Louis Aug 14th 1824	$ 97.81 1/4
70 Bushels Charcoal @ 12 1/2	8.75
Duplicate	106.56 1/4

Recd payment Scott & Rule[5]

The United States pr Genl Atkinson To David Prentice

To 28 Gudgeons 811 pounds at 4 1/2 cents $ 36.49 1/2

4
3244
405 1/2
36.49

Recd payment of Br Genl H. Atkinson

Duplicate David Prentice[6]

---

5. Voucher 2, Commission Accounts, 10987/1824–25, RG 217. Alexander Scott and William K. Rule remained partners until 1831. *St. Louis Beacon*, Dec. 29, 1831. Advertisements in St. Louis newspapers show the company provided a wide variety of goods.

6. Voucher 1, Commission Accounts, 10987/1824–25, RG 217.

Brig General Henry Atkinson	To Peter Lindell & Co Dr
For three Keel boats with their tackle purchased for transportation of Military escort at $500	$1500
St Louis 16th August 1824	
Recd of Gen Genl Henry Atkinson fifteen hundred Dollars in full of the above	
	Peter Lindell & Co
St. Louis 16th Augt 1824	(Duplicate)[7]

St. Louis Mo Sept 2, 1824

The U. States pr Genl Atkinson Dr.

To R. Alexander

for	Hauling up Keel Boat No. 5	$ 10.00
	Raising boat on Blocks	6.00
	Turning Boat	5.00
	Seventeen days work Caking [caulking] Boat	34.00
	pitch for the Boat	10.00
	Oackum for the Boat	6.00
	Dead wood & Rudder for the Boat	50.00
	Trapping twenty Blocks	8.00
	Launching Boat	6.-
		$135.00

Ruben Alexander

St. Louis Septemb 2, 1824.

Received of Br. Genl. H. Atkinson one hundred and thirty five dollars in full of the above account.

Signed duplicates Ruben Alexander[8]

U States pr Gen H. Atkinson	To George Casner		Dr.
For two sets Rudder irons	110 1/2	25	$ 27.62 1/2
For 200 Staples		12 1/2	25.00
			$ 52.62 1/2

St. Louis Sept 14th 1824.

Recd of Br. Genl. H. Atkinson fifty two dollars & 62 1/2 cents in full of the above acct.

Signed duplicate his

Witness George X Casner

Jas Wanton mark[9]

7. Voucher 3, ibid. Peter Lindell and Jesse G. Lindell dissolved their partnership in 1826. *Missouri Republican*, Jan. 12, 1826.

8. Voucher 4, Commission Accounts, 10987/1824–25, RG 217.

9. Voucher 5, ibid.

The United States	To J Hawkins	Dr

1824 sept 14 For Casting four brass Boxes weighg 25 lb at 75 cents per pound $ 18.75

Received Saint Louis 14 September 1824 for Brigadr. Genl Henry Atkinson Eighteen Dollars seventy five cents in full of the above account.

Signed Duplicate Jacob Hawken[10]

The United States	To Sylvester Labadie	Dr
1824 Sept 15	For 3794 feet of Plank and	
	Scantling at 2 cents per foot	$ 75.88
	Sawing two logs into small Scantling	2.25
		$ 78.13

Received Saint Louis 15 Sept 1824 of Brig Genl Henry Atkinson Seventyeight dollars and thirteen cents in full of the above account

Signed Duplicates S. Labadie[11]

The United States	To R B Powell		Dr
1824 Sept 15	For 166 feet cherry scantling	a 3c	$ 4.98
	885 feet Maple plank	" 2c	17.70
	40 pounds Iron	" 9	3.60
	22 pounds Nails	" 12 1/2	2.75
	1 Diamond Wrench		50
	1 Key Wrench		3 -
	1 Hammer		1 -
	1 Axe		2 -
	1 Step gudgeon 31 1/2 pounds 8		2.52
	The use of Black smith shop		
	and tools 1 month		12 -
	The use of the Mill grindstone axes &c		8 -
		Dr	58.05

Received Saint Louis 15 Sept 1824 of Brigadr Genl Henry Atkinson Fifty Eight Dollars and five cents in full of the above account

Signed Duplicates R. B. Powell[12]

The United States pr Genl Atkinson To W. Walter & Co

For 5 sheet-iron stoves 125 30 [illegible word] $ 36.00

St. Louis 15th Sept. 1824 Recd of Br Genl. H. Atkinson thirty six dollars in full of the above acct.

Signed duplicate W. Walter & Co[13]

---

10. Voucher 6, ibid.
11. Voucher 8, ibid.
12. Voucher 7, ibid.
13. Voucher 11, ibid.

The United States	To John Shackford	Dr
1824 Sept 15	For sundries for the boats employed for transportation of Military Escort as follows	
	38 blocks assorted measuring 273 inches at 12 1/2 cents per inch	$ 34.12
	24 pounds Cordage at 11 cents	2.64
	12 Fishlines at 75 cents	9
	2 bales Oakum weighg 125 lb at 10 c pr lb	12.50
	Dollars	58.26

Received Saint Louis 2nd December 1824 of B General Henry Atkinson Fifty eight Dollars and twenty six cents in full of the above account
Signed Duplicates J W Shackford[14]

United States Genl Atkinson To James Byrnes

1824				
Augt	19	To Drayage on Linnen $		25
"	20	" Stripping Keil Boat & lowering mast	3	00
"	21	" Drayage & Rigging purchase to Keil Boat	2	25
		" Ditto to Mill		25
		" Spunyarn	2	00
		" Drayage to the mill 2 loads		50
		" Rigging the Cordell Mast & wheels	23	00
		" 5 [illegible word] cleets for masts	2	50
		" Making 5 Orneans [?] $13 each	75	00
		" Sail Twine	5	00
		Dollars	113	75

Saint Louis Sept 16, 1824 Recd of Br Genl. H. Atkinson one hundred and thirteen dollars & seventy five cents in full of the above account
signed duplicate James Byrnes[15]

The United States per Genl Atkinson	To Scott & Rule	Dr
for 71 lbs Pitman Irons	25 ct	17.75
" 80 1/2 " Do Do	2 1/2	20.12 1/2
" 4 pounds of Hoop Iron	16 2/3	.67
" 2 large Iron Bolts & Nuts	4 1/2 at 25	1.14

14. Voucher 22, ibid.
15. Voucher 9, ibid.

" 2 pound large spikes	25		.50
" 1 Band and five spikes	3	25	.75
" 1 Screw Bolt & Nut	2 1/4	25	.56
" 2 large 12 lb spikes	3	25	.75
" 5 small do	2	25	.50
" 1 large Screw Bolt & Nut	4 1/2	25	1.12 1/2
			$ 43.85 3/4

Saint Louis Sept 16th 1824
Recd of Genl H Atkinson forty three Dollars and Eighty five and three fourth cents in full for the Above account.
(Duplicate) Scott & Rule
Witness Jas Wanton[16]

The United States

	To Laveille & Morton	Dr	
1824 Sept 16	For 4136 feet of boards at	2 1/4 cents	$ 93.06
	5311 " Ditto	2 1/2 "	132.77
	400 " Ditto	2 "	8
	400 " Ditto	1 1/4 "	5
	103 " 1 1/2 in plank	3 1/2 "	3.61
	179 " 2 Ditto	5 "	8.95
	2 Oars	$1	2
	Drayage of the above		12.25
	Workmanship on 5 boats		130
	Making 5 Steering wheels & frames at $14 each		70
	Materials for same		29.11
		Dollars	494.75

Received Saint Louis 16 September 1824 of Brigadier General Henry Atkinson Fourhundred nintyfour Dollars and seventy five cents in full of the above account
Signed Duplicates Laveille & Morton[17]

The U. States pr Genl Atkinson Dr To W. H. Pacack
For Lettering five public transport Boats at 100 cents $ 5.00
St. Louis. Sept 22, 1824 Reck of Br Genl H Atkinson five dollars in full of the above account
signed duplicate Wm H Pacoike[18]

16. Voucher 10, ibid.
17. Voucher 12, ibid.
18. Voucher 13, ibid.

The United States
pr Genl Atkinson To William McGinniss
for Repairs on [illegible word] Boats Viz

Boat Raccoon	Hawling out boats	$100.00	
	Putting 2 new plank bottom	10.00	
	Nails and Spikes	2.50	
	Caulking of butts	6.00	
	Ditto of decks	8.00	
	putting on dead wood	10.00	
	Making of Rudder	12.00	
	Launching boat	6.00	
		$ 64.50	
Boat Beaver	Caulking the decks	4.00	
	Repairing Rudders	4.00	
			8.00
Boat Muskrat	Caulking of Decks	8.00	
	putting new blade on Rudder	7.00	
	Drayage on do	.50	
			15.50
Boat Mink	Repairing of Decks	8.00	
	" dead wood	10.00	
	" new Rudder	12.00	
			30.00
			$118.00
Paid Drayage of [illegible words]		.50	
Building 5 Skifts		15.00	
Sails for Skifts		5.50	
Ocum and pitch		3.50	
5 Pair of Oars		3.75	
			28.25
			$146.25
St Louis September 25, 1824			
Caulking deck <*Constitution*> Otter			8.00
			$154.25

St Louis. Sept. 23, 1824 Recd of Br Gen. H. Atkinson one hundred and fifty four dollars & twenty five cents in full of the within acct

signed duplicate William McGinniss[19]

19. Voucher 15, ibid.

The U. States pr Genl Atkinson	To Asa Wilgers	dr.
For 9 1/2 days labor painting public Keel boat $2 pr day		$ 19.00
"small quantity of flour to paste awning of the Boats before painting them		37 1/2
"furnishing eighteen lights and glazing the same [illegible words] Keel Boats	20 ct ea.	3.60
		$ 22.97 1/2

St. Louis Sept 23, 1824. Recd of Br. Genl. Atkinson twenty two dollars & 97 1/2 / 100 in full of the above acct
Signed duplicates Asa Wilgers[20]

The United States		To H L Hoffman		Dr
1824 Sept 24 For	1 Keg Saltpetre	100 lb	20	$ 20 -
	1 Keg Sulpher	60	20	12 -
	1 Demijohn contg spirits of Wine	3 gallons a 2.25 per gallon		6.75
				$ 38.75

Received Saint Louis 24 Sept 1824 of Brigadier General Henry Atkinson Thirty eight Dollars and seventy five cents in full of the above account.
Signed Duplicates H L Hoffman[21]

The United States	To Trach & Wahrendorff	Dr	
1824 Sept			
	For 917 1/4 yds Towel Cloth	@ .20	$ 183.45
	" 213 lb assorted bar iron	" 8	170.80
	" 8 lb Hoop Iron	" 15	1.20
	" 180 lb Boiler Iron	" 18 3/4	33.75
	" 21 lb English Crowby Steel	" 25	5.25
	" 3 1/4 lb English Cast Steel	" 50	1.62
	" 417 lb assorted Nails	" 11	45.87
	" 10 lb wrought Nails	" 25	2.50
	" 12 gross assorted wood Screws from 1 3/4 to 2 3/4 inch	" 1.50	18.00
	" 4 2/3 doz assorted Files	" 6.12 1/2	28.55
	" 2 dozen Butt Hinges	" 1.50	3.00
	" 1 2/12 dozen Tall Hinges	" 4.50	9.75
	" 1 Foreplane	"	3 -
	" 1 Smoothing plane	"	1.25

20. Voucher 14, ibid.
21. Voucher 16, ibid.

"	3 double iron plane bits	"	.75	2.25
"	3 iron Squares	"	.75	2.25
"	2 Hand Saws	"	2.	4.
"	2 pair Carpentry Compasses	"	.25	.50
"	3 Foot adzes	"	1.75	5.25
"	2 best Shingling hatchets	"	1.	2.
"	1 W M Felling axe & handle	"		5.
"	2 large steel hammers	"	75	1.50
"	2 two foot Carpenters Rules	"	75	1.50
"	2 C V Drawing knives	"	1	2.
"	1 Key hole saw	"		1.
"	1 broad axe	"		4.50
"	1 hand axe	"		3.50
"	1 brace and bitts (12 pairs)	"		6.
"	2 dozen Assorted Gimblets	"	1	2.
"	3 Spike gimblets	"	25	.75
"	1 Sledge hammer 10 lb	"	25	2.50
"	2 hand hammers 8 oz	"	25	2.
"	1 pair Smith bellows	"		35.
"	1 Smiths vice 51 lb	"	18 3/4	9.56
"	1 Smiths Anvil 123 lb	"	15	18.45
"	14 Screw Augers 57 [illegible words]	"	12 1/2	7.12
"	3 3/4 lb Chalk	"	12 1/2	.47
"	5 Chalk Lines	"	12 1/2	.62
"	6 Paint Brushes	"	62 1/2	3.75
"	1 barrel Linseed oil 34 gallon per gal 1.12 1/2			38.25
				$ 667.74

Amount brought over				$ 667.74
For	8 Kegs White Lead in Oil	"	5.	40.
"	2 papers lampblack	"	25	.50
"	1 bottle olive oil	"		1.
"	2 bottle Spirits turpentine	"	62 1/2	1.25
"	2 lb Red Lead	"	37 1/2	.75
"	1/4 lb Amber	"		.38
"	1 lb Lothrage	"		.50
"	1/2 lb white copperas	"	25	.12
"	1 Cast iron pot	"		1.25
"	1 Tea Kettle	"		1.75
"	9 Coil Cordage	"	11 & 12	10.23
"	5 Cables			
"	2 Coils Spun yarn 39lb	"	12 1/2	4.87
"	10 lb Twine	"	50	5.00
"	1 doz Sail needles	"		.50

"	6 Socket Chissels assorted	"	50	3.00
"	2 Firers Chissels	"	37 1/2	.75
"	212 lb Tallow	"	8	16.96
"	5 Kegs Lard 182 lb including Keg	"	10	18.20
"	2 Kegs Pitch	"	3.25	6.50
"	1 Oilstone weighing 2 1/4	"	1.25	2.81
"	1 Grindstone 23 in	"	20	4.60
"	1 patent Lall Lock	"		.75
"	400 3 Bar Lead	"	64	25.
"	848 feet boards	"	2 1/4	19.08
"	Drayage to Steam Mill			4.38
"	6 lb Lamp Black	"	5 1/4	2.25
"	25 lb Venetian Red	"	10	2.50
"	110 Bushels Coal	"	8	8.50
		Dollars		961.42

Received Saint Louis 25 September 1824 of Brigadier Genl Henry Atkinson -------- Nine hundred sixty one Dollars and forty two cents in full of the above account

Signed Duplicate Trach & Wahrendorff[22]

The United States per General Atkinson & Major O'Fallon Dr
Bought of the American Fur Company

			Sterling			New York		Fixed
15 North West Guns		$11.40						171
45 pairs Blankets 3 points		15/	33	15	1			
29 ------------ 2 1/2		11/5	15	11	1			
3 pp Com blue Strouds broad Cord								
3 ------------------ narrow "		78/	23	8				
1 Coverlet Wrapper to Strouds								75
2 pp Scarlet Cloth 66 & 67	40 3/4	5/2	10	10	7			
2 -------------- 69 & 70	45	5/10	15	8	4			
---- Green ---- 333	25	5/2	6	9	2			
1 -------------- 344	23 3/4	6/	7	2	6			
20 --- Indian Calico		26/	26	"	"			
2 --- Cotton Bandanoes doz	3 8/12	2.40				8	80	
4 --- Blue Do "	4 1.87	1/2				7	50	
1 --- Mock Madrass Hkfs	8/12	1.75				1	17	
1 --- Turkey Red do	1 4/12	3 -				4		

22. Voucher 17, ibid.

8 --- Black Silk do		6.25				50			
2 --- Mock Madrass do	2	2.25				4	50		
5 lbs black Thread c#	10	2/3		11	3				
5 --- All Coloured C	"	2/6		12	0				
1 --- Nankeen	"	2/2		2	2				
4 --- All Coloured	16	3/		12					
11 --- Stitching	50	3/3		13					
1 --- C	60	3/8		3	8				
3 dozen Foxtail Feathers		20/	3	"	"				
2 " red cock " white tops		225				4	50		
1 " " " "						2	25		
67 Indian calico Shirts									
5 Printed Cotton do		1.20				86	40		
1 Gross Iron Jews Harps		3/7		3	7				
2 ----- Finger Rings		2/6		5					
1 ----- Gun Worms		1/10		1	10				
2 3/12 ---- Fire Steels		12/	1	11					
3 dozens Womens Scissors		2.75				8	25		
1/2 ---- ---- Do ----		5/6		2	9				
1/2 ---- ---- Do ----		4/		2					
2 Gross Brass Bells		10/6	1	1	"				
6 ----- Indian Awls		3/6	1	1	"				
4 Thousand Gunflints		12/	2	8					
2500 White Chapel Needles pr M		1.25				3	12		
Carried forward			149	15	5	180	49	171	75

[Continued]

Brot Forward L			149	15	5	$180	49	$171	75
12 dozen Scalping Knives		4/6	2	14	-				
12 " Cartouche "		4/	2	5	-				
24 " Green Handled		8/3	9	18	0				
24 " Papered Looking Glasses		25				6	-		
3 " Files flat Bastard	8 in	1.32				3	96		
2 " do 1/2 round	10	2.62				5	24		
1 " do "	"	2.07				2	07		
1 " do "	8	1.32				1	32		
2 " do X cut		3/5		7					
3 " do pit saw		1.32				3	96		
52 Lbs Sky blue Beads		1/2	3	0	8				
47 1/2 " White		1/6	3	11	3				

35 ------------------		1/1	1	17	11				
21 Masses Blue		22 1/2				4	72		
58 Lbs Green & blue		1/2	3	7	8				
1 Box Vermillion 66 2/3 lbs		75				50	-		
3 Setts Pierced Broaches	No 1	4.38				13	14		
3 " -------- do ------	2	3.47				10	41		
24 Eambossed do	1st use	42 1/4				10	14		
24 " -------- do ----	2d	33				7	92		
10 Pairs Wristbands	1 1/2 in	1.40				14	-		
10 do	1 1/4	1.25				12	50		
4 do	1	86				3	44		
4 Arm Bands	3	4.50				18	-		
3 do	"	5.25				15	75		
3 do	2	3.50				10	50		
2 do	"	2.62				5	24		
9 Dz Verdigris		.44				3	96		
12 --- Collar Wire		56 1/4				6	75		
11 --- White Pipe Beads		31 1/4				3	44		
2 Nests Tin Kettles 15 in a Nest		39	3	18					
26 Wampum Hair Pipes 102 inches		3				3	06		
7000 Black Wampum		3.25				22	75		
1 Box Pipes 4 Gr		82 1/2				3	30		
3 Dz Ingrained Worsted		1.62				4	86		
4 " Yellow & Green do		1.12				4	48		
1 Qt Cask Port Wine 31 1/2 Gals		3.25						102	42
1 " Teneriffe	31 "	3 -						93	-
2 English Trunks		4 -						8	-
1 New York do								3	-
8 Boxes		38 1/2						3	-
2 Bale Cloths & Cords		1 -						3	-
5 English do		1.50						7	50
Carting to Boat									75
Forward		L	180	17	11	$433	90	$391	42

Amount of Sterling Goods brot Forward	L	180.17.11		
Advance 100 pr Cent		180.17.11		
	L	361.15.10	$ 1167.96	
Amount of New York Goods brot forward		$ 433.90		
Advance 33 1/3 pr Cent		144.63	578.53	
Amount of Goods at fixed price brot forward			831.42	
			2577.91	

1 Bbl Loaf Sugar 120 17 105 net	25	25.75	
12 bottles Lime Juice	62 1/2	7.50	
1 Bbl Mackarel		13 -	
1 Bag Coffee 113 lbs	25	28.25	
12 doz Claret Wine	4.50	54 -	
2 Boxes Mould Candles 66 1/2	16	10.64	
2 " Soap 101	8	8.08	
12 Bottles Sweet Oil	$1	12 -	
2 dozen English Mustard	2.50	5 -	
1/2 lb Nutmegs	3 -	1.50	
1 Bbl Rice 220 17 203	10	20.30	
1 do Sugar 232 17 215	11	23.65	
4 Bottles Bitters	75	3 -	
2 Chests Young Hyson Tea 22	1.25	27.50	
6 Boxes Table Salt	37 1/2	2.25	
10 lb Pepper	50	5 -	
5 " Alspice		2.50	
4 Bottles Cayenne		2 -	
1 Bbl Teneriffe Wine 30 Gals	$2	60 -	
14 Gallons Molasses	1	14 -	
12 Kegs Tobacco 1818 lbs		109.08	
1 " Do 162	14	22.68	
1 Keg		1 -	
6 Boxes	37 1/2	2.25	
2 Do	25	50	
1 Do	75	75	
3 Bbl	37 1/2	1.12	
Carting to Boat		1.38	464.68
		DS	3042.59

Errors &c Excepted Saint Louis Sept 28th 1824

Saint Louis Sept 29th 1824 Recd of Genl H. Atkinson & Maj Beng O'Fallon three thousand and forty two 59/100 Dollars in full of the above a/c O. N. Bostwick

Agt Am Fur Co[23]

St. Louis Sept. 29th 1824

Sir, Agreeably to your letter of instructions of the 1st of June last we have this day drawn upon you in favor of Mr. O. N. Bostwick, of this place, for three thousand and ninety four dollars and ninety nine cents, on acct of goods purchased of him for Indian presents, authorized by the act of Congress of the 26th May last.

23. Voucher 1, Commission Accounts, 9534/1824–25, RG 217.

With very great respect Sir we have the honor to be

Your Mo. ob Servts
Benjn O.Fallon
H. Atkinson
Br Gen. U.S. Army

To the Honb.
J. C. Calhoun
Secy of War
W City[24]

The United States pr Genl Atkinson To Joseph Siddons Dr
for 2 1/2 days work as carpenter on the public
Keel Boat, Otter, at 1 50/100 pr Day --------- $3.75
St Louis Sept 30th 1824 Recd of Genl. H. Atkinson
three dollars and 75/100 in full of the above account
Signed duplicates Jos H Siddons[25]

The United States To Wm. Mcginniss Dr
1824 Oct 1 For reparing a Rudder for a Keel boat
for use of Military Escort $ 5 -
Received Saint Louis 1 October 1824 of Brigad Genl Henry Atkinson
Five Dollars in full of the above account
Signed Duplicate William McGinniss[26]

The United States To Gregg McDanniel Dr
1824 Oct 4 For Amount of Workmanship Wages and Materials on
Boats fitted up and constructed for the use of the Military Escort
by order of Brigadr Genl Henry Atkinson as follows

Carpenters Work Prepair	30 1/2	days at	1.50 per day	$ 45.75
Oliver Bergmann	24	"	1.50	" 36
A. Sutton	12 1/2	"	1.50	" 18.75
Jones	12	"	1.50	" 27
Johnsen	26	"	1.50	" 39
Dickersan	35 1/2	"	1.50	" 48.81
J. Skidders	19	"	1.50	" 18.50
Roy	11	"	1.50	" 5
Bruster	20 1/2	"	1.	" 20.50
W Earl	16 1/2	"	1.50	" 24.75
J. Robinson	9	"	2.	" 18.00
Marlin	22	"	1.	" 22.00
R. Pursy	27	"	1.50	" 40.50
J. Russell	32	"	2.50	" 80
A. Shearer	34	"	1.	" 34

24. Letters Received, M234, roll 429, 107-8.
25. Voucher 18, Commission Accounts, 10987/1824–25, RG 217.
26. Voucher 19, ibid.

G. House	22	"	1.50	" 33	
J. Bates	8	"	1.50	" 12	
					577.31
Sergt Davis	24	"	50 pr day	$ 12	
Private Long	29	"	50 "	14.50	
" OBrian	21 1/2	"	50 "	10.75	
" Farrent	5	"	50 "	2.50	
" Graft	31	"	50 "	15.50	
" Fitzgerald	30	"	50 "	15	
" Cabbet	30	"	50 "	15	
" Kearns	4	"	50 "	2	
" Austin	30 1/2	"	50 "	15.25	
" Hitel	21	"	50 "	10.50	
" Presson	17	"	50 "	9.50	
" Brechmond [?]	25	"	50 "	12.50	
" Glenfirst	27	"	50 "	13.50	
" Ayres	27 1/2	"	50 "	13.75	162.25
					$ 739.56

Carried over

1824 Oct 4 The United States
To Gregg McDanel Dr
Amount brot over $ 739.56

Carpenters Work Continued

Private Thomas	23 1/2 days at 50c pr day	$ 11.75	
" Riley	10 " 50 "	5	
		16.75	

Mill Wright Work
Ames Hill for 37 1/2 days Work at $2.50 pr day $93.33
The same for 8 days Work on board of boats being found in Provisions at $2. pr day 16 109.33
My Services as principal Millwright
and Superintendant 74 days at $3.50 pr Day 259

For one Jackplane		$ 1.25	
one handsaw		1.50	
blacksmith work on boat at Ft Charles		1.50	
6 Dozen Woodscrews	12 1/2	.75	
25 pounds Tallow	8	2.	
Dollars			1131.64

Received Saint Louis 4 October 1824 of Brigadier Genl Henry Atkinson Eleven hundred thirty one dollars and Sixty four cents in full of the above account

Signed Duplicates Gregg McDanel[27]

27. Voucher 20, ibid.

The United States	To	John Boone		Dr
			Dolls.	Cts.
Oct 17th 1824	For			
	One Skiff as a tender to the			
	U. States Keel Boat Otter		12	00

Qr. Master will pay the above account
E Shaler Capt 6 Infy Comg
Received, Franklin Oct 17th 1825 of Lieut Thomas Noel, Act. Asst Coms of Sub. twelve —— dollars and —— cents, in full of the above account. Signed duplicates.
J. Boone[28]

The U. States to Bt. Major S. W. Kearny 1st U.S. Infy
October 1, 1825 Dr
For plank, cartage, wrenches, spikes & screws
Sockets for poles purchased at Franklin (Mo)
for the use of the Boats under his Command $ 27.75
Received from Brigd Genl H. Atkinson U.S. Army this 2d Nov. 1824 Twenty seven dollars & seventy five cents in full of the above account
S. W. Kearny
Bt Maj 1st Inf[29]

The United States per General H Atkinson
To Jean Mousette For 63 days Services as Pilot to Council Bluffs to Major Kearneys command at $3.- per day $198. -
Received at Fort Atkinson Council Bluffs 4 Nov 1824 of General Henry Atkinson One hundred eightynine Dollars in full of the above account
Test Signed Duplicate his
Chas Warendorff Jean X Mousette
mark[30]

The United States	To Ely & Curtis		Dr
	For	$	Cts
December	Six Quires of fools cap paper at 37 1/2 cts pr	2	25
15th	Six do Letter do 37 1/2 " "	2	25
1824	Three papers of Ink Powder at 18 3/4 cts		56 1/4
	Six Norvell [?] cast steel Axes $4.25	25	50

28. Voucher 1, Commission Accounts, 4418/1825, RG 217.
29. Voucher 50, Commission Accounts, 10987/1824–25, RG 217.
30. Voucher 21, ibid.

One pit saw & Tiller	13	00
1/2 doz pit saw files	2	00
One box of Wafers		12 1/2
	$ 45	68 3/4

Received Liberty Missouri December 15th 1824 of Lieut Thomas Noel A. A. C. Subsistence Forty five dollars and Sixty eight and threeforths cents in full of the above account Eley & Curtis The Qr Master will pay the above account

E Shaler Capt 6 Inf comg[31]

The United States pr Genl H Atkinson To Tunis Roberdeau Dr

1824 For one Horse. Bay 14 hands
6 years old ------------ $ 35 -

Received Saint Louis Dec. 20th 1824 of Brig Genl H. Atkinson U.S. Army Thirty five Dollars and ------- cents in full of the above account Duplicated

Witness
Geo K. McGunnegle

His
Tunis X Roberdeau
mark[32]

The United States To Ely & Curtis Dr

		Dolls.	Cts.
Jan 13th 1825	For One Load of Hay	15	"
	One Wrench and one dozen		
	Wedges for the use of the Keel		
	Boat Otter acending the Missouri		
	River under the command of		
	Captain E. Shaler 6th Inf		

Qr. Master will pay the above account
E Shaler Capt 6 Infy Comg

Received, Liberty (Misso) Jany 13th 1825 of Lieut Thomas Noel, Act. Asst Coms of Sub. Seventeen dollars and fifty cents, in full of the above account. Signed duplicates.

Eley & Curtis[33]

The United States pr Genl H Atkinson To J Reed & Co Dr
1825 Febry 19 For 63 yards Russia Sheeting at 31 1/4 cents $ 19.68 3/4

31. Voucher 3, Commission Accounts, 4418/1825, RG 217.
32. Voucher 55, Commission Accounts, 10987/1824–25, RG 217.
33. Voucher 2, Commission Accounts, 4418/1825, RG 217.

Received Saint Louis 19 February 1825 of Br General Henry Atkinson
Nineteen dollars and sixtyeight and three fourth Cents in full of
the above account
Signed Duplicates James Reed & co[34]

The United States per Genl H Atkinson To Peter Burtlow Dr
1825 Feby 28 For making a sail for Boat employed for
military escort $ 10.
Received Saint Louis 28 February 1825 of Genl Henry Atkinson
Ten Dollars in full of the above account Signed Duplicates
his X
Test Peter Burtlow
Chas Wahrendorff mark[35]

The United States To Charles Bosseron Dr

1825	
28th Febr For Shoeing 21 Public Horses, all round at $2	$ 42.00
" 2 New Shoes and 2 removed	1.50
" removing all round on 3 Horses	3.00
	$ 46.50

Saint Louis, Feb 28th 1825 Received of Br. Genl. H. Atkinson U.S.
Army, Forty Six Dollars and fifty cents in full of the above account.
Duplicates, Charles Bosseron[36]

The United States To Eley & Curtis Dr

For One load of Hay	$15.00
" Eight pounds of nails	1.60
" Three quires paper	75
" Twenty five pounds Hog Lard	2.50
" Forty one pounds of Rope 20 cts	8.20
	$ 26.05

Received of Ths. Noel Lt. & a.a.c. sub.USA. Twenty Eight
dollars and five cents In full of the above account on the 28th
day Feby 1825 Eley & Curtis
Signed duplicates
The Qr Master will pay the above account
E Shaler Capt 6 Inf comg[37]

34. Voucher 23, Commission Accounts, 10987/1824–25, RG 217.
35. Voucher 24, ibid.
36. Voucher 25, ibid.
37. Voucher 4, Commission Accounts, 4418/1825, RG 217.

	United States	To Thornton Grimsley	Dr
1825			
March 4	For Making 27 Halters @ 00.30 -------		8.10

Recd payment in full for the Above Account of General Henry Atkinson
signed duplicates
St. Louis March 10 - 1825 Thornton Grimsley[38]

The United States per General Atkinson
1825 To W. Walter & Co Dr
March 12th

For One Sheet Iron Cooking Stove weighing		
115 pounds at 30 cents per pound		$ 34.50
One tin Roaster		3.00
Ten pounds Sheet Iron	20	2.00
Twelve tin Cups	6 1/4	75
Four tin pans	37 1/2	1.50
One Glass Lantern		1.25
One Tin do		50
Two wash basins	50	1.00
One Coffee Pot		75
One Coffee Boiler		1.25
One Black tin Teapot		1.50
		$ 48.00

Received St. Louis March 12 1825 of Brig General H. Atkinson forty eight dollars in full of the above account
(Signed Duplicates) Washington Walter & Co[39]

The Commissioners Genl Atkinson & Maj O Fallon
To Essex & Hough Dr
1825

March 7	To 1 Ream folio post		9.50
	1 Ream Letter paper		4.50
	4 three gr Blk Books e 2		8.00
	3 Bottles Ink	37 1/2	1.12 1/2
	1/2 Doz. Ink powder		75
	2 Doz. Lead pencils		2.00
	2 Ink stands 1/75	1/25	1.00
	2 lbs Sealing Wax	2	4.00
	3 Boxes Wafers	.25	75
	1 Bottle Gum arabac		50

38. Voucher 26, Commission Accounts, 10987/1824–25, RG 217.
39. Voucher 27, ibid.

2 Sand Boxes	25	50
300 quills	1.25	3.75
1 Ruler		1.00
1 Ream Enrolling paper		15.00
1 Bottle Red Ink		1.00
1 Piece Sponge		25
1 Piece India Rubber		12 1/2
		$ 53.75

Rec Saint Louis March 12, 1825 of Genl Atkinson and Maj O.Fallon Fifty three dollars & seventy five cents in full of the above account
Duplicates Essex & Hough[40]

St Louis March 14, 1825
The United States Br Genl Henry Atkinson To John Shackford Dr

For 1 5/8 lb Serving Twine	@ 75	1.25
1/2 dz Sail needles	@ 25	.12 1/2
5 Blocks 27 1/2 inches	@ 12 1/2	3.43 3/4
4 Fishing Lines	@ 25	1.
1 [illegible] Saddlers Sacks	@	.50
1 [llegible] (formast)	@	.50
4 Coils of Cordage	0.34.34.18=136	
1 Cable	32	
1 piece of white rope	14	
1 " Tarred do	11	
	193 @ 10	19.30
Drayage of cordage to the "Antelope"		.25
		24.36 1/4

Received Saint Louis 14th March 1825 of Br General Henry Atkinson Twenty Six dollars thirty six and a fourth cents in full of the above account Signed Duplicates John Shackford[41]

The United States To Lewis Oldenbury Dr

1825			Dolls cets
12th Feb	For 1 Grey	Horse	65 "
14th "	1 Sorrel	do	45 "
18th "	1 Sorrel	do	65 "
18th "	1 Roan	do	65 "
18th "	1 Grey	do	50 "
18th "	1 Black	do	50 "
18th "	1 Bay	do	45 "

40. Voucher 2, Commission Accounts, 9534/1824–25, RG 217.
41. Voucher 28, Commission Accounts, 10987/1824–25, RG 217.

18th "	1 Bay	do	45 "
19th "	1 Brown	do	67 "
19th "	1 Bay	do	50 "
21th "	1 Sorrel	do	60 "
21th "	1 Dark Brown	do	45 "
21th "	1 Dark Brown	do	65 "
22th "	1 Sorrel	do	45 "
22th "	1 Bay	do	70 "
22th "	1 Sorrel	do	40 "
22th "	1 Sorrel	do	70 "
23th "	1 Sorrel	do	50 "
23th "	1 Cream Col	do	65 "
23th "	1 Bay	do	35 "
23th "	1 Sorrel	do	50 "
23th "	1 Black	do	45 "
24th "	1 Sorrel	do	45 "
24th "	1 Grey	do	55 "
24th "	1 Dapple Grey	do	75 "
25th "	1 Bay	do	50 "
26th "	1 Sorrel	do	70 "
28th "	1 Grey	do	75 "
	28		
	Keeping the above Horses 83 Weeks at $1 per week a head		83 "
			1640 "

Saint Louis, March 16th 1825. Received of Br. Genl. H. Atkinson of the U.S. Army, Sixteen Hundred and forty Dollars in full of the above account. Lewis Oldenbury Duplicates[42]

The United States pr Genl Atkinson To Peter Bartlow Dr
for 3 1/2 days labor rigging keel Boat - 1 /50 pr day $5.25

Recd - St Louis March 16th 1825 of Br. Genl. H. Atkinson five dollars & twenty five cents in full of the above acc.
Lewis Oldenbury duplicate his
Peter X Bartlow
mark[43]

42. Voucher 30, ibid.
43. Voucher 29, ibid.

United States per Genl Henry Atkinson To Tracy Wohrendorff

1825		Dr		
March 16	For	10 bushels charcoal at	10 c	$ 1 -
		20 bushels Stonecoal	18 3/4	3.75
		34 yards Flaxliners	28	9.52
		1 hundred Needles		25
		1 pound Thread		50
		6 Dozen Curtain screws	37 1/2	2.25
		34 pounds Cordage for halters	10	3.40
		7 1/2 yards Linen for Foragebags	25	1.88
		5 horse blankets	1	5 -
		10 pounds Tallow	10	1 -
		25 pounds Lard	10	2.50
			Dollars	31.05

Received Saint Louis 16 March 1825 of General Henry Atkinson
Thirty one Dollars and five cents in full of the above account
Signed Duplicate Tracy & Wohrendorff[44]

The United States pr Genl. Atkinson To VonPhul & McGill

1825			Dr
March 9	For 5 Common saddles	@ 8$	$ 40.00
	4 " snaffle Bridles	@ 75	3.00
			$ 43.00

Received St. Louis March 17th 1825 of Genl Henry Atkinson
Forty three Dollars in full of the above account
Signed Duplicate VonPhul & McGill[45]

The United States To Reuben Davis Dr

1825 Mar 17	For 15 pounds Pitch	12 1/2	1.87
	10 " Oakum	12 1/2	1.25
			$ 3.12

Received Saint Louis 17 March 1825 of General Henry Atkinson
Three Dollars and twelve cents in full of the above account
Witness — Signed Duplicates
William P. Tilton — his
Reuben X Davis
mark[46]

44. Voucher 31, ibid.
45. Voucher 32, ibid.
46. Voucher 33, ibid.

The United States	To Ames Hill	Dr
1825		
17th Mar For Building the Keel boat Antelope with		
Machinery complete for running with wheels		$ 692.00
Putting on an upper deck & finding materials		88.00
Painting the Boat & her Cabbins & finding materials		63.42
		$ 843.62

Saint Louis March 18th Received of Br Genl. H. Atkinson U.S. Army, Eight hundred forty three Dollars and Sixty two cents, in full of the above account

Duplicates Ames Hill[47]

The United States	To David Workman	Dr
For 5 pack saddles	at $3 ea	$ 30.00

21 March 1825. Franklin Mo. Recvd of Brig Gr H Atkinson thirty dollars in full of the above acct

Signed Duplicate David Workman[48]

The United States pr Genl Atkinson & Major O'Fallon

Bot of the Am. Fur Compy

10 Guns half stock	no 12	$ 8	$ 80.00
10 " stockd	10	$ 6.66 2/3	66.67
20 " do		6.53	130.60
40 North West Guns		$ 8	320.00
			$ 593.

Received Saint Louis March 24th 1825 from Major Benjamin O'Fallon commissioner to treat with the tribes of Indians, on the upper Missouri Five hundred and ninety three dollars in full of the above bill

(Signed duplicates) O. N. Bostwick
Agt. Am. Fur Co[49]

United States	To Eley & Curtis	Dr
	For 1 Bay Horse	$ 42.00
	" 1 Gray ditto	45.00
	" 1 Sorrel ditto	55.00
		$142.00

47. Voucher 34, ibid. In the 1820s newspapers, such as the St. Louis *Missouri Gazette*, regularly advertised keelboats for sale ranging from fifteen to sixty tons. A mid-sized boat could be purchased for $400.

48. Voucher 35, Commission Accounts, 10987/1824–25, RG 217.

49. Voucher 3, Commission Accounts, 9534/1824–25, RG 217.

Liberty April 9th 1825. Received of Brig. H. Atkinson
One hundred and forty two dollars in full of the above
account Signed Duplicate Eley & Curtis[50]

The United States To William L. Smith Dr
For one sorrel Horse $ 80.00

Liberty, Missouri. April 9th 1825. Recd of Br. Genl.
H. Atkinson eighty dollars in full of the above account.
Duplicate William L. Smith[51]

The United States To Ruben R Reynolds Dr
For one Bay Horse $ 70.00

Liberty Missouri. April 9th 1825 Recvd of Br. Genl.
H. Atkinson Seventy dollars in full of the above acct.
duplicate Ruben R Reynolds[52]

The United States To William Lamme & Co
For 909 lb Bar iron ------------ 12 1/2 $ 113.62 1/2
Liberty, Missouri, April 9th 1825 Recd of Bri Genl
H. Atkinson one hundred and thirteen dollars and 62 1/2 /100 in
full of the above account Duplicate
William Lamme & Co[53]

The United States To Singleton Vaughn Dr
For one pied Horse $ 60.00
Liberty. April 9th 1825 Recvd of Genl. H. Atkinson Sixty dollars
in full of the above acct.
duplicate Singleton Vaughn[54]

The United States To Daniel Monroe Dr
For one Sorrel Horse $ 45.00

Liberty, Missouri April 9th 1825 Recvd of Br. Genl.
H. Atkinson forty five dollars in full of the above acct.
duplicate Samuel Monroe[55]

50. Voucher 36, Commission Accounts, 10987/1824–25, RG 217.
51. Voucher 37, ibid.
52. Voucher 38, ibid.
53. Voucher 39, ibid.
54. Voucher 40, ibid.
55. Voucher 41, ibid.

The United States
pr Genl Atkinson and Commos
Maj O Fallon To W. B. Culver Dr
1825 April 20 For freighting 7844 pounds of Merchandise from Saint Louis to Fort Atkinson Council Bluffs for the use of the Commission appointed to treat with the Indians West of the Mississippi under Act of Congress 25 May 1824.
at 3 cents per pound $ 235.32
Received of Genl Henry Atkinson and Major Benjam O Fallon Commissioners Two hundred thirty five Dollars and thirty two Cents in full of the above account Fort Atkinson Council Bluffs 20 April 1825 Signed Duplicates Wm B. Culver[56]

Council Bluffs, April 21st 1825
The United States To Samuel McRee Dr
For one Sorrel Horse $ 60.00
Recvd of Br. Genl. H. Atkinson this 21st April 1825 Sixty dollars in full of the above acct.
S. McRee Duplicate[57]

The United States To William Armstrong Dr

1825		
15 March	For Corn and Hay for Public Horses at St. Charles $	1.50
" "	" Ferriage " " " "	5.75
" "	" Corn & Fodder " " at Pitmans	1.00
16 "	" Corn & Hay " " at Prondles	2.50
" "	" Corn & Fodder " " at Farrars	1.25
17 "	" Corn, Hay and Keeping " " at Kebbeys	3.75
18 "	" Corn and Hay " " at	3.75
" "	" Corn and Hay " " at Harrisons	1.25
19 "	" Corn and Hay " " at	2.75
" "	" Corn and Fodder " " at Sextons	1.75
20 "	" Corn and Hay " " at Robinsons	2.00
22 "	" Corn and Pasture " " at Jon [illegible]	5.50
" "	" Farriage at Arrow Rock	2.15
23 "	" Corn and Hay " " at Reeds	2.50
24 "	" Corn Hay and Stabling " at	10.25
" "	" Farriage at at Tabo	1.50
26 "	" Corn and Hay " " at Lexington	1.50

56. Voucher 4, Commission Accounts, 9534/1824–25, RG 217.
57. Voucher 42, Commission Accounts, 10987/1824–25, RG 217.

" "	"	Farriage " " at Jacks	3.25
" "	"	Corn and Hay " " at Bluffton	1.25
27 "	"	Farriage " " at Tealing Creek	1.75
" "	"	Corn " " at Tealing Creek	1.50
30 "	"	Fodder " " at Liberty	4.50
6 April	"	2 Axes for the use of the party on their way to Fort Atkinson	6.00
7 "	"	80 Bushel of corn fed to Public Horses at Liberty	27.00
8 "	"	Salt for Public Horses	1.00
" "	"	17 1/4 yards Towling to make Bags	5.00
" "	"	9 Bed Cords for Packing rope	3.50
" "	"	1 Bridle	1.00
" "	"	12 lbs Salt for Public Horses	" 50
" "	"	2 Bed Cords for Packing ropes and halters	" 75
" "	"	1 1/2 yds Towling	" 50
" "	"	Making Bags	2.00
10 "	"	Corn for Public Horses at Paymasters Camp	5.00
11 "	"	Corn " " at Smiths	4.50
		Amount $	120.25

[Continued on reverse]

I Certify that the within is a correct account of expenses incurred by me in bringing twenty six Public Horses from St Louis (Mo) to Fort Atkinson.

Fort Atkinson Wm Armstrong
24th April 1825[58]

The United States John Welch Dr

For eight bushels of corn at 50c per bushel	4.00
	4.00

Received Fort Atkinson April 25, 1825 of Brig Genl Atkinson four dollars in full of the above account

Signed Duplicate John Welch[59]

58. Voucher 43, ibid.
59. Voucher 44, ibid.

The United St To John Welch Dr
May 8, 1825 For three hundred pounds of
Tallow at 12 1/2 ct per pound $ 37.50
Received Fort Atkinson May 8, 1825 of Brig Genl H. Atkinson Thirty seven dollars and fifty cents in full of the above account Duplicate John Welch[60]

The United States To Joseph Bates Dr
For his services from the 20th Decmb. 1824 to the 16th May 1825 in constructing machinery for the flotilla of the Missouri expedition, being 4 months & 20 days at 64 per month $ 304.00

Council Bluffs May 10th 1825
Received of Br Genl. H. Atkinson three hundred & four dollars in full of the above account. Signed duplicates Jos Bates[61]

The United States To Joseph Greenwood Dr
For two Horses purchased by Genl Atkinson and Maj O'Fallon for two Ottoe Indians & employed to accompany them on the expedition up the Missouri river at thirty seven Dollars & fifty cents acct. $ 75.00
Council Bluffs May 10th 1825
Received of Genl H. Atkinson and Maj O'Fallon seventy five Dollars in full of the above account.
witness Signed duplicates

his
[illegible words] Joseph X Greenwood
mark[62]

The United States	To Michael Eley	Dr
For one sorrel Horse	----------------- $ 60	$ 60.00
one bay mare	----------------- $ 40	40.00
		$ 100.00

Fort Atkinson. May 11th, 1825. recd of Br Genl. H. Atkinson one hundred dollars in full of the above account
duplicate Michael Eley[63]

60. Voucher 45, ibid.
61. Voucher 46, ibid.
62. Voucher 5, Commission Accounts, 9534/1824–25, RG 217.
63. Voucher 47, Commission Accounts, 10987/1824–25, RG 217.

The United States	To James Kennerly	Dr
For two sorrel Horses at $ 75 ea		$ 150.00
For one sorrel horse --- $ 50		50.00
		$ 200.00

Council Bluffs, May 14th, 1825 Recvd of Br. Genl. H. Atkinson two hundred dollars in full of the above acct
duplicate Jas Kennerly[64]

The Unites States for Genl Atkinson	To Ely & Curtis	Dr
1825 May 11 For the following furnished for the use of the Military Escort by order Genl H Atkinson		
1 Mainyard for one of the Keelboats 43 ft a 37 1/2 c		$16.12
3 Blocks for same 20 inches	at 12 1/2	2.50
6 do Cordage for same		.75
		$19.37

Received Fort Atkinson council Bluffs 14 May 1825 of Br Genl Henry Atkinson Ninteen Dollars and thirty seven cents in full of the above account Signed Duplicates Eley & Curtis[65]

Fort Atkinson May 14, 1825

I certify that it became necessary for me to purchase for the use of the Keel boat Antelope whilst on her voyage from St. Louis to Council Bluffs the following articles.

89	Cordel rope	12 1/2 cents	$ 11.12 1/2
3	Hinge screws	25 "	.75
	Window glass and putting the same in the cabin windows		1.50
1	[illegible word] black		1.00
6	nails		1.00
			$ 15.37 1/2

for which said purchases I advanced the sum of fifteen dollars & 37 1/2/100 Wm Bloodgood Lt U.S. Infy

May 14, 1825 Recd of Br H. Atkinson fifteen dollars & 37/100 in full of the above acct

duplicate Wm Bloodgood Lt U.S. Infy[66]

64. Voucher 48, ibid.
65. Voucher 56, ibid.
66. Voucher 49, ibid.

The United States per Genl Henry Atkinson To J B Mousette Dr
1825 May 14 For services as pilot on board the Keelboat Antelope from Saint Louis to Fort Atkinson Council Bluffs 69 days at $3 per day $ 207
Received 14 May 1825 of Br General Henry Atkinson Two hundred and seven Dollars in full of the above account
Signed Duplicate Rects. his
Witness Jean Baptiste X Mousette
J. Dougherty mark[67]

The United States To Peter Primo
For my Services as Interpreter for the Puncar tribe of Indians in Council with the Commissioners at there Vilage $ 10.00

Puncar Vilage June 9th 1825 Received of Genl Atkinson & Maj O Fallon Commissioners Ten Dollars in full of the above acct
witness Signed Duplicates his
P Payne Peter X Premo
mark[68]

The U States to Mr Sire DN

		$	cts
Fort			
Kiawa	For one hundred eight for Macasins at 25/100 pr ps	17	00
June 23	For sixty bushels of charcoal at 12/100 pr Bu	7	50
1825	For fifty lbs of iron at pr pnd	8	55
	Total	43	05

The a. a. Q.M will pay the above acct
H. Atkinson Br Gen U.S. Army
Recd Fort Kiowa June 23, 1825 of Lt. R Soting [?] a. a. Qr. M. 6 Inf forty three & five cents in full of the above acct.
(Signed duplicates) Jos. A Sire[69]

The United States To Edwin Rose
For my Services as Interpreter & Express for the Commissioners on the Expedition up the Missouri for the 1st of April to the 30th day of June 1825 at one dollar pr day $ 91

67. Voucher 53, ibid.
68. Voucher 6, Commission Accounts, 9534/1824–25, RG 217.
69. Voucher 2, Abstract A, Commission Accounts, 5020/1825, RG 217.

Received of Genl Atkinson & Maj B. O Fallon commissioners Ninety one dollars in full of the above account
witness Signed Duplicates
P Payne Edw J Rose[70]

Lt. R. Holmes a. a. Qr Mr. In consequence of a deficiency of shoes among the troops will issue to the Brigade Commanded by Brigdr Genl H. Atkinson Three Hundred & Ninety three pairs of Buffaloe Mockasins as an extra issue.
Mandan Village H. Atkinson
Aug. 31, 1825 Br Gen U.S. Army[71]

The United Stated pr Genl Atkinson To Jas Kennerly Dr
1825

For 168 Cordell Rope	@ 25.0	$ 42.00
1 1/2 doz flat files	@ $ 9	13.50
1 1/2 " 1/2 round ditto	6	9.00
4 " hand saw ditto	1.50	6.00
35 yd red flannel	50	17.50
1 Book [?] muslin		1.50
		$ 89.50

Fort Atkinson Council Bluffs October 6th 1825 Recevd of Brg Gen H Atkinson Eighty nine dollars & fifty cents in full of the above account Jas Kennerly[72]

The United States To Moses Harris Dr
For his services as a guide & for carrying expresses form the 6th of May 1825 to the 6th of October at $15 pr month $ 75.00

Council Bluffs. October 6th 1825 Recd of Brig Genl. H. Atkinson Seventy five dollars in full of the above acct.
Witness Signed duplicate
[illegible words] His
Lt. 6th Infy Moses X Harris
mark[73]

70. Voucher 7, Commission Accounts, 9534/1824–25, RG 217.

71. Atkinson to Holmes, an enclosure from Holmes to "Sir," Oct. 5, 1827, Commission Accounts, 12969/1829, RG 217.

72. Voucher 51, Commission Accounts, 10987/1824–25, RG 217.

73. Voucher 52, ibid.

The United States In Act with Collin Camble

For services rendered the Commissioners as Interpreter for the various Tribes of Sioux from the 18th of June to the 9th of Sept 1825 at one Dollar per Day $ 84.00

Received Fort Lookout Sept 10th 1825 of Genl. H Atkinson & Majr B. O Fallon commissioners, Eighty four Dollars in full of the above account

Witness (Duplicate)

P Payne Colin Campbell[74]

Brigadier General Atkinson and Major O'Fallon commissioners of the United States on the Missouri

1825	To the Acting Asst Commissary of Subsistance		D.	B.
June 28	To 1 Bl. Flow	$12.15	$ 12	15
30	" " " Whiskey 32 gallons	79 ct per gallon	25	28
July 4	" 5 Gallons 28 gills whiskey	" per Brown	4	44
11	" 48 Gills Whiskey	"	1	14
15	" 5 Gallons and 28 gills	"	4	44
23	" 1 Bll. Flour	$12.15	12	15
Augt 1	" 40 pounds Flour from [?]	5 gallons 18 gills wh	4	57
19	" 50 - - - - - -	9 - 8 " "	10	73
"	" 4 lb Bread to men of Genl Ashley's party			42
Sept 4	" 1/2 Gallon Salt 18 3/4 B qts Vinigar	12 cts		30 3/4
			$ 78	3 1/4

Received Fort Atkinson September 1825 of Brigadier General Atkinson and Major O'Fallon United States Commissioners Seventy Eight Dollars and thirty three and fourth cent in full of the above account

Signed Duplicate Jas W Kingsbury Lt 1 Reg Inf & aa CS[75]

Genl H. Atkinson & Majr O Fallon U.S. Commissioners to Liet Holmes Act & Asst Commissionary Dr

For	230 3/4 pounds pork	@ 8 3/4 cts pr lb	$ 20.00
	1 Bushel & 10 quarts Salt	@ $3.00 pr Bushl	3.94
	90 Pounds hard Bread	@ 7 ct pr lb	6.30
	7 Quarts Vinegar	@ 16 ct pr gill	8.28
	1 Barrell Flour		12.15
	1/2 Bushel Beans	$2.50	1.25
	47 Gallons Whiskey	@ 79 ct	37.13
			$ 81.05

74. Voucher 8, Commission Accounts, 9534/1824–25, RG 217.

75. Voucher 9, ibid. This seems to be the only time the addition on the bill was incorrect.

Received Fort Atkinson September 1825 of Brig. Genl. H. Atkinson & Maj. O Fallon U. States Commissioners Eighty one Dollars five cents in full of the above account R Holmes
(Signed Duplicates) Lt. [illegible] of Sub. 6 Inf[76]

The United States To Charles Magrain Dr
For my services in going express to the different Villages of the Panis Nation of Indians and conducting the chiefs and leading men to the Council Bluffs on a visit to the Commissioners at that place $ 15.00
Received Fort Atkinson 2d October 1825 pr Genl Atkinson & Maj O Fallon Commissioners fifteen Dollars in full of the above account
witness Signed Duplicate his
C Pentland Charles X Magrain
Capt 6 Inf mark[77]

The United States pr the Commissioners To Jas Kennerly Dr
1825

For	397 lb Bacon	@	15	$ 59.55
	45 lb Cheese	@	25	11.25
	6 Kegs crackers	@	1.50	9.00
	3 Boxes salt Fish	@	2.50	7.50
	2 large Tin pitchers	@	1	2.00
	1 pr Decanters			2.50
	1 1/2 Wine glasses	@	3	4.50
	2 Candlesticks	@	1	2.00
	2 Waiters	@	2	4.00
	5 Gals Chery bounce	@	1	5.00
	1 large Demi john			2.50
	10 yd Rucia Sheeting	@	62 1/2	6.25
	2 Brls & 98 lb Flour	@	$ 12.15 pr br	30.37
	3 1/4 bushels Beans	@	2.25	7.31
	96 lb Butter		26 1/4	6.00
	3 Brass cocks	@	75	2.25
				$ 161.98

Fort Atkinson Council bluffs Oct 7 1825
Recd of Gr Gen H Atkinson & Maj B. OFallon commissioners One hundred & sixty one dollars ninety eight cents in full of the above account
Jas Kennerly[78]

---

76. Voucher 10, ibid.
77. Voucher 11, ibid.
78. Voucher 12, ibid.

2 November 1825	St. Louis, Mo.	B. Pratte & Co.	
$46.50			
1 Mast			$10.
1 Sail and Rigging			25.
1 Cordelle & 1 Warp			5.
4 poles with Sockets			5.
2 Oars			1.50[79]

79. Voucher 13, ibid.

BIBLIOGRAPHY

Abel, Annie Heloise, ed. *The Fort Clark Journal of F. A. Chardon.* Iowa City, Iowa: Athens Press, 1932.

Alwin, John A. "Pelts, Provisions, and Perceptions: The Hudson's Bay Company Mandan Indian Trade, 1795–1812." *Montana The Magazine of Western History* 29, 3 (1979): 16–27.

American Fur Company. Records. Missouri Historical Society, St. Louis.

Anderson, Harry H. "An Investigation of the Early Band of the Saone Group of Teton Sioux." *Journal of the Washington Academy of Sciences* 46, 1 (1956): 87–94.

———. "The Letters of Peter Wilson, First Resident Agent among the Teton Sioux." *Nebraska History* 42, 4 (1961): 237–64.

Atkinson, Henry. "Letter from General Atkinson to Colonel Hamilton." *Nebraska History* 5, 1 (1922): 9–11.

Baldwin, Leland D. *The Keelboat Age on Western Waters.* Pittsburgh: University of Pittsburgh Press, 1941.

Barry, Louise. *The Beginning of the West: Annals of the Kansas Gateway to the American West, 1540–1854.* Topeka: Kansas State Historical Society, 1972.

Bemis, Samuel Flagg. *John Quincy Adams and the Foundations of American Foreign Policy.* New York: Alfred A. Knopf, 1956.

Billon, Frederick L. *Annals of St. Louis in Its Territorial Days.* 2 vols. St. Louis: n.p., 1888.

Blenkenson, Willis. "Edwin Rose." In vol. 9 of *The Mountain Men and the Fur Trade of the Far West.* Ed. Leroy R. Hafen. Glendale, Calif.: Arthur H. Clark Co., 1972.

Bonner, T. D. *The Life and Adventures of James P. Beckwourth.* Ed. Bernard DeVoto. New York: Alfred A. Knopf, 1931.

Brackenridge, H. M. *Journal of a Voyage up the Missouri, Performed in 1811.* Vol. 6 of *Early Western Travels, 1748–1846.* Ed. Reuben Gold Thwaites. Cleveland: Arthur H. Clark Co., 1904.

Bradbury, John. *Travels in the Interior of America.* Vol. 8 of *Early Western Travels, 1748–1846.* Ed. Reuben Gold Thwaites. Cleveland: Arthur H. Clark Co., 1904.

Bray, Kingsley M. "Teton Sioux Population History, 1655–1881." *Nebraska History* 75, 2 (1994): 165–90.

Brower, J. V. *The Missouri River and Its Utmost Sources.* St. Paul, Minn.: Pioneer Press, 1896.

Carlson, Gayle F. *Archeological Investigations at Fort Atkinson (24WN9), Washington County, Nebraska, 1956–1971.* Lincoln: Nebraska State Historical Society, 1979.

Carter, Clarence Edwin, ed. *The Territorial Papers of the United States.* 29 vols. Washington, D.C.: GPO, 1934.

Catlin, George. *Letters and Notes on the Manners, Customs, and Condition of the North American Indians.* 2 vols. New York: Wiley and Putman, 1841.

———. *O-Kee-Pa: A Religious Ceremony and Other Customs of the Mandans.* Ed. John C. Ewers. New Haven, Conn.: Yale University Press, 1967.

Charbonneau Family. Papers. Missouri Historical Society, St. Louis.

Chittenden, Hiram M. *The American Fur Trade of the Far West.* 3 vols. New York: Francis P. Harper, 1902.

———. *History of Early Steamboat Navigation on the Missouri River.* 2 vols. 1903. Reprint, Minneapolis: Ross and Haines, 1962.

Clarke, Dwight L. *Stephen Watts Kearny, Soldier of the Old West.* Norman: University of Oklahoma Press, 1961.

Clow, Richmond L. "General William S. Harney on the Northern Plains." *South Dakota History* 16, 3 (1986): 229–48.

Collins, Ethel A. "Pioneer Experiences of Horatio H. Larned." *Collections of the State Historical Society of North Dakota* 7 (1925): 1–58.

Colt, Katherine Gideon. *The Letters of Peter Wilson.* Baltimore: Wirth Brothers, 1940.

Conrad, Howard L., ed. *Encyclopedia of the History of Missouri.* 6 vols. New York: Southern History Co., 1901.

Cooke, Philip St. George. *Scenes and Adventures in the Army.* Philadelphia: n.p., 1859.

Cooling, Benjamin Franklin, ed. *The New American State Papers: Military Affairs.* 19 vols. Wilmington, Del.: Scholarly Resources, Inc., 1979.

Coues, Elliott, ed. "Letters of William Clark and Nathaniel Pryor." *Annals of Iowa* 1 (1893–95): 613–20.

Daily National Intelligencer (Washington, D.C.)

Dale, Harrison Clifford. *The Ashley-Smith Explorations and the Discovery of a Central Route to the Pacific, 1822–1829*. Cleveland: Arthur H. Clark Co., 1918.

Denig, Edwin Thompson. *Five Indian Tribes of the Upper Missouri*. Ed. John C. Ewers. Norman: University of Oklahoma Press, 1961.

Dorsey, Dorothy B. "The Panic of 1819 in Missouri." *Missouri Historical Review* 29, 1 (1935): 79–91.

Dunbar, Seymour. *A History of Travel in North America*. Indianapolis: Bobbs-Merrill Co., 1915.

Edwardsville (Illinois) *Spectator*

Ewers, John C. *The Blackfeet: Raiders on the Northwestern Plains*. Norman: University of Oklahoma Press, 1958.

Foreman, Grant. "River Navigation in the Early Southwest." *Mississippi Valley Historical Review* 15, 1 (1928–29): 34–55.

Frost, Donald McKay. *Notes on General Atkinson, the Overland Trail, and South Pass*. Barre, Mass.: Barre Gazette, 1960.

Gregg, Kate L. "The History of Fort Osage." *Missouri Historical Review* 34, 4 (1940): 439–88.

———. "The War of 1812 on the Missouri Frontier. *Missouri Historical Review* 33 (October 1938): 3–22; 34 (January 1939): 184–202; 34 (April 1939): 326–48.

Grinnell, George Bird. *The Cheyenne Indians*. 2 vols. New York: Cooper Square, 1962.

Haines, Aubrey L. "John Colter." In vol. 8 of *The Mountain Man and the Fur Trade of the Far West*. Ed. Leroy R. Hafen. Glendale, Calif.: Arthur H. Clark Co., 1971.

Hanson, James A. "The Keelboat." *Museum of the Fur Trade Quarterly* 30, 1 (1994): 9–25.

Heitman, Francis B. *Historical Register and Dictionary of the United States Army*. 2 vols. Washington, D.C.: GPO, 1903.

Hemphill, W. Edwin, ed. *The Papers of John C. Calhoun*. 20 vols. Columbia: University of South Carolina, 1963–65.

Holmes, Reuben. "The Five Scalps." Missouri Historical Society *Glimpses of the Past* 5 (1938): 3–54.

Houck, Louis. *A History of Missouri from the Earliest Explorations and Settlements until the Admission of the State into the Union*. 3 vols. Chicago: R. R. Donnelley and Sons, 1908.

Hulbert, Archer Butler, and Dorothy Printup Hulbert. *Marcus Whitman, Crusader*. Vols. 6 and 7 of *Overland to the Pacific*. Denver: Stewart Commission of Colorado College, 1936.

Hutchins, James S. "'Dear Hook': Letters from Bennet Riley, Alphonso Wetmore, and Reuben Holmes, 1822–1833." *Bulletin of the Missouri Historical Society* 36, 4 (1980): 203–20.

Jackson, Donald, ed. *Letters of the Lewis and Clark Expedition*. Urbana: University of Illinois Press, 1962.

Jackson, John C. "Old Traders in a New Corporation: The Hudson's Bay Company Retreats North in 1822." *North Dakota History* 55, 3 (1988): 22–28.

James, Edwin. *Account of an Expedition from Pittsburgh to the Rocky Mountains*. Vol. 1 of *Early Western Travels 1748–1846*. Ed. Reuben Gold Thwaites. Cleveland: Arthur H. Clark Co., 1905.

Jensen, Richard E. "Bellevue: The First Twenty Years, 1822–1842." *Nebraska History* 56, 3 (1975): 339–74.

———. *The Fontenelle and Cabanné Trading Posts: The History and Archeology of Two Missouri River Sites, 1822–1838*. Lincoln: Nebraska State Historical Society, in press.

Jesup, Thomas Sidney. Papers. Library of Congress, Washington, D.C.

Johnson, Allen, ed. "John C. Calhoun." In vol. 3 of *Dictionary of American Biography*. New York: Charles Scribner's Sons, 1943.

Johnson, Sally Ann. "The Sixth's Elysian Fields: Fort Atkinson at the Council Bluffs." *Nebraska History* 40, 1 (1959): 1–38.

Kappler, Charles J., ed. *Indian Affairs, Laws and Treaties*. 3 vols. Washington, D.C.: GPO, 1904.

Kennerly, James. Papers. Missouri Historical Society, St. Louis.

Lavender, David. *The Fist in the Wilderness*. 1964. Reprint, Lincoln: University of Nebraska Press, Bison Book, 1998.

Lecompte, Janet. "Auguste Pierre Chouteau." In vol. 9 of *The Mountain Men and the Fur Trade of the Far West*. Ed. Leroy R. Hafen. Glendale, Calif.: Arthur H. Clark Co., 1972.

———. "Gantt's Fort and Bent's Picket Post." *Colorado Magazine* 41, 2 (1964): 111–25.

———. "Pierre Chouteau, Junior." In vol. 9 of *The Mountain Men and the Fur Trade of the Far West*. Ed. Leroy R. Hafen. Glendale, Calif.: Arthur H. Clark Co., 1972.

Long-Island (New York) *Star*

Louisville (Kentucky) *Public Advertiser*

Lowrie, Walter, ed. *American State Papers: Documents, Legislative and Executive of the Congress of the United States; Indian Affairs*. 38 vols. Washington, D.C.: Gales and Seaton, 1834.

Luttig, John C. *Journal of a Fur-Trading Expedition on the Upper Missouri, 1812–1813*. Ed. Stella M. Drum. St. Louis: Missouri Historical Society, 1920.

Malone, Dumas, ed. "Bennet Riley." In vol. 16 of *Dictionary of American Biography*. New York: Charles Scribner's Sons, 1943.

———. "George C. Sibley." In vol. 17 of *Dictionary of American Biography*. New York: Charles Scribner's Sons, 1943.

———. "Henry Leavenworth." In vol. 11 of *Dictionary of American Biography*. New York: Charles Scribner's Sons, 1943.

———. "Richard Barnes Mason." In vol. 12 of *Dictionary of American Biography*. New York: Charles Scribner's Sons, 1943.

———. "William Selby Harney." In vol. 13 of *Dictionary of American Biography*. New York: Charles Scribner's Sons, 1943.

Mattes, Merrill J. "Joseph Robidoux." In vol. 8 of *The Mountain Men and the Fur Trade of the Far West*. Ed. Leroy R. Hafen. Glendale, Calif.: Arthur H. Clark Co., 1971.

Mattison, Ray H. "Kenneth McKenzie." In vol. 2 of *The Mountain Men and the Fur Trade of the Far West*. Ed. Leroy R. Hafen. Glendale, Calif.: Arthur H. Clark Co., 1965.

Maximilian [Prince of Wied], *Travels in the Interior of North America*. 3 vols. Cleveland: Arthur H. Clark Co., 1905.

McDonald, Marshall. Papers. William R. Perkins Library. Duke University, Durham, North Carolina.

Merk, Frederick. *Fur Trade and Empire: George Simpson's Journal*. Cambridge: Harvard University Press, 1931.

Mississippi Free Trader and Natchez Gazette

Missouri Advocate (St. Louis)

Missouri Gazette and Public Advertiser (St. Louis)

Missouri Intelligencer (Franklin)

Missouri Republican (St. Louis)

Morgan, Dale L. *Jedediah Smith and the Opening of the West*. Indianapolis: Bobbs-Merrill Co., 1953.

———. *The West of William H. Ashley*. Denver: Old West Publishing Co., 1964.

Morgan, Dale L., and Eleanor Towles Harris. *The Rocky Mountain Journals of William Marshall Anderson*. San Marino, Calif.: Huntington Library, 1967.

Moulton, Gary, ed. *The Journals of the Lewis and Clark Expedition*. 11 vols. Lincoln: University of Nebraska Press, 1986–97.

Nasatir, Abraham P. "The International Significance of the Jones and Immell Massacre and of the Aricara Outbreak in 1823." *Pacific Northwest Quarterly* 30, 1 (1939): 77–108.

———. *Spanish War Vessels on the Mississippi, 1792–1796*. New Haven, Conn.: Yale University Press, 1968.

National Archives and Records Administration. Journals of the Commissioners Under the Act of Congress approved May 25, 1824. Journals of Commissions, 1824–39. Records of the Bureau of Indian Affairs. Record Group 75.

———. Letters Received by the Office of Indian Affairs, 1824–81 (National Archives Microfilm Publication M234). Records of the Bureau of Indian Affairs. Record Group 75.

———. Consolidated Correspondence File, 1794–1890. Records of the Office of the Quartermaster General. Record Group 92.

———. Letters Received by the Office of the Quartermaster General. Records of the Office of the Quartermaster General. Record Group 92.

———. Letters Sent by the Office of the Quartermaster General (Main Series), 1818–83. Records of the Office of the Quartermaster General. Record Group 92.

———. Fort Atkinson Post Returns, 1821–27. Returns from U.S. Military Posts (National Archives Microfilm Publication M617). Records of the Adjutant General's Office. Record Group 94.

———. Letters Received by the Office of the Adjutant General (Main Series), 1822–60 (National Archives Microfilm Publication M567). Records of the Adjutant General's Office. Record Group 94.

———. Letters Sent by the Office of the Adjutant General (Main Series), 1800–90 (National Archives Microfilm Publication M565). Records of the Adjutant General's Office. Record Group 94.

———. Muster Rolls of the Sixth Infantry, 1824–25. Muster Rolls of Regular Army Organizations, 1784–1912. Records of the Adjutant General's Office. Record Group 94.

———. Register of Enlistments in the U.S. Army, 1798–1914 (National Archives Microfilm Publication M233). Records of the Adjutant General's Office. Record Group 94.

———. Register of Post Traders. Records of the Adjutant General's Office. Record Group 94.

———. Letters Received by the Office of the Secretary of War (Registered Series), 1801–70 (National Archives Microfilm Publication M221). Records of the Office of the Secretary of War. Record Group 107.

———. Letters Sent by the Secretary of War Relating to Military Affairs, 1800–89 (National Archives Microfilm Publication M6). Records of the Office of the Secretary of War. Record Group 107.

———. Court Martial Case Files. Records of the Office of the Judge Advocate General (Army). Record Group 153.

———. Atkinson-O'Fallon Commission Accounts. Records of the Accounting Officers of the Department of the Treasury. Record Group 217.

———. Descriptive Books, Sixth Infantry. Records of the Infantry, 1815–1942. Records of United States Regular Army Mobile Units. Record Group 391.

———. Orders Issued, Sixth Infantry. Records of the Infantry, 1815–1942. Records of United States Regular Army Mobile Units. Record Group 391.

———. Orders Received, Sixth Infantry. Records of the Infantry, 1815–1942. Records of United States Regular Army Mobile Units. Record Group 391.

———. Letters Received by Henry Atkinson, 1825–31. Records of Named Departments. Records of U.S. Army Continental Commands. Record Group 393.

———. Letters Sent, Headquarters, Western Department, 1821–37. Records of Named Departments. Records of U.S. Army Continental Commands. Record Group 393.

———. Orders and Special Orders Issued, Western Department, 1820–53. Records of Named Departments. Records of U.S. Army Continental Commands. Record Group 393.

———. Orders and Special Orders Issued by Bvt. Brig. Gen. H. Atkinson, June 1819–Jan. 1826. Records of Named Departments. Records of U.S. Army Continental Commands. Record Group 393.

———. Orders and Special Orders Received from the War Department. Records of Named Departments. Records of U.S. Army Continental Commands. Record Group 393.

Ney, Virgil. *Fort on the Prairie: Fort Atkinson on the Council Bluff, 1819–1827*. Washington, D.C.: Command Publications, 1978.

Nichols, Roger L., "The Arikara Indians and the Missouri River Trade: A Quest for Survival." *Great Plains Quarterly* 2, 2 (1982): 77–93.

———. "Army Contributions to River Transportation, 1818–25." *Military Affairs* 33, 1 (1969): 242–49.

———. *General Henry Atkinson, A Western Military Career*. Norman: University of Oklahoma Press, 1965.

———, ed. "General Henry Atkinson's Report of the Yellowstone Expedition of 1825." *Nebraska History* 44, 12 (1963): 65–82.

———. *The Missouri Expedition 1818–1820: The Journal of Surgeon John Gale with Related Documents*. Norman: University of Oklahoma Press, 1969.

Nielsen, George R. *The Kickapoo People*. Phoenix: Indian Tribal Series, 1975.

Niles Weekly Register (Baltimore)

O'Fallon, Benjamin. Letterbook, 1823–29. Beinecke Library of Rare Books and Manuscripts. Yale University, New Haven, Connecticut.

Oglesby, Richard Edward. *Manuel Lisa and the Opening of the Missouri Fur Trade*. Norman: University of Oklahoma Press, 1963.

Osgood, Ernest Staples, ed. *The Field Notes of Captain William Clark*. New Haven, Conn.: Yale University Press, 1964.

Ottoson, Dennis R. "Toussaint Charbonneau, A Most Durable Man." *South Dakota History* 6, 2 (1976): 152–85.

Parker, Donald Dean, ed. *The Recollections of Philander Prescott*. Lincoln: University of Nebraska Press, 1966.

Parks, Douglas R. "Bands and Villages of the Arikara and Pawnee." *Nebraska History* 60, 2 (1979): 214–39.

Perry, John Perry. *American Ferryboats*. New York: Wilfred Funk, Inc., 1957.

Peters, Richard, ed. *Public Statutes at Large of the United States of America*. Boston: Little Brown and Co., 1861.

Peterson, William J. "Up the Missouri with Atkinson." *Palimpsest* 12, 8 (1931): 315–25.

Phillips, Paul Chrisler. *The Fur Trade*. 2 vols. Norman: University of Oklahoma Press, 1961.

Porter, V. Mott, ed. "Journal of Stephen Watts Kearny." *Missouri Historical Society Collections* 3, 1 (1908): 8–29.

Pratt, Julius W. "Fur Trade Strategy and the American Left Flank in the War of 1812." *American Historical Review* 40, 2 (1935): 263–73.

Prucha, Francis Paul. *A Guide to the Military Posts of the United States*. Madison: State Historical Society of Wisconsin, 1964.

Reed, Russell, and Clell G. Gannon, eds. "Journal of the Atkinson-O'Fallon Expedition." *North Dakota Historical Quarterly* 4, 1 (1929): 5–56.

Robinson, Doane. *A History of the Dakota or Sioux Indians*. Minneapolis: Ross and Haines Co., 1956.

———. "Official Correspondence Pertaining to the Leavenworth Expedition into South Dakota in 1823." *South Dakota Historical Collections* 1, 7 (1902): 181–241.

Settle, Raymond W. "Nathaniel Pryor." In vol. 2 of *The Mountain Men and the Fur Trade of the Far West*. Ed. Leroy R. Hafen. Glendale, Calif.: Arthur H. Clark Co., 1965.

Sheldon, Addison E. "Records of Fort Atkinson, 1819–1827." 6 vols. Nebraska State Historical Society, Lincoln.

Shomette, Donald G. "Heyday of the Horse Ferry." *National Geographic* 176 (1989): 548–56.

Smith, Elbert B. *Magnificent Missourian: The Life of Thomas Hart Benton*. Philadelphia: J. B. Lippincott Co., 1958.

St. Louis Beacon

St. Louis Enquirer

Steiger, John W. "Benjamin O'Fallon." In vol. 5 of *The Mountain Men and the Fur Trade of the Far West*. Ed. Leroy R. Hafen. Glendale, Calif.: Arthur H. Clark Co., 1968.

———. *Benjamin O'Fallon and the Indian Frontier, 1815–1830*. Master's thesis, San Diego State College, 1963.

Stewart, Frank H. "Mandan and Hidatsa Villages in the Eighteenth and Nineteenth Centuries." *Plains Anthropologist* 19, 1 (1974): 287–302.

Sunder, John E. *Joshua Pilcher: Fur Trader and Indian Agent*. Norman: University of Oklahoma Press, 1968.

Thiessen, Thomas D. "Historic Trading Posts near the Mouth of the Knife River." In *The Phase I Archeological Research Program for the Knife River Indian Villages National Historic Site, Part II*. Lincoln, Nebr.: National Park Service Midwest Archeological Center, 1993.

Thurman, Melburn D. "The Little Missouri River: A Source of Confusion for Plains Ethnohistory." *Plains Anthropologist* 33, 1 (1988): 429–77.

Thwaites, Reuben Gold, ed. *Original Journals of the Lewis and Clark Expedition*. 8 vols. New York: Dodd, Mead, and Co., 1905.

Tyson, Robert A. *History of East St. Louis*. East St. Louis: n.p., 1875.

Unrau, William E. *The Kansa Indians: A History of the Wind People*. Norman: University of Oklahoma Press, 1971.

U.S. Congress. "James Monroe, Message to Congress, December 17, 1819." *Annals of the Congress of the United States, 16th Congress, 1st Session*. Washington, D.C.: Gales and Seaton, 1855.

———. "Documents in relation to the Claim of James Johnson for Transportation on the Missouri and Mississippi Rivers." *Annals of the Congress of the United States, 16th Congress, 2nd Session*. H. Doc. 110. Washington, D.C.: Gales and Seaton, 1855.

———. *Annals of the Congress of the United States, 17th Congress, 1st Session.* Washington, D.C.: Gales and Seaton, 1855.

———. *Annals of the Congress of the United States, 18th Congress, 1st Session.* Washington, D.C.: Gales and Seaton, 1856.

———. *Expedition up the Missouri, 19th Congress, 1st Session.* H. Doc. 117. Serial 136. Washington, D.C.: Gales and Seaton, 1826.

Wallace, Agnes. "The Wiggins Ferry Monopoly." *Missouri Historical Review* 42, 1 (1947–48): 1–19.

Weese, A. O., ed. "The Journal of Titian Ramsay Peale, Pioneer Naturalist." *Missouri Historical Review* 41 (1947): 147–63, 266–64.

Wesley, Edgar B., *Guarding the Frontier: A Study of Frontier Defense from 1815–1825.* Minneapolis: University of Minnesota Press, 1935.

———. ed. "Diary of James Kennerly." *Missouri Historical Society Collections* 6, 1 (1928): 41–97.

White, James Haley. "Reminiscences, 1822–1823." St. Louis Reminiscences Envelope. Missouri Historical Society, St. Louis.

White, John Barber. "The Missouri Merchant One Hundred Years Ago." *Missouri Historical Review* 13 (1919): 91–111.

Wilhelm, Paul [Duke of Wurttemburg]. *Travels in North America.* Ed. Savoie Lottinville. Trans. W. Robert Nitske. Norman: University of Oklahoma Press, 1973.

Williams, Walter, ed. *A History of Northeast Missouri.* 3 vols. Chicago: Lewis Publishing Co., 1911.

Wood, W. Raymond, ed. *Papers in Northern Plains Prehistory and Ethnology: Ice Glider 32OL110.* Special Publication No. 3. Sioux Falls: South Dakota Archeological Society, 1986.

Wood, W. Raymond, and Thomas D. Thiessen. *Early Fur Trade on the Northern Plains: Canadian Traders among the Mandan and Hidatsa Indians, 1738–1818.* Norman: University of Oklahoma Press, 1985.

INDEX